RANGEFINDER

Equipment, history, techniques

RANGEFINDER

Equipment, history, techniques

Roger Hicks and Frances Schultz

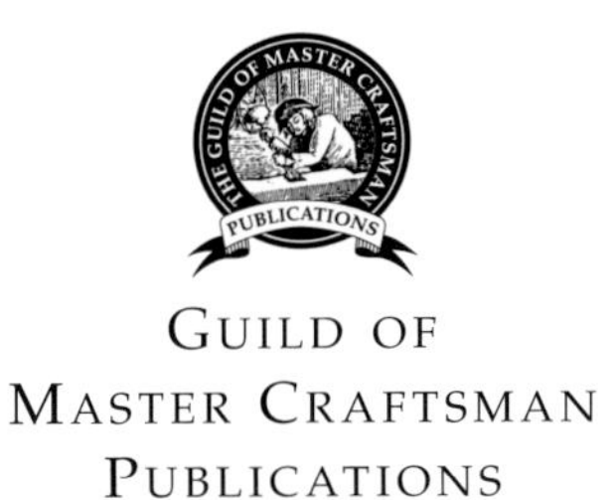

GUILD OF
MASTER CRAFTSMAN
PUBLICATIONS

First published 2003 by
Guild of Master Craftsman Publications Ltd,
166 High Street, Lewes, East Sussex, BN7 1XU

ISBN 1 86108 330 0

British Cataloguing in Publication Data
A catalogue record of this book is
available from the British Library.

Publisher: Paul Richardson
Art Director: Ian Smith
Production Manager: Matt Weyland
Managing Editor: April McCroskie
Editor: Dominique Page
Designers: Francis and Partners
Illustrator: Simon Rodway

Typeface: Stymie and Machine

Colour origination by
Viscan Graphics Pte Ltd (Singapore)
Printed and bound by Kyodo (Singapore)
under the supervision of MRM Graphics,
Winslow, Buckinghamshire, UK

For Hirofumi Kobayashi

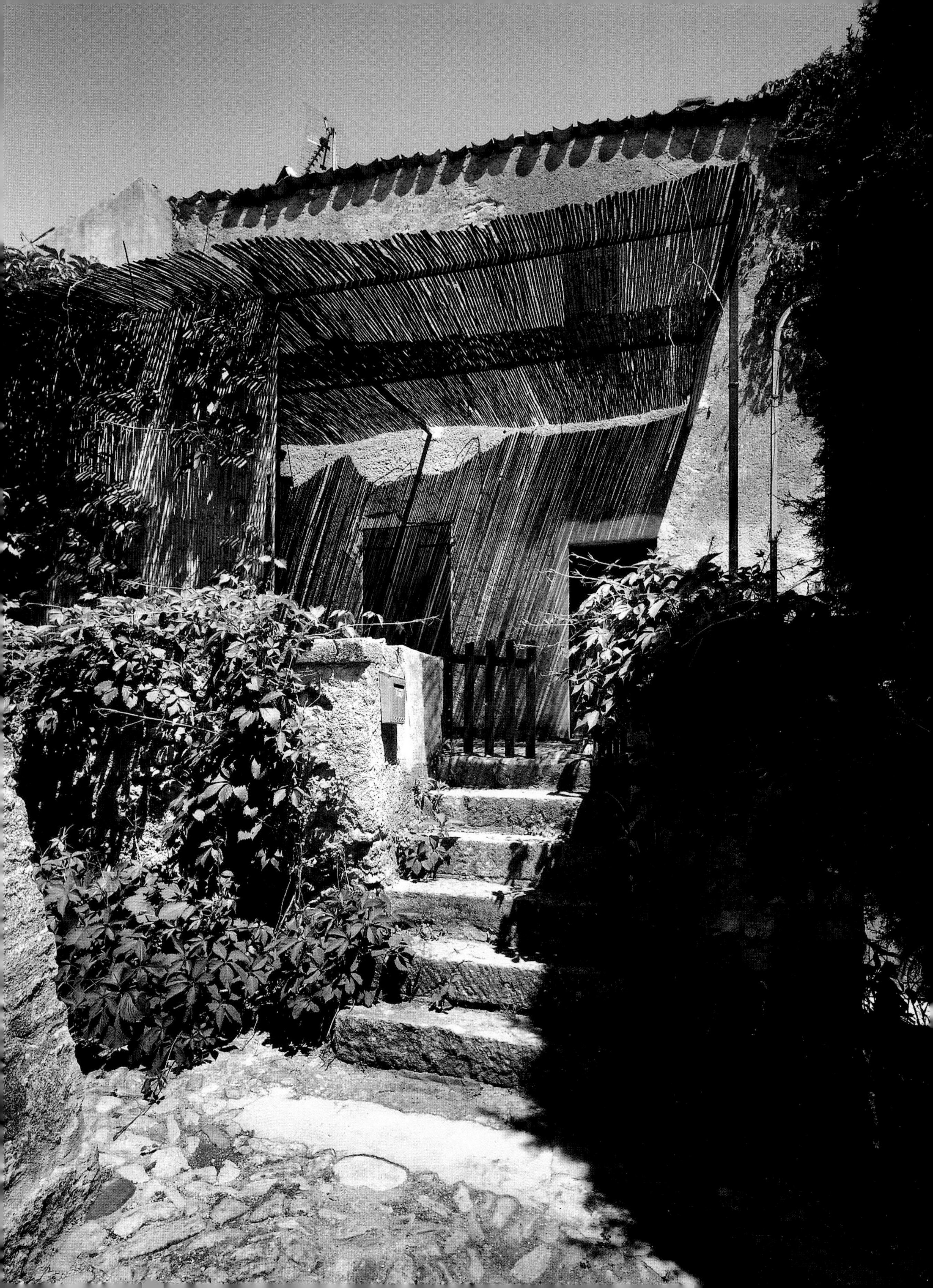

ACKNOWLEDGEMENTS

Some of the people we'd particularly like to thank include:
Jenny Glanfield, widow of Colin Glanfield, who was one of the
greatest authorities of all time on old cameras. If Colin had
lived, he would have co-authored this book. As it is, there are
quite a lot of Colin's pictures in these pages.

Malcolm Glanfield, Colin's brother, for the generous loan of
numerous old cameras and for freely sharing his considerable
knowledge.

Paul-Henry van Hasbroeck and Photo-Historical Publications.
If your interest is in historical cameras, look for books by
Paul-Henry.

Christie's, who provided the picture on page 47: this is *the*
place to buy rare old cameras at auction.

Stuart Heggie loaned us a lot of stock from his shop in The
Borough in Canterbury – a place well worth visiting – and
Brian Cowley at Canterbury Cameras was very helpful too.

Steve Fan at Prisma is a real enthusiast for Voigtländer and
made available new equipment as (and sometimes before) it
came on the market. Alpa could not have been more helpful;
Hasselblad kindly loaned an XPan; Alpa, Fuji, Johnsons
Photopia, Leica, Nikon and Konica all provided pictures.

R indicates Roger speaking

F indicates Frances speaking

Sunshade, South of France

F *Many users of rangefinders and direct-vision cameras find that
they do their best work with a minimum of equipment. This is one of my
favourite pictures. My 'outfit' for the day's shooting was one camera
(Alpa 12 S/WA), one lens (35/5.6 Apo-Grandagon) and a 6 x 9cm back
loaded with HP5 (at 500 in DD-X). The only other things I was carrying
were my spot meter (which I used) and my tripod (which I didn't). MG
Warmtone in selenium*

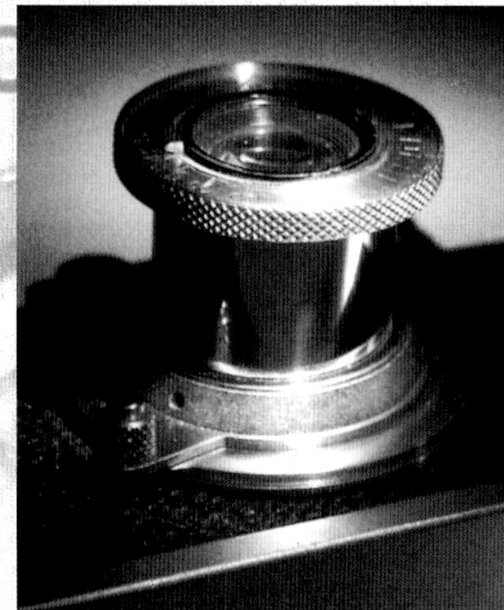
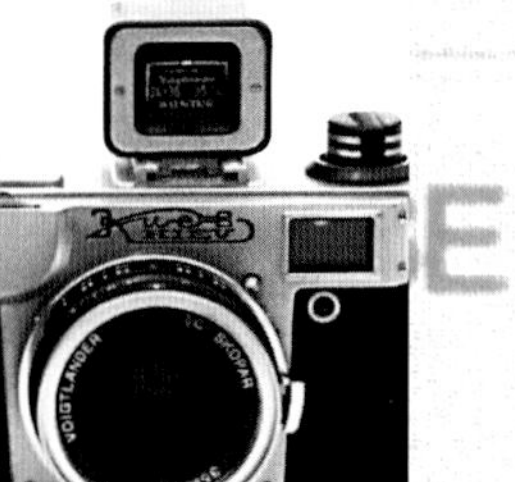
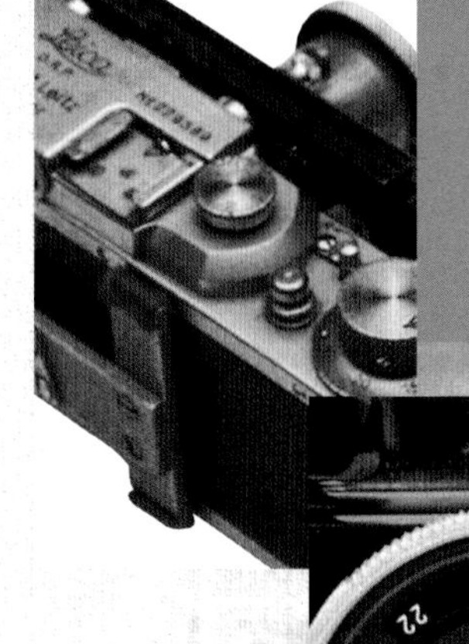
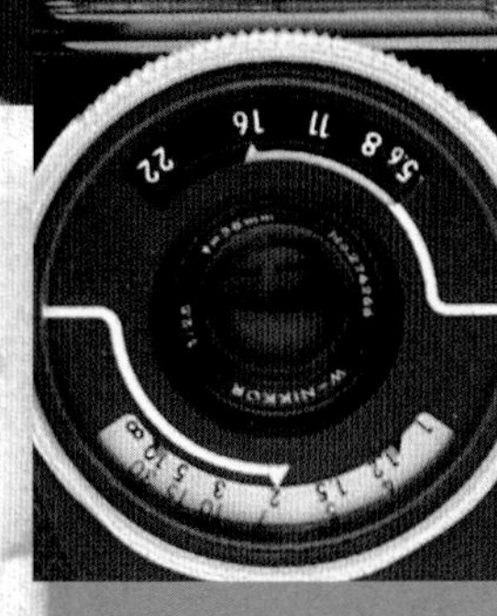

CONTENTS

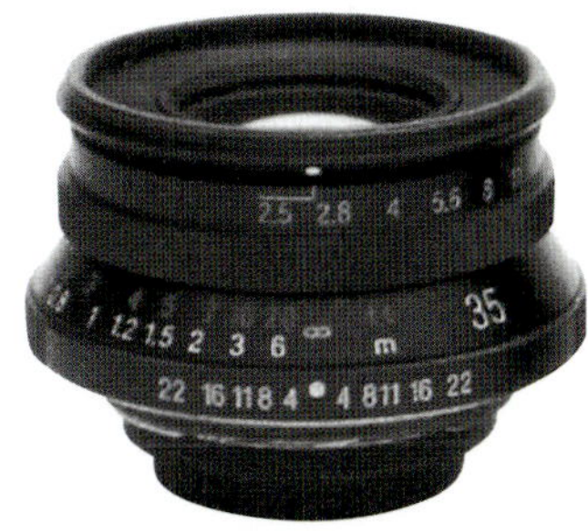

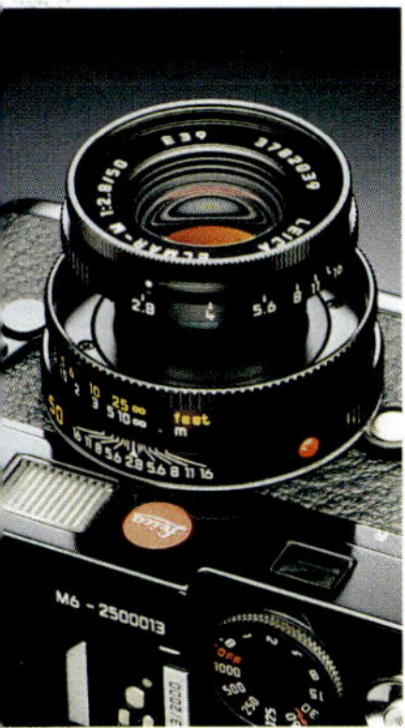

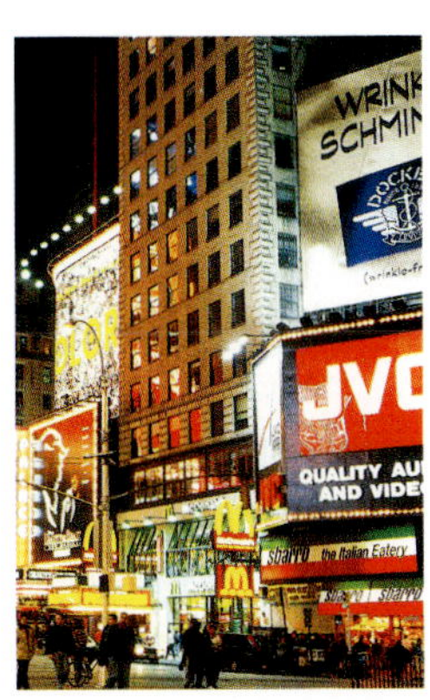

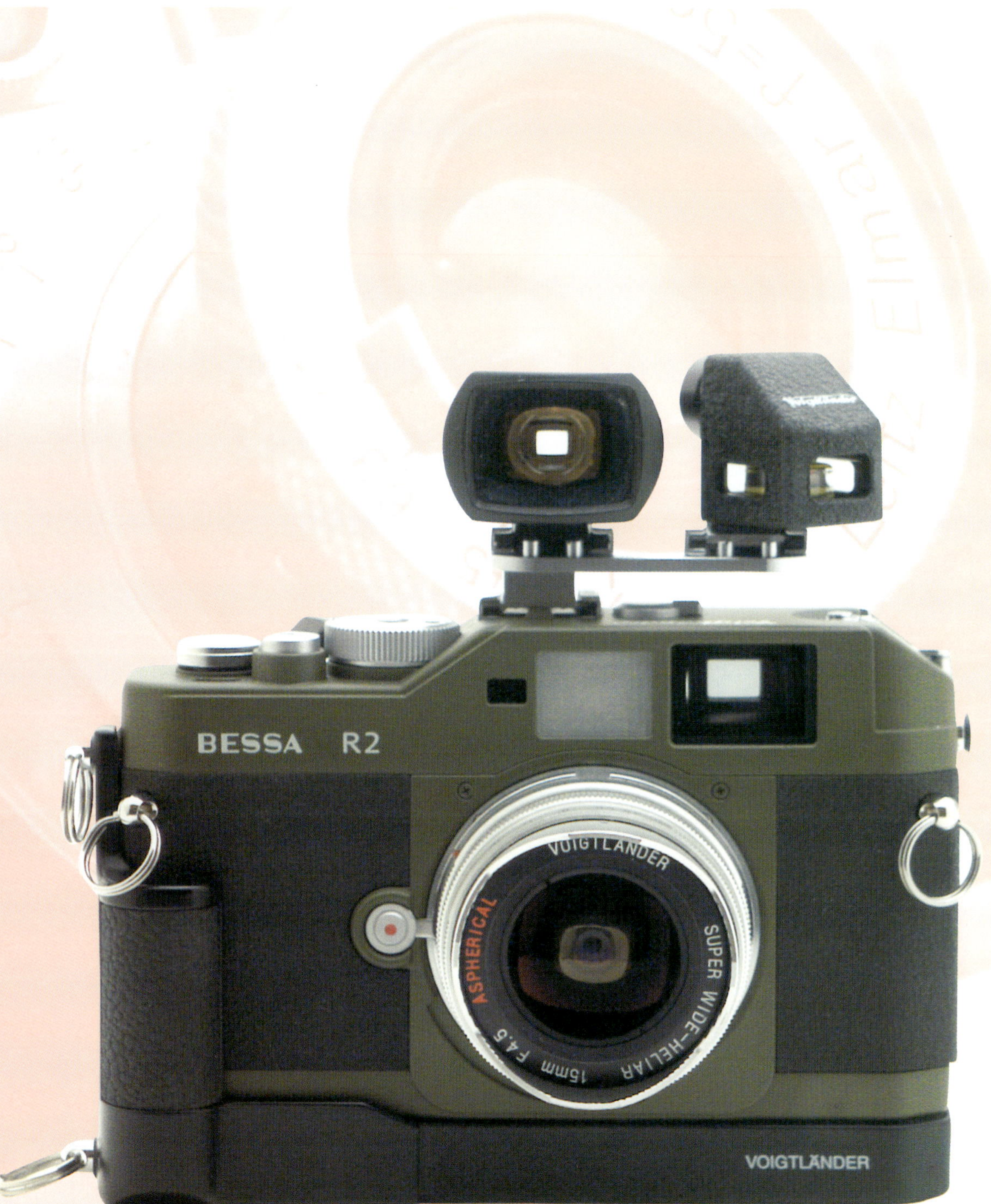

BESSA   R2
VOIGTLÄNDER
ASPHERICAL
SUPER WIDE-HELIAR
15mm F4.5
VOIGTLÄNDER

INTRODUCTION

The rangefinder camera is like Joe Hill: it never died. It may have been overshadowed by the ubiquitous single-lens reflex, but it has always had its devotees. Its darkest days were in the 1980s and early 1990s, but even then the M-series Leica retained an unbroken lineage back to 1925, via the M3 of 1954 and the Leica II of 1932; and aficionados nursed elderly rangefinder Nikons and Canons from the 1950s and early 60s.

For that matter, there have always been those who loved high-quality, mechanical direct-vision cameras – that is, cameras with separate viewfinders, though without a rangefinder. For years these were personified by the Rollei 35, but there were also idiosyncratic roll-film cameras such as the Linhof 617 and 612. They could hardly have been more basic, but they delivered the very highest quality results.

Then, a strange thing happened. Towards the end of the twentieth century, there was a sudden upwelling of sentiment for high-quality rangefinder (RF) and direct-vision (DV) cameras: cameras that could deliver results that were the equal of any SLR, while retaining unique advantages of their own. Models were introduced in roll film and 35mm, with and without autofocus, often with interchangeable lenses, and their success sometimes took even their manufacturers by surprise.

Whether you are contemplating the purchase of an RF/DV camera, wondering how to get the best from one you have already bought, or simply reminiscing about the great RF cameras you owned in the past; whether you like your cameras ancient or modern, simple or complex, cheap and cheerful or exclusively expensive, this is a book for you.

We have concentrated on 35mm, because that is what the vast majority of RF and DV cameras have been, but there is more to it than that. In these pages you will find a surprising range of formats from sub-miniature to 8 x 10in (20 x 25cm) – yes, you can get an 8 x 10in DV camera, though the biggest RF models (no longer in production) were a mere 5 x 7in (13 x 18cm). And 4 x 5in (9 x 12cm) RF and DV cameras are downright commonplace, even new. All have their own charms, their own advantages, their own unique qualities; and they are there to be enjoyed.

Because the field is so vast, it is impossible to be comprehensive about the older equipment; therefore, some of your favourite cameras may be omitted. Don't worry about it. Likewise, you may feel that we've got the balance wrong with new kit. Again, don't worry about it. This is a book by enthusiasts, for enthusiasts.

The Bessa R2 from Voigtländer was in large measure the inspiration for this book, which is dedicated to Hirofumi Kobayashi, saviour of the Voigtländer name.

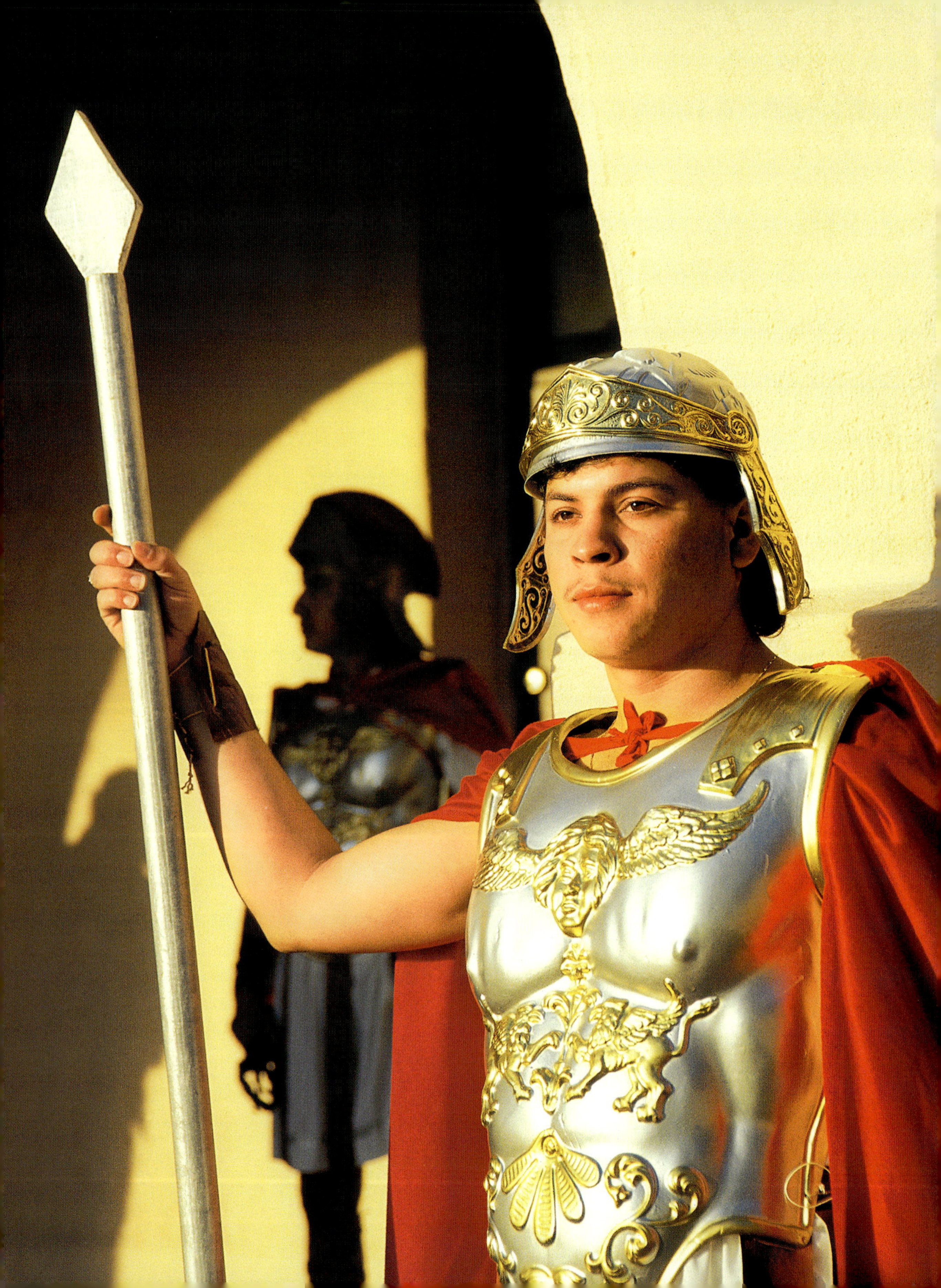

1
WHY RANGEFINDER?

Devotees of RF and DV cameras tend to take on an almost religious fervour when they start to describe the advantages of their favourite marque. Their eyes begin to sparkle; the pitch of their voices begins to rise. Impugn their choice at your peril: there are those who would start a fist-fight over Leica versus Contax, Fuji versus Linhof.

They talk of the immediacy of the RF/DV camera, and of the way that it is 'transparent': there is no barrier between the photographer and the subject. They speak of compactness, unobtrusiveness, silence, ease of operation.

Others, more historically minded, invoke the ghosts of the great photojournalists of the 1950s, with their M-series Leicas, their Nikon SPs and Canon 7s. Yet others recall Bailey's 1960s fashion shots, the immortal Shrimp, A-line dresses and Mary Quant. Others again conjure up the spectre of the Vietnam war photographer, with his two Leicas – one black, one chrome – and his black Nikon F.

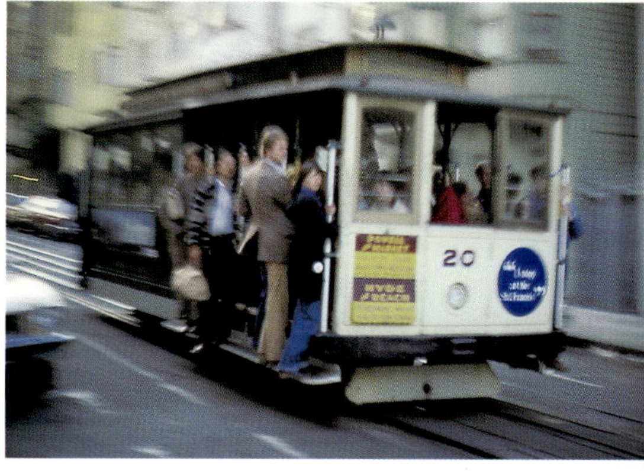

Cable car

I shot this one-handed while hanging off another cable-car going in the opposite direction. Try doing that with the current generation of big, heavy SLRs! It's blurry, sure, but this seems to me to emphasize the speed and motion. M4-P, 35/1.4 Summilux, Kodachrome 64

Roman soldier, Guadalupe passion play

Many longtime RF users cultivate the trick of working with both eyes open, one scanning what is going on in the scene overall and the other looking through the viewfinder. It takes practice, but it's not that hard. M2, 90/2 Summicron, Fuji RF ISO 50

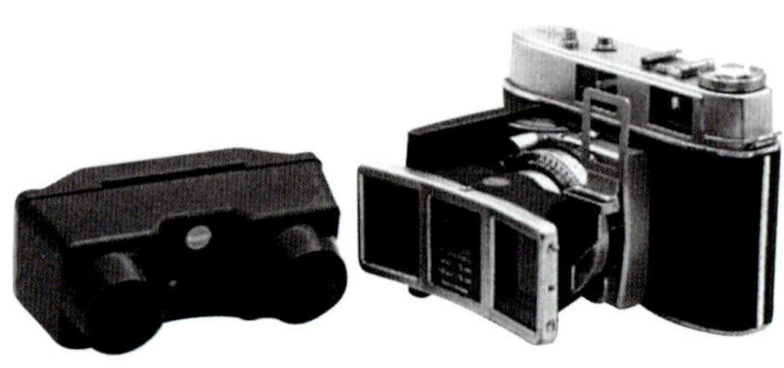

Stereo attachments were made for a surprising range of RF cameras, including the Retina

Then there are the collectors. Old cameras are gadgets par excellence, quite apart from the fact that it is fascinating to trace the evolution of today's cameras through earlier models and marques, some long gone. That is why, although this book is aimed primarily at the user, there is a whole chapter devoted to older cameras, and there are other collectors' cameras dotted through its pages. They are just so hard to resist.

Without doubt, then, there is a mystique to the RF/DV camera that is lacking with reflexes. There are also technical advantages: up to seven – a suitably mystical number. Not all cameras will have all seven advantages, and it is true that DV cameras do have a couple of quite significant disadvantages compared with reflexes, so it is a question of filtering out hype and fashion and deciding what is best for you.

Continuous viewing

There is no blackout during the exposure. You can see whether the subject has pulled a face, or fallen over, or whatever. Advocates of DV maintain that this alone is a strong enough argument for avoiding reflexes, though advocates of twin-lens reflexes will fight their corner on this one.

The granddaddy of 35mm RF cameras: the prototype Ur-Leica

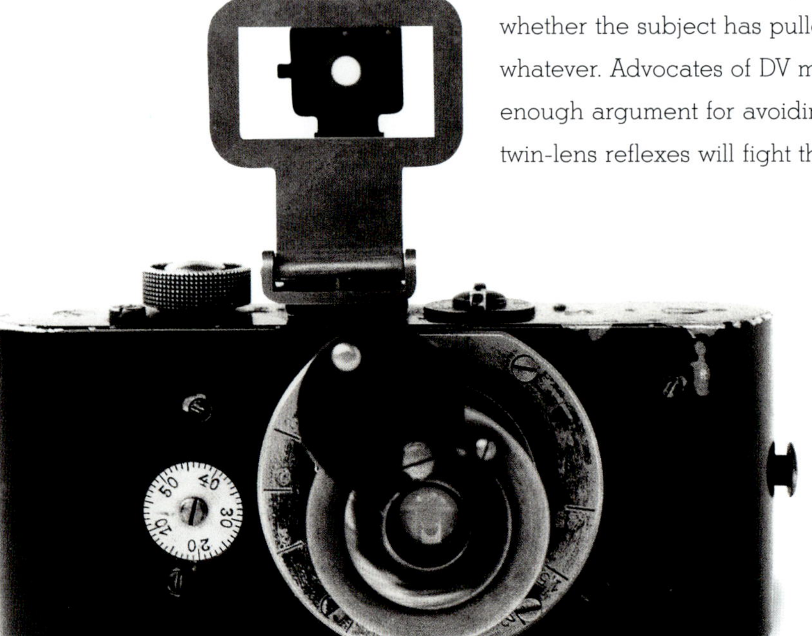

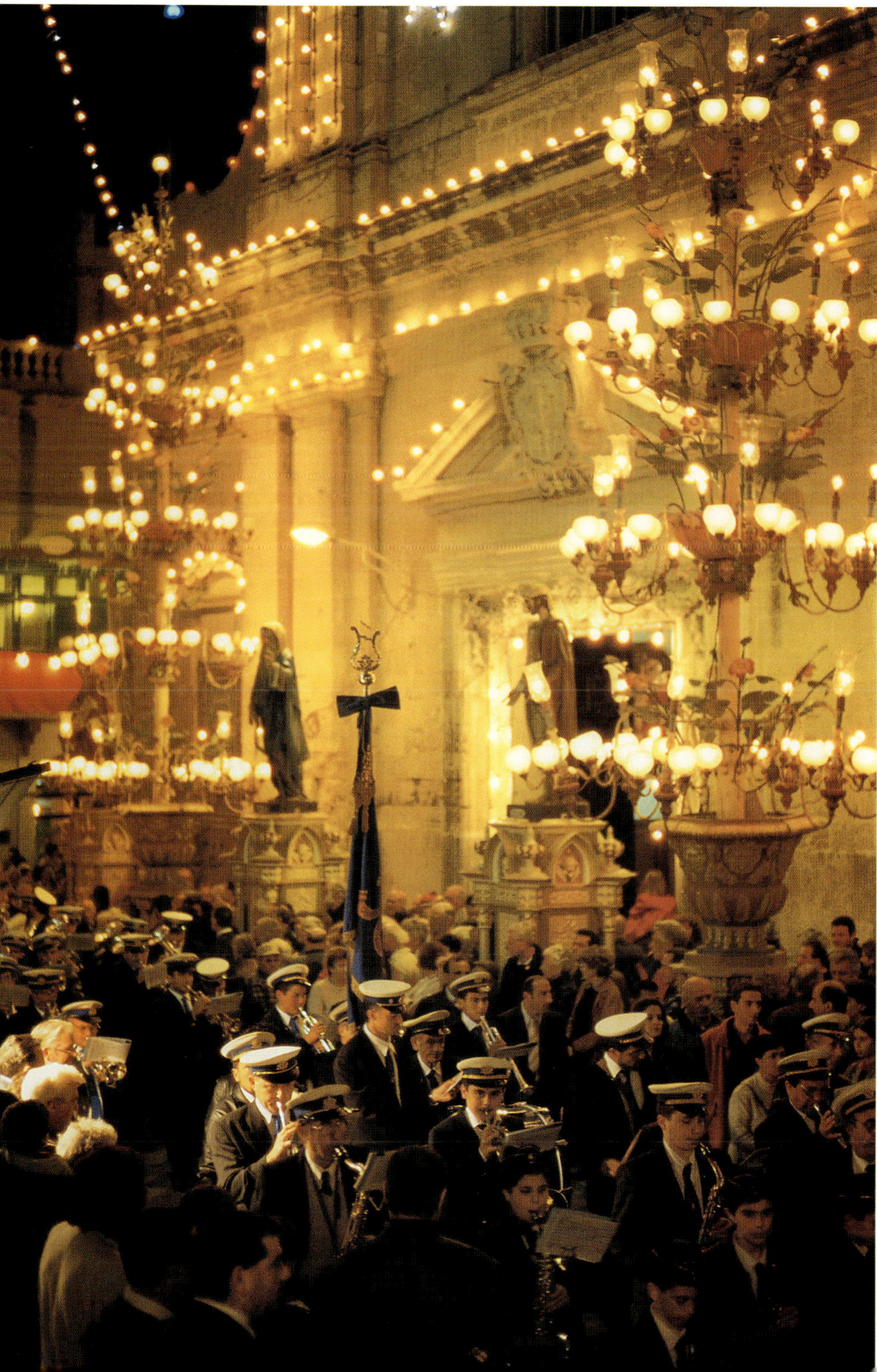

Festa San Giuzepp

The Feast of St Joseph (March 19th, Frances's birthday) is a major event in Rabat and Mdina in Malta. With modern fast films (this is Kodak E200 pushed to 1000), it is relatively easy to take handheld pictures even in colour at very low light levels – though depth of field with the 90/3.5 Apo-Lanthar wide open on the Bessa-R is limited

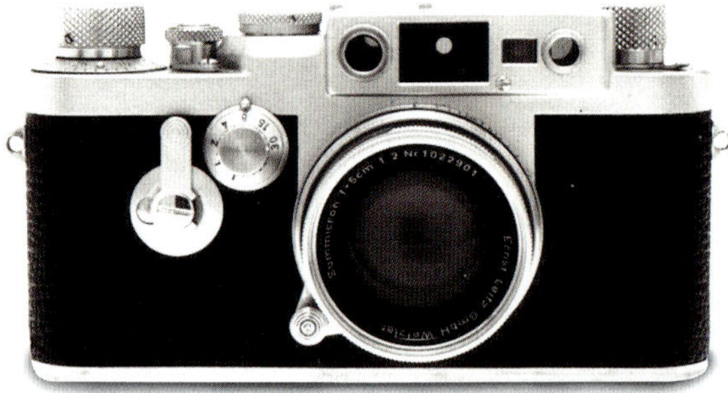

The Leica IIIg: the last of the screw-mount Leicas

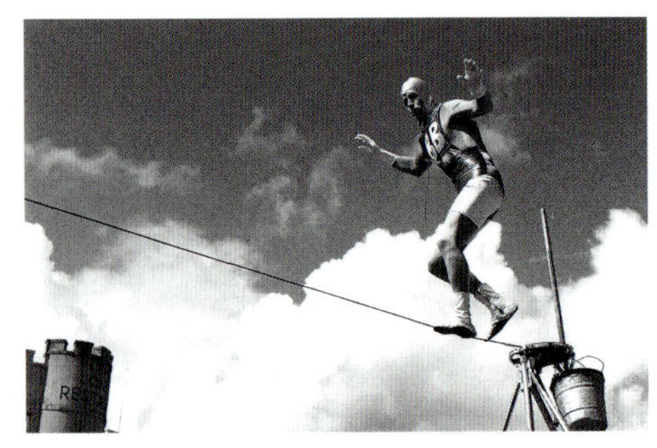

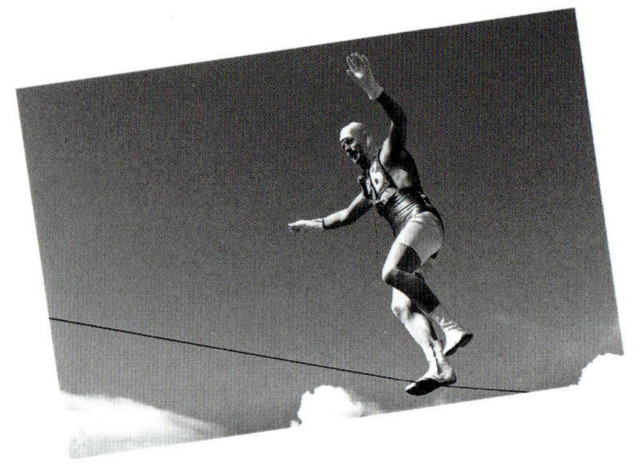

Brighter viewing

Direct-vision finders can be made much brighter than reflex viewing screens. For working in poor light, some photographers even go so far as to attach DV finders to their SLRs, just to make framing easier.

Smaller, lighter, simpler cameras

Without a mirror chamber, cameras can be smaller and lighter, though not necessarily less complex: either a rangefinder or an autofocus mechanism is a spectacularly complex piece of precision engineering. The reduced size is a boon when you are packing for travel, and the reduced weight is very welcome when you have to carry the camera far. Some modern 35mm SLRs, after all, are as bulky and heavy as a medium-format camera.

No RF/DV camera offers an enormous range of modes and metering patterns: you don't need to wade through an instruction book that weighs nearly as much as the camera. Many offer no automation at all: you set focus, aperture and shutter speed yourself. Quite a few do not even have meters: they are real purists' cameras. Very few are battery dependent: mechanical shutters are the order of the day, and if the meter battery gives out, you just guess the exposures, or use a separate meter.

Of course, there are automatic DV cameras, even autofocus, if you prefer to work that way. But for anyone contemplating the change from automation to fully manual operation, there is a good deal of advice and reassurance in Chapter 8.

Wire Walker

With a rangefinder camera, it is a lot easier to see the decisive moment in time and space – and to know that you have captured it, because you can see what's happening when you hear the shutter go off. Bessa-T, 50/1.5 Nokton, yellow filter, XP2, on MG Cooltone

Smaller, sharper wide-angles

Wide-angle lenses for non-reflexes are much easier to design than wide-angles for reflexes. They can therefore be sharper or smaller or lighter or cheaper or faster. Many combine several of these advantages.

In order to make room for the flipping mirror in an SLR, a 'Retrofocus' design is needed, with a negative lens or lens group in front of the image-forming group to increase the back focus. This makes the lens bigger, heavier and more expensive than the non-Retrofocus, and does nothing for sharpness.

Smaller, cheaper standard and short tele lenses

Almost all lenses for 35mm SLRs have an automatic diaphragm, making the lens larger, bulkier, heavier and more expensive. But although lenses for RF cameras are smaller, they often incorporate more brass, steel and light alloy, and less plastic, so they are sometimes surprisingly heavy for their diminutive size.

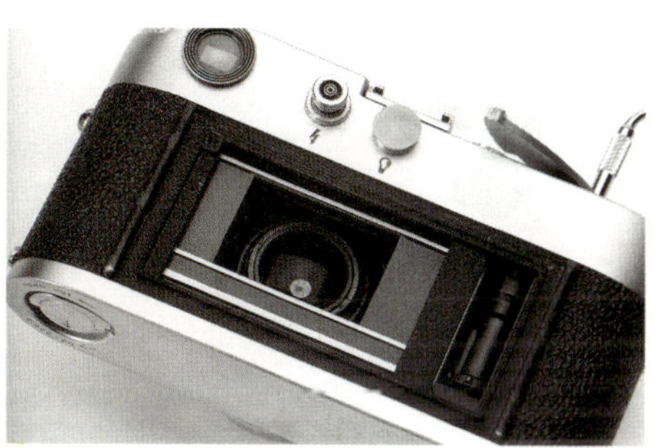

Wide-angles for RF cameras – this is a 21mm Biogon – can protrude deep into the body

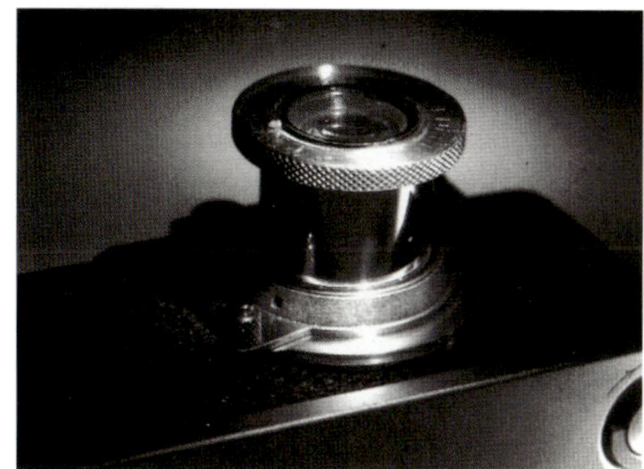

Our ancestors' concern for compactness extended to making collapsible lenses

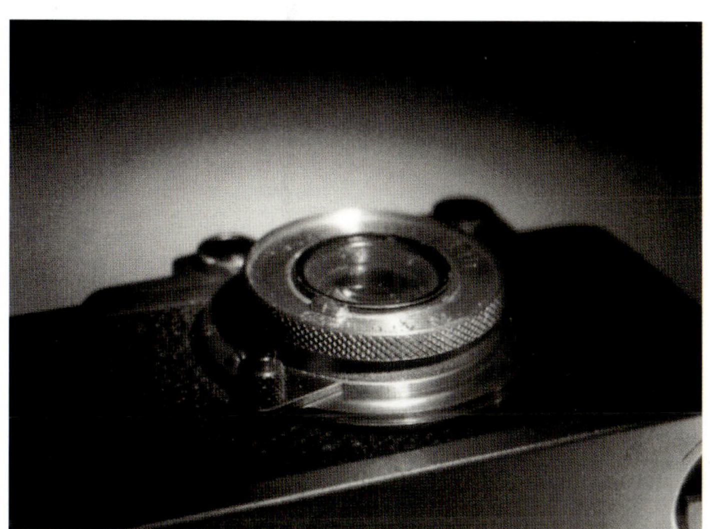

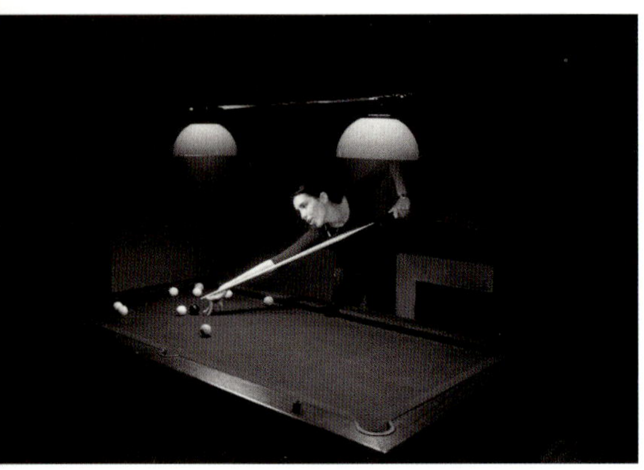

Pool player, Paulmy

This looks posed, but it isn't: she was just impossibly graceful. With a quiet, unobtrusive camera and no flash, she soon began to ignore me and I could wait for the sort of picture that I really wanted. M4-P, 28/1.9 Ultron, Delta 3200 at 3200 in DD-X, on MG warmtone, brief selenium toning

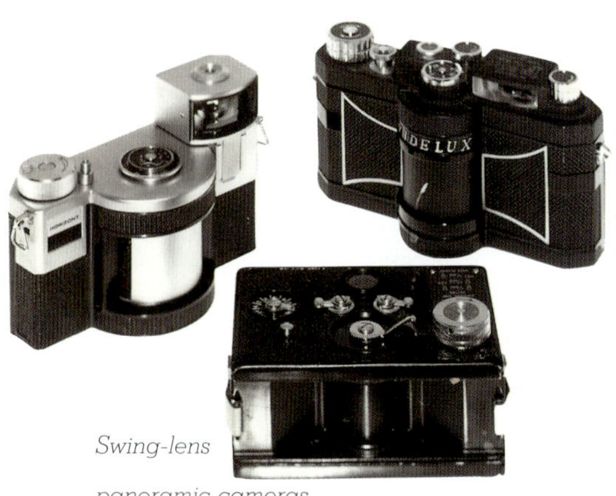

Swing-lens

panoramic cameras

are an unusual

sub-species of DV.

L to R: Horizont,

FT-2, Widelux

Ease of focusing

With a rangefinder, focusing in poor light or with slow or wide-angle lenses is as quick and easy as it is in good light or with longer lenses. With a reflex, the wider the angle of view of the lens, or the lower the light level, or the slower the lens, the harder it is to focus on the screen.

With a scale-focus camera, focusing is just as easy and accurate (or difficult and inaccurate) in any light, or with any lens, but at least with wide-angles, depth of field covers up focusing errors better than with long lenses. Of course, you can scale-focus wide-angles on reflexes, but most people don't.

With passive autofocus cameras, the autofocus just stops working at low light levels, and you have to scale-focus anyway. Active autofocus should work all right, but projecting spots of red light onto people can be a bit obtrusive. One White House photographer found this out in the interval between taking a picture of President Clinton and the time when both he and the Secret Service worked out where the 'gunsight' came from. Of course, the spot is a lot bigger than a laser sight, but it can take a fraction of a second to work that out…

Quieter cameras

Because there is no moving mirror, DV cameras can be a lot quieter than SLRs. This is far less important than in the past, partly because SLRs are now much quieter than they used to be, and partly because some current DV cameras have unreasonably noisy shutters and motordrives. But there are still some DV cameras that are so quiet as to be all but inaudible, even when you are expecting to hear them, let alone when you are not, and on average, direct-vision cameras remain quieter than SLRs.

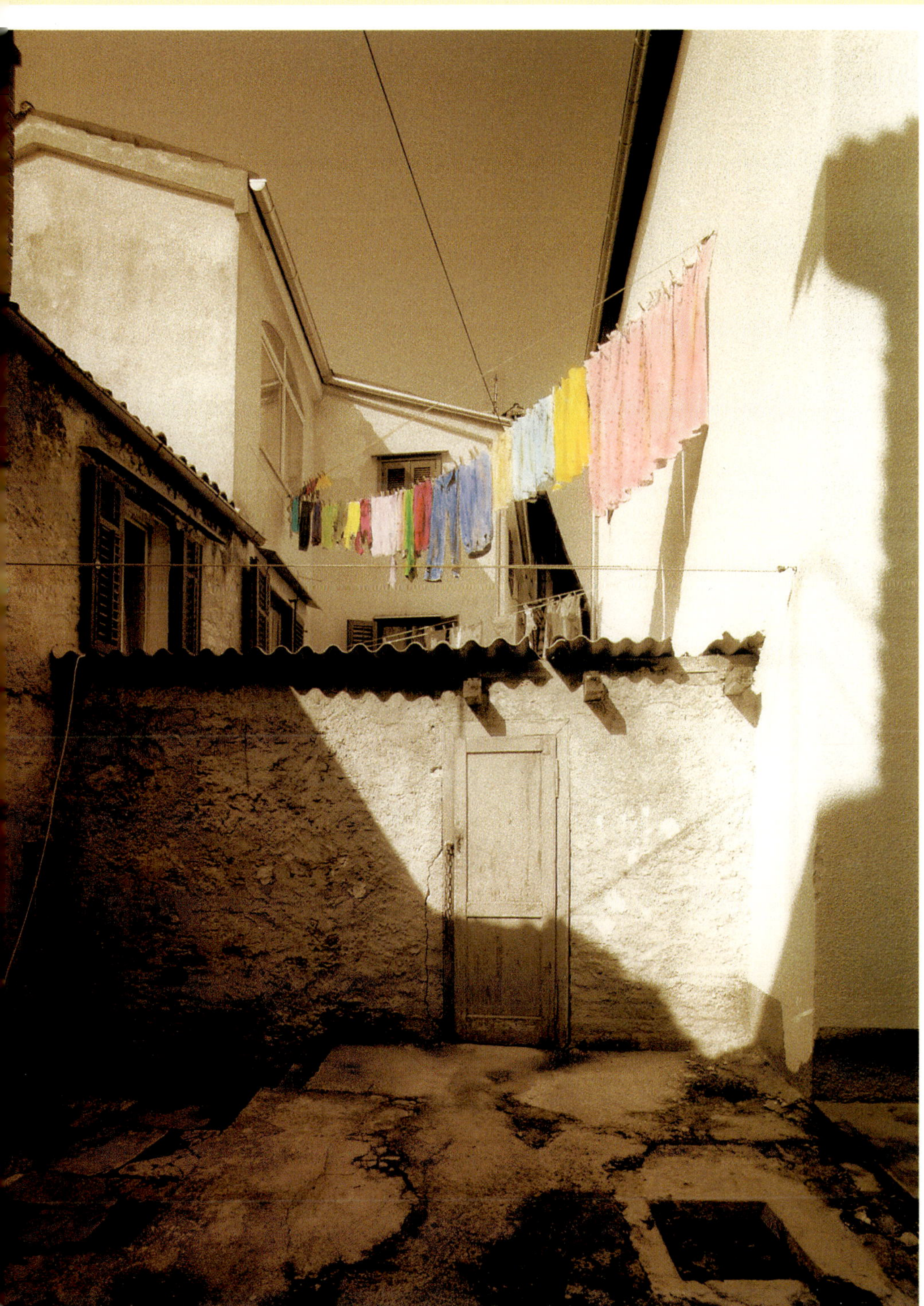

Washing, Capodistria

F *I shot this with hand colouring in mind. I really like the way that in silver halide photography I can raid 150 years of technology and aesthetics. I cropped the bottom ten per cent or so: I wanted to hold the 21/4 Color-Skopar dead level to avoid 'drunken' verticals. Bessa-T, XP-2, MG Warmtone in sulphide, coloured with Zig Pens and Marshall's Hand Coloring Wands*

Thin Red Line

It's silly, really, but somehow, it seems easier to shoot old-fashioned subjects with an old-fashioned (manual, zoom-free) camera – even though this uniform was current decades before the original Leica appeared. M4-P, 90/2 Summicron, HP5 at 500 in DD-X, on MG Warmtone

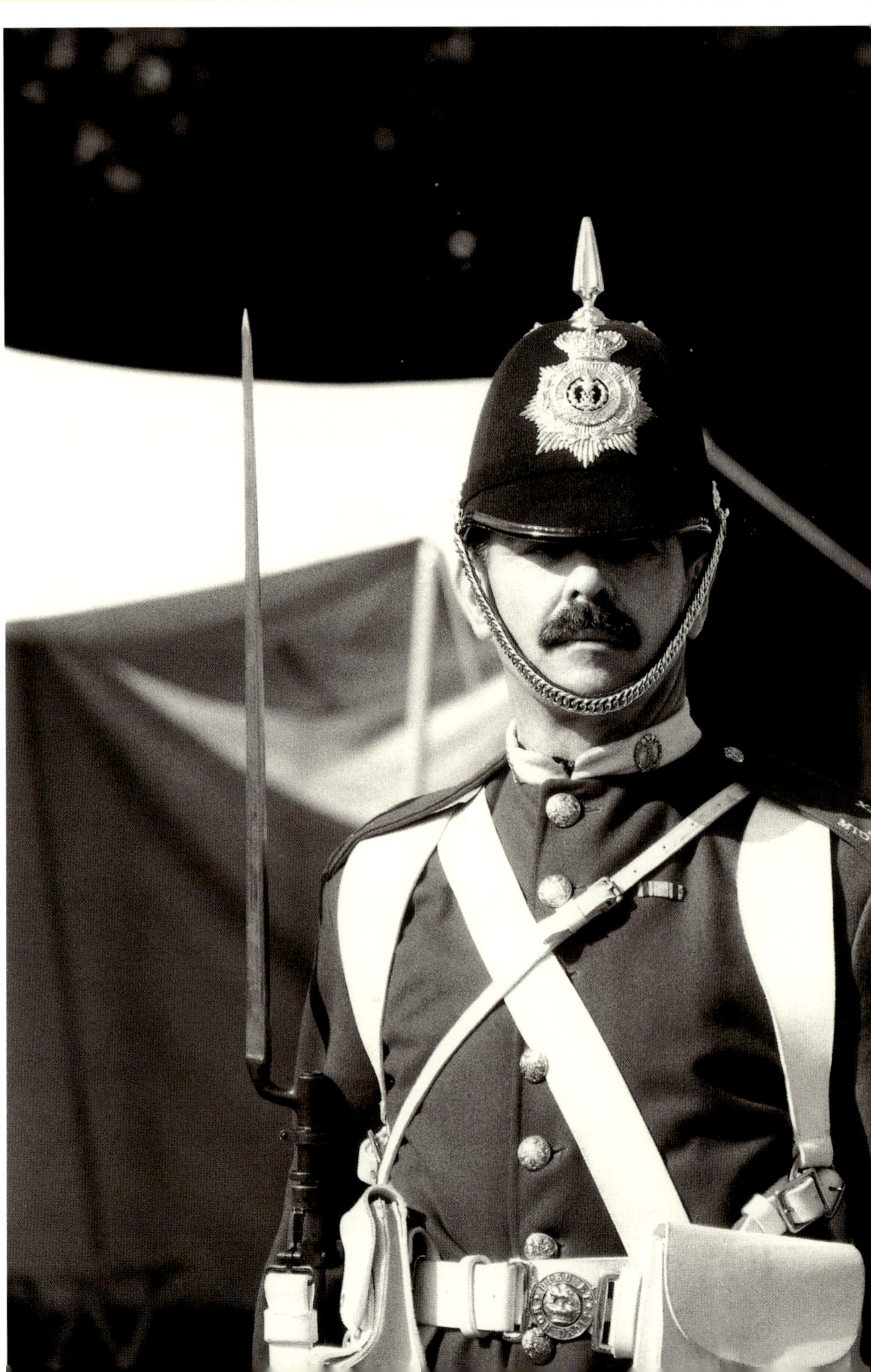

DISADVANTAGES

The non-reflex has two enormous disadvantages over the reflex: parallax, and an inability to work well with long lenses. Lesser disadvantages are that precise framing to the very edge of the picture is more difficult; that different lenses may require supplementary viewfinders; and, though few even think about it, that shift lenses are something of a trial.

Parallax

Parallax – the fact that the viewfinder can never have precisely the same viewpoint as the lens – is obviously of more and more importance as you get closer to the subject. Depending on the focal length, it can safely be ignored at anything above 1½–3m (5–10ft). With a well-designed viewfinder, it can be substantially compensated for down to less than 1m (3ft): the viewfinder frame moves as the lens is focused closer, either automatically or via a manual adjustment. There have been close-focusing devices for RF cameras, down to 30cm (12in) or less, but they are, for the most part, a very inferior alternative to reflex viewing for close-ups.

Supplementary finders (see overleaf) often use a simpler system, with a main bright-line and a supplementary dotted line for the range between 1 and 2m (3 and 6ft).

Long lenses

There are two main problems with long lenses. One is that it is very difficult indeed to make a rangefinder that will couple adequately, especially with long, fast lenses. On a 35mm camera, even a 135/2.8 is pushing things to the limit. Although a 180/2.8 Sonnar was offered for the 1936 Olympics, trying to use a lens of this speed and focal length on an RF camera is foolish in the extreme.

The second objection is that it is difficult to make a convenient viewfinder for long lenses. With a built-in finder, 135mm is inconvenient enough; with an accessory finder, which will almost certainly have a tiny amount of movement in the accessory shoe, it is next to impossible to make one which sits accurately enough for anything much beyond 135mm. In practice, something between 85mm and 105mm is the longest that most people are comfortable using with an RF camera.

Composition

Composition to the edge of the frame is less of a problem than it might appear, not least because most modern SLRs do not have particularly accurate viewfinders. Typically, around 1mm (1/16in) is cropped off on all sides and often the focusing screen is slightly offset vertically or horizontally, or both.

A little-considered problem, though, is the way that the angle of view decreases as a lens is focused closer. This is obviously taken care of with a reflex, but a DV finder must either choose a particular distance at which the viewfinder is strictly accurate, so that it shows a little more at infinity and a little less at 1m (3ft), or build an extremely complex rangefinder in which the field of view diminishes as the lens is focused closer.

As far as we know, only one camera has ever taken the last approach, the Linhof Technika 70, though there have been at least some (fixed-lens) Konicas with an ingenious compromise: the inner and lower bright-lines in the viewfinder remain stationary, while the outer and upper bright-lines move inwards, simultaneously correcting for parallax and reduction in the field of view. There have, however, been zoom accessory finders with two indices: one for infinity and one for 1m (3ft), and we used to have a magisterial Linhof 4 x 5in finder that both tilted and zoomed as the parallax correction was made; it can be seen on top of the Linhof Technika on page 91.

Supplementary viewfinders

Many top-flight RF cameras have switchable, parallax-compensated bright-line finders for several focal lengths. Most current Leicas, for example, provide six as three pairs (28/90, 35/135 and 50/75), while the Bessa-R and R2 offer 35/90 as a pair, plus individual settings for 50 and 75. Other lenses require separate finders, which vary widely in size, weight, bulk and accuracy. For example, we have separate finders for 15mm, 21mm, 28mm, 35mm and 90mm, plus an old Tewe 'zoom' finder for 35–200mm.

Most other cameras have only one finder (usually 50mm or 35mm), while a few have no finder at all: all lenses require supplementary finders. Examples include some Leica I-series, the Reid I-series, and the Voigtländer Bessa-L and Bessa-T.

A very few use interchangeable masks or front components on the viewfinder. Alpas, for example, have masks that are matched to the range of lenses available (principally 35mm, 38mm, 47mm, 58mm) and the formats (66 x 44mm, 6 x 6cm, 6 x 7cm, 6 x 8cm, 6 x 9cm). There is more about accessory viewfinders in Chapter 7, Accessories.

Shift lenses

With shift lenses, surprisingly accurate composition is possible with a little guesswork, even with a conventional viewfinder. There is more about this in Chapter 7. A very few cameras offer 'shift' finders: one Linhof has a permanent shift built in, the finder on the Corfield WA67 moves, and Alpa offers special viewfinder masks with gradations corresponding to the degree of shift.

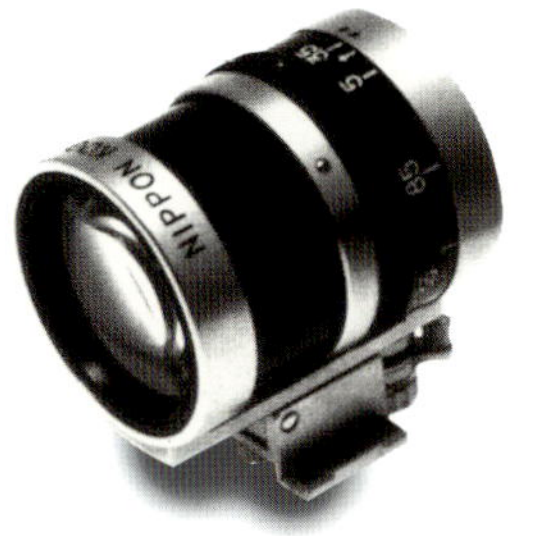
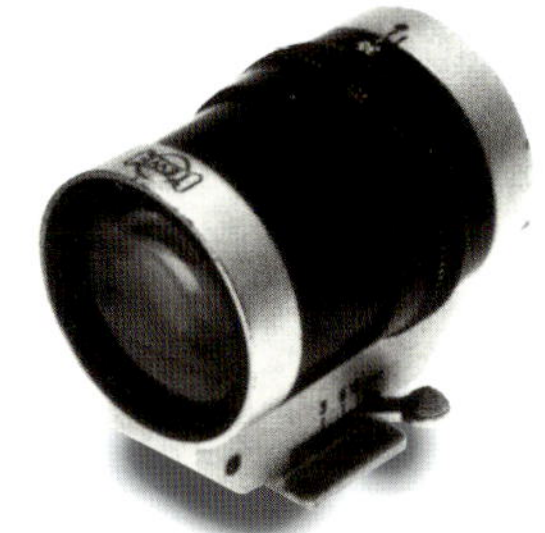

Convergent evolution? Nikon's zoom finder (left), next to a Tewe

DO YOU NEED AN RF/DV CAMERA?

There are some things that a DV camera cannot do. If you want anything longer than a short tele lens, they are not for you. If close-up and macro figure large in your work, you will certainly do better with a reflex – though you can convert some DV cameras into reflexes with mirror housings (see page 132), and many medium-format and most large-format DV cameras can also be used with a ground glass.

But there are some things that RF/DV cameras do sublimely well. Reportage is the classic example, but if you want to shoot landscapes or travel, there is a great deal to be said for light, easily carried DV cameras. And when it comes to ultra-wides, for whatever application, they are hard to beat.

There is also the point that old fixed-lens leaf-shutter RF cameras from the 1960s and 1970s can still deliver quality comparable with current, state-of-the-art reflexes, but at prices which make them all but disposable. If you want to go anywhere that there is any danger of being mugged or of having your camera damaged, a cheap RF could be the obvious answer.

Nor should you forget formats that are larger than 35mm. In all honesty we cannot, with a clear conscience, recommend such legendary folders as the Super Ikonta – there is more about why on page 30 – but there are plenty of others we can recommend. After all, why do you suppose that press photographers used to shoot everything on 4 x 5in? The simple answer is that it was very hard to get a picture that was so technically inadequate that it wouldn't print.

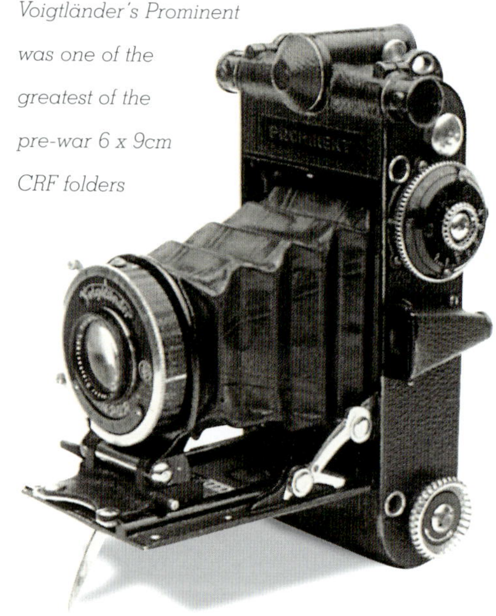

Voigtländer's Prominent was one of the greatest of the pre-war 6 x 9cm CRF folders

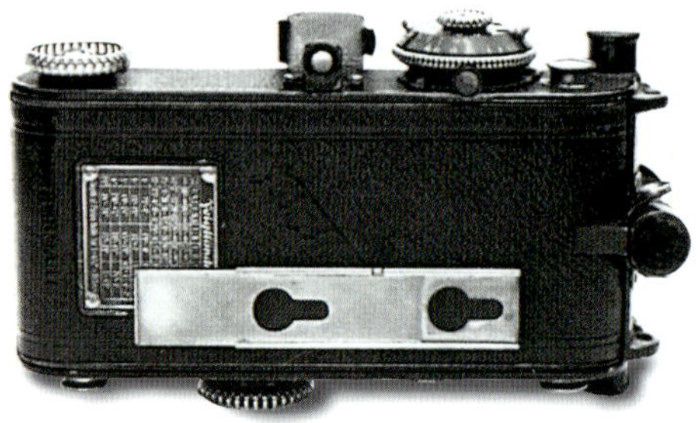

The back of the Prominent, showing the red-window dual-format film advance

And, of course, there is that indescribable mystique: the sense
of being a part of a history that stretches back for more than
three-quarters of a century; the chance to join a lineage that
includes Erich Salomon, Henri Cartier-Bresson, Eugene Smith,
and countless more – even Weegee the Famous, because,
after all, the 4 x 5in Speed Graphic is a rangefinder camera.
If that doesn't stir your blood – well, maybe there's not enough
of the artist in your soul for you to be a photographer anyway.

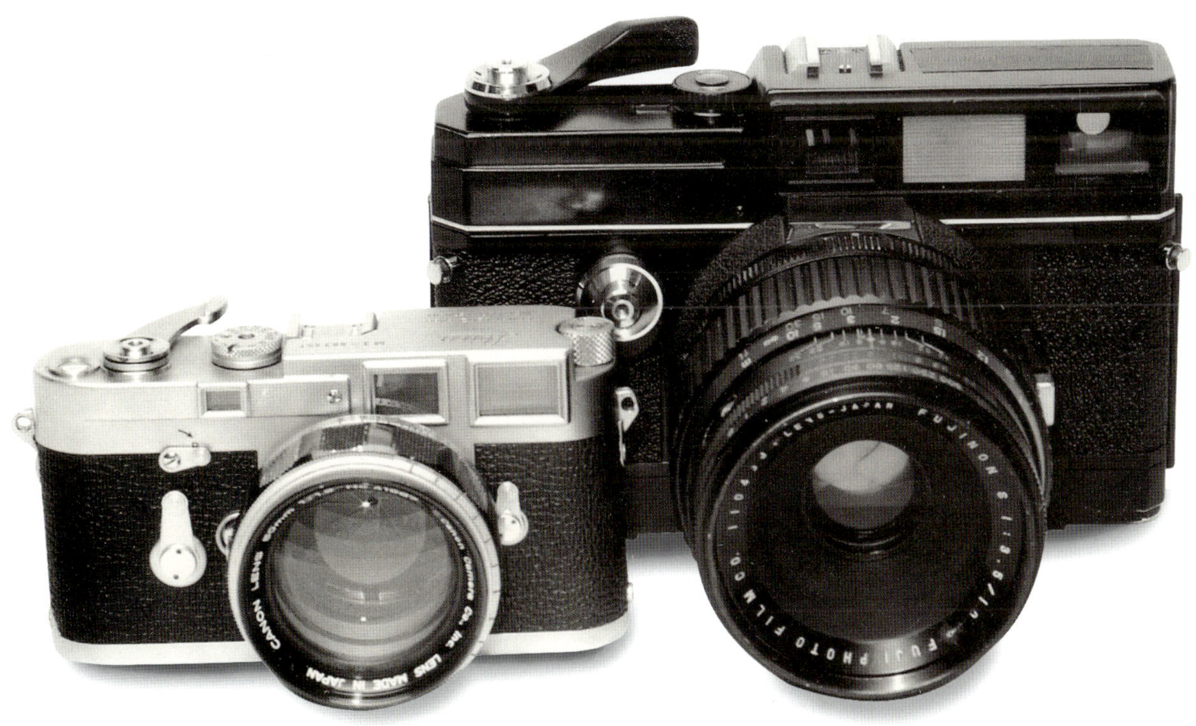

*The 'Texas Leica' (Fuji
690) next to a real
M-series for comparison*

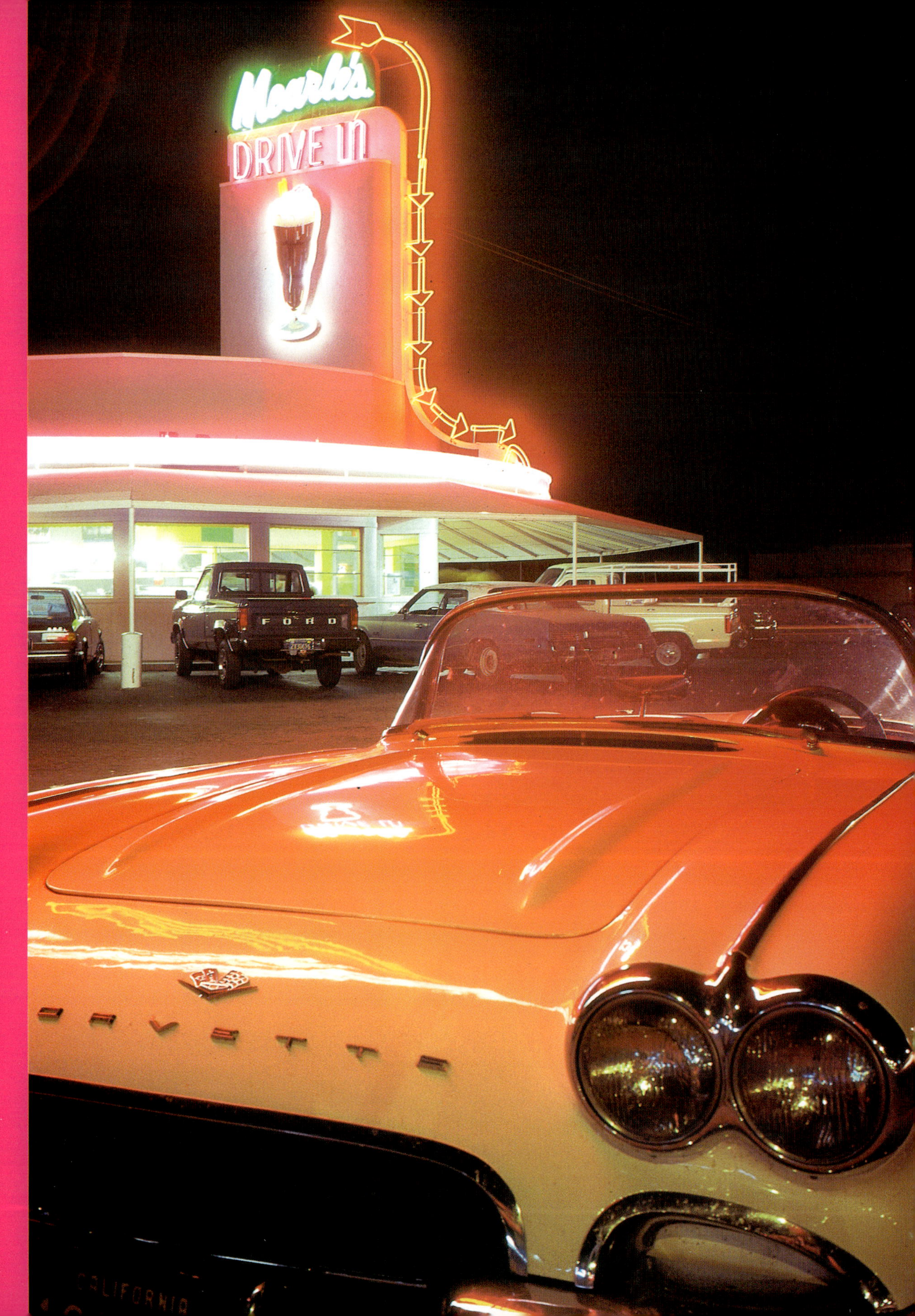
Mearle's
DRIVE IN
CORVETTE
CALIFORNIA

A BRIEF HISTORY

Rangefinders were devised in the nineteenth century, principally for artillery ranging. They were huge, typically with a rangefinder base about a yard (90cm) long. The first camera with a coupled RF (CRF) was the Kodak Autographic 3A of 1916; the first 35mm CRF cameras appeared in 1932, the Leica II in February, the Contax a little later.

On most early RF cameras, the CRF was separate from the viewfinder – sometimes all too separate, to the detriment of ease of use. But the best were very good: a separate RF can easily be magnified, which makes it much easier to see exactly when the images fuse, and it is also easier to incorporate dioptric eyesight compensation. The only modern separate-RF camera; the Voigtländer Bessa-T, is unexpectedly easy to use.

There have also been a few cameras with built-in but uncoupled rangefinders: you measure the distance with the RF, then transfer the setting to the lens. Then there have been even fewer where the rangefinder is coupled to the standard lens, but readings have to be transferred when you change lenses. And, of course, there have been plenty of accessory, non-coupled rangefinders.

Direct-vision cameras, without rangefinders, date back to the dawn of photography. The simplest 'viewfinders' were no more than sighting lines inscribed or impressed on the camera body, or three pins to give a rough idea of the angle of view. These were found on the original Kodak and, intriguingly, are still found on the Robert Rigby pinhole cameras of today. There is a lot more about finders in Chapter 7.

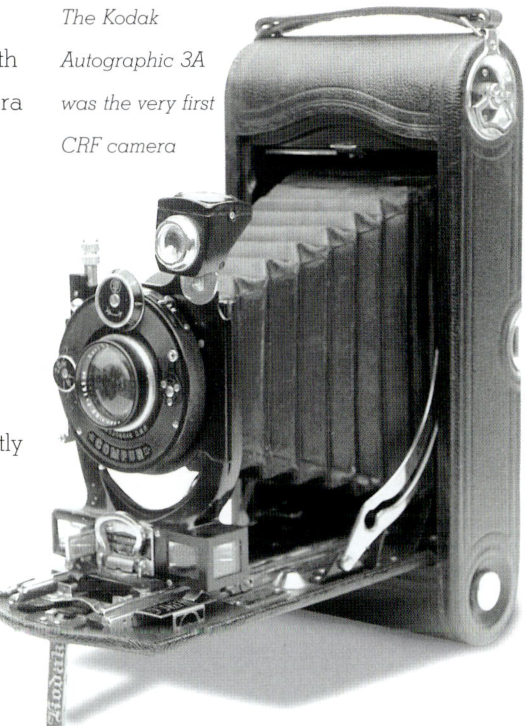

The Kodak Autographic 3A was the very first CRF camera

The rangefinder of the Autographic 3A was extremely inconvenient, set at the base of the front standard

Corvette

This is a glorious mishmash of ancient and modern. In the early 1990s I used my 1960s M2 with a 1950s Zeiss Biogon 21/4.5 to shoot this classic late 1950s/early 1960s scene of a 'Vette outside a diner. Shooting on Kodachrome (introduced in 1936) added another historical dimension

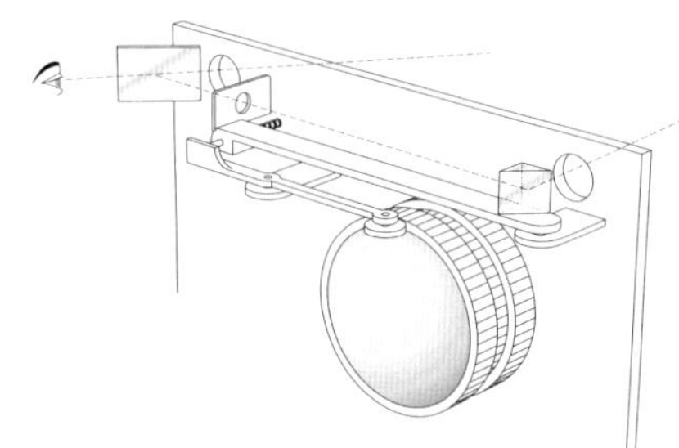

Figure 1.1

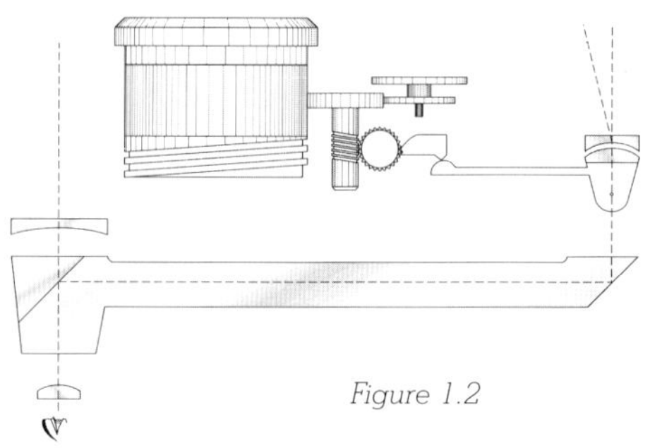

Figure 1.2

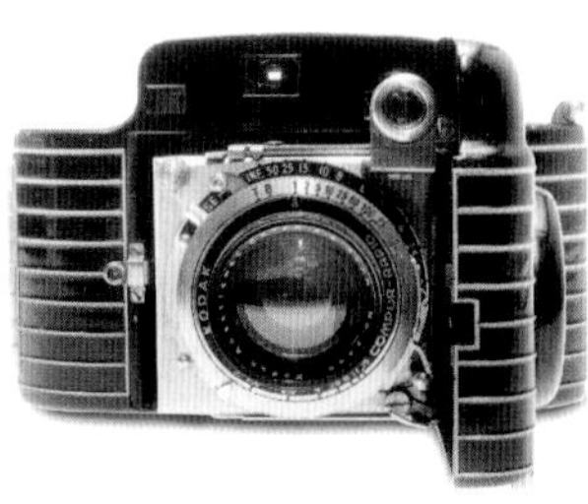

Kodak's Bantam Special looks gorgeous, but was designed for Kodak's 828 'Bantam' roll film

Art deco architecture, Pecs

In colour, modern lenses deliver better contrast and saturation, though of course, there is nothing to stop you putting new lenses, such as the screw-fit 90/3.5 Apo-Lanthar that I used for this shot, onto significantly older cameras. Bessa-R, EBX

RANGEFINDER DESIGNS

The sheer variety of ways that have been devised to build a rangefinder is amazing. The simplest is the swinging-mirror (or swinging-prism) viewfinder, as employed on the original Leica. This works by reflection (see Fig. 1.1). The Autographic 3A used a completely different principle, with a moving wedge, and rotating-wedge and swinging-wedge rangefinders were always preferred by Zeiss. These work by refraction: a block of optical glass is split in two, and the two parts can be moved relative to one another so that the parallelism of the front and rear surfaces is destroyed and the image is displaced. In the swinging-wedge type illustrated, the wedge is on the extreme right (see Fig. 1.2). As the front component swings, the image is displaced. This is a Kiev, a direct copy of the Contax. Rotating-wedge finders use a similar principle, with two contra-rotating circular wedges. Then there was the Bantam Special, which employed a sort of double telescope, and moved one of the objectives.

In a coincidence rangefinder, two identical images are superimposed, one on the other. With a split-image rangefinder, any convenient line can be used as a reference, and when it is continuous, the image is in focus. Most rangefinders have an image patch in the middle, so they can be used either coincident or split-image, but for many years, beginning in the 1930s, Agfa split the entire viewfinder.

Rangefinders with clear, bright, hard-edged rectangular patches are easiest to use, and this is what most (though far from all) RF cameras of the last two or three decades have offered. Circular patches are almost as good, though the lozenge-shaped patch in a Retina is a poor third. But even a fuzzy-edged RF patch (as on the Zorkii) can be surprisingly easy to use, both as split-image and as coincident.

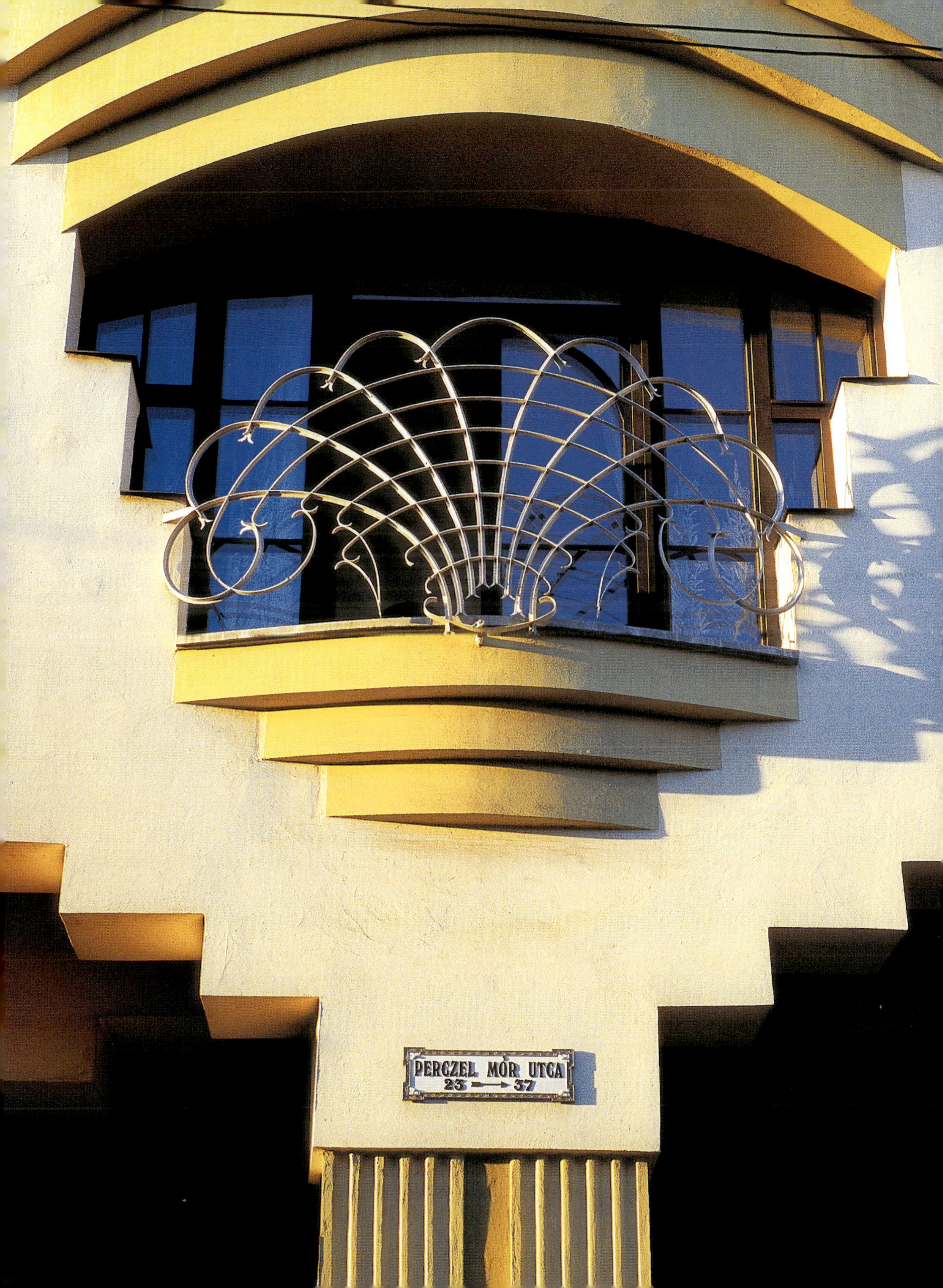
PERCZEL MÓR UTCA
23 ⟶ 37

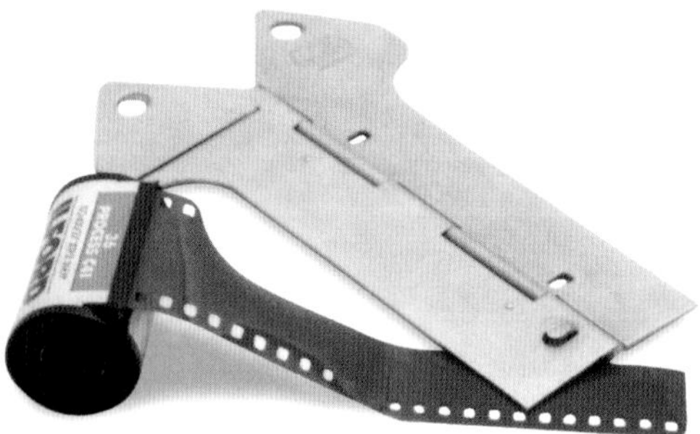

The Leica Nullserie was a pre-production run designed to test the concept of 35mm

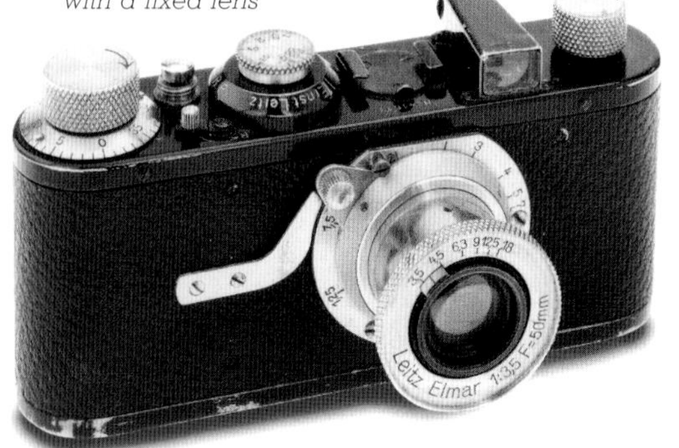

Film for old Leicas must be trimmed with an extra-long leader

The Leica A was the first production Leica, with a fixed lens

THE SCREW LEICA FAMILY

It may seem that we have devoted a disproportionate amount of space to screw-mount Leicas, production of which ceased in 1960, but there is a good reason for this. They are in many ways the camera that popularized the CRF and made the 35mm RF camera a legend; there are an awful lot of them around – and they are frequently misadvertised because non-aficionados cannot tell them apart. On the one hand, this raises the possibility of buying rare and extremely valuable cameras for a song, though this is ever less easy nowadays. And on the other, it raises the possibility of paying far too much for a camera that is described as 'rare and collectable' when it's nothing unusual.

Although they are very usable cameras, screw Leicas fit best in this chapter because they tend to be worth more to a collector than to a user. If you want to use one, do – Roger uses his 1936 IIIa to this day – but always be aware that without the sentimental or historical dimension, you might well do better with something cheaper and more modern.

If you decide to use one, always cut a film leader with a long tongue, as illustrated. Modern short-tongue films may cause loading difficulties, including (in the worst case) film chips that break off the leader and get loose in the works. The shape of the leader is not very critical, but you do need about 10cm (4in) of film cut to about half its width. All screw Leicas, of course, load through the base.

The original Model A production Leica of the 1920s had no RF and a simple reverse-Galilean finder; a rangefinder was available as an accessory. The shutter was speeded from 1/20 of a second to 1/500 and the lens was initially fixed, though interchangeable lenses were available unofficially in the late

1920s and from the factory from 1930. The actual dimensions of the now-classic Leica screw thread, as introduced in 1930, are 39mm diameter x 26tpi (turns per inch), not 39 x 1mm as is often reported.

On the very earliest interchangeable-lens Leicas, lenses were matched to individual bodies: the last three digits of the camera serial number were engraved on the lenses. After a few months, the film-to-flange distance was standardized at 28.80mm and an 'O' was engraved on the lens flange. These were known as the Model C, or Leica Standard or Leica I.

The Leica II (Leica D in the United States) was introduced in 1932, essentially a I with a CRF on top. The RF window was about 2cm (⅘in) to the left of the viewfinder, a layout followed in the 1933 III or Leica F (a II with slow speeds from 1 to 1/20) and the 1935 IIIa or Leica G (a III with a top speed of 1/1000 instead of 1/500). This I – II – III classification is the key to all later Leicas: I-series have no RF, II-series have an RF but no slow speeds, and III-series have an RF and slow speeds.

The 1938 IIIb was a transitional model, with the two eyepieces (rangefinder and viewfinder) much closer together, but still with a fabricated shutter crate similar to the earlier models. In 1940, the IIIc appeared with a much superior die-cast chassis: film-to-flange tolerance was halved from 0.05mm to 0.025mm, and the likelihood of this being maintained under the hurly-burly of general use was much increased.

Production of the IIIc continued after the war, but it was supplanted by the 1950 IIIf, effectively a IIIc synchronized for flash. Early models had a black synch dial (IIIf BD), while later versions had a red dial (IIIf RD). Then there is the IIIf RD DA with self timer (DA = Delayed Action). The last screw-mount

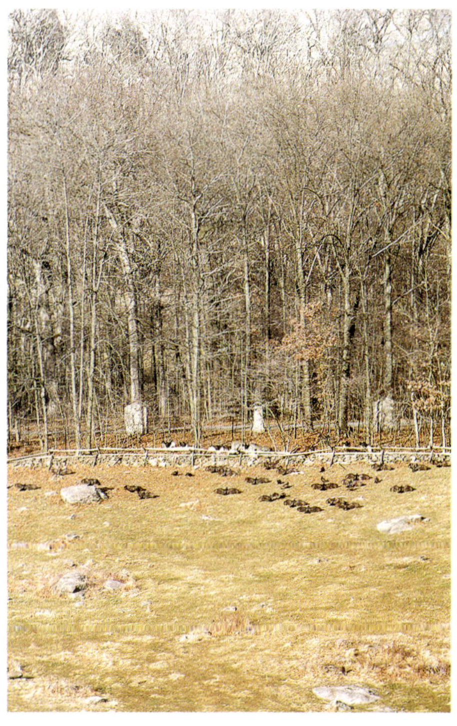

Buzzards

OK, it's not the most beautiful picture in the world, but it was taken with a 400/5 Telyt on a Visoflex III. These buzzards are sunning themselves in the rising sun. This suddenly becomes rather chilling when you know that it was taken at Gettysburg, the great Civil War battlefield. Think of the buzzards on the day after that battle... Leica M2, Kodachrome 64

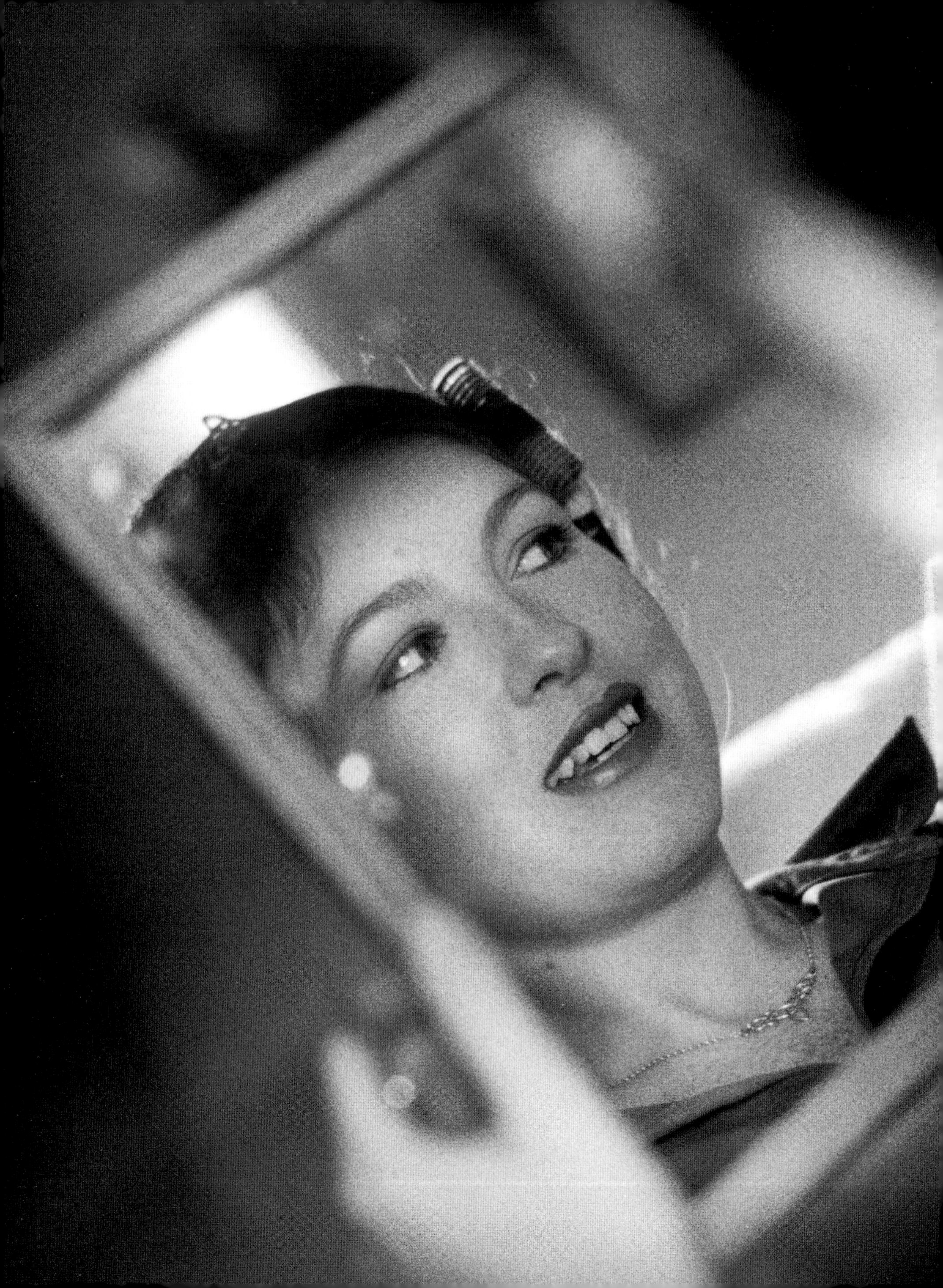

Leica, the IIIg, appeared in 1956 with parallax-compensated bright-line finders for both 50mm and 90mm (all previous models were reverse-Galilean).

For the user, the IIIc is probably the best bet. Many thousands were made and, as already noted, they were more robust than earlier models. Even so, a III, IIIa or IIIb can be an affordable, usable camera. A IIIf tends to be more expensive, and a IIIg is so expensive that it is best left to the collectors.

The II-series tend to cost more than the III-series because they are less common. Even so, there were 11,000 IIc cameras made, so they should be affordable too. There never were IIa or IIb models. And although plenty of IIf cameras were made (27,000 RD alone), they don't seem to come up as often as they should. The IIg was only ever a prototype, though some Ig cameras were reputedly converted. On all screw Leicas the slow speeds (1 second to 1/20 of a second or 1/30) are set by a separate slow-speed dial on the front, which can also be added to I or II models.

The I-series is very much a camera for the purist. They existed as I, Ic, If and Ig only: no Ia, and if you think about it, there couldn't be a Ib. Although there were plenty of If models (well over 20,000 were made), they seem not to turn up as often as one might expect. The Ig not only basks in the reflected glory of the IIIg, but also has a slow-speed train as standard.

There are many rare and expensive variants among early Leicas. Among fixed-lens cameras, for example, the very earliest models have f/3.5 Elmax lenses, not f/3.5 Elmars; a few have lenses in Compur shutters, which was a way of getting slow speeds in the early days (this is the Model B, if you noted the gap between A and C above); about 1000 have

The photographer was more nervous than the bride! This was the first 'real' (unrepeatable) shoot I did with the Bessa-R. When I first went through the contact sheets I didn't even notice it – but when I did notice it, I loved it. 50/1.5 Nokton, Delta 3200 at 3200 in DD-X, on MG WT selenium-toned

the faster f/2.5 Hektor; there is the oft-faked gold-plated Luxus, with lizard-skin body covering; and the Ig Special has no synch, shoes, lugs or slow speeds.

Otherwise, there are grey 'Lufwaffe' finishes, mostly on IIIc cameras; red (wartime) blinds; 250-exposure models, with bulbous film chambers; the very rare IIId, also known as a IIIc DA; half-frame versions of the IIIa; black Swedish If and IIIf cameras engraved with three crowns; Post Office instrument recording versions, often 24 x 27mm format with fixed lenses; presentation cameras, typically with memorable numbers (e.g. 25,000, Sven Hedin; 150,000 and 175,000, Godowsky and Mannes of Kodachrome fame; 375,000, Erwin Rommel; 555,555, HH Dalai Lama) and numerous more.

Many have been faked: several fake IIId cameras exist, including an 'Afrika Korps' IIId, finished in khaki/sand paint, made by the late George Carr in the 1970s.

Screw Leica derivatives

Many, many cameras were made that used the Leica 39mm x 26tpi lens mount, right up to the Voigtländer Bessa series that was in large measure responsible for the genesis of this book. Some are almost exact copies of the Leica and of comparable quality: first among these is the British-made Reid.

Others look similar, but were built nothing like as well: early Feds from the Soviet Union are an excellent example. Yet others share next to nothing with the Leica except the lens mount: the Corfield Periflex, with its strange periscopic reflex focusing (hence Peri-flex), is about as far as you can get from a Leica and still trace the ancestry. Then there's the Leningrad (1958) with its built-in clockwork (but sprocketless) motordrive, multiframe finder, and Leica-fit lenses.

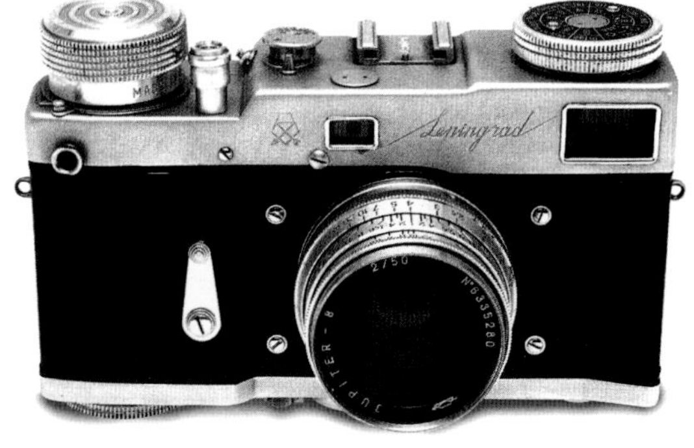

The Leningrad took Leica screw-fit lenses and had a built-in spring-driven film advance

A few Leica derivatives are arguably improvements on contemporary Leicas, and of these the most famous came from Canon. The original 1935 Kwanon did not share the Leica screw mount, but after about 1942 they switched to 39mm x 26tpi. The greatest Canons were the VT, with a built-in trigger base wind, or the selenium-metered 7 and CdS-metered 7s of the late 1950s and early 1960s. Many reckon that the 7 and 7s, with multi-frame parallax-compensated bright-line finders and conventional opening backs (unlike the Leica's base off-loading), were the finest screw-mount cameras ever made. Even today, if you can afford one, they are superb.

Most others are best left to collectors, if only because you can buy yourself anything from a new Voigtländer to a new M-series Leica for the same money: the Ilford Witness, the American Kardon, the Czech Meopta, the Japanese Leotax, Minolta, Nikka and Yashica YF, and more. Getting these old cameras repaired can be fun too.

THE CONTAX FAMILY

The original Contax I (right) was introduced in the spring of 1932. It was a curious, blocky, black beast with the shutter-speed dial on the front of the camera, concentric with the film wind. The earliest models had no slow speeds, but by 1933 they managed to add a slow-speed train down to 1/2 a second.

In 1936 the camera was completely redesigned as the II, with the shutter-speed dial on top, still concentric with the wind-on. It was also a true single-speed dial, instead of using two separate settings (range and speed), as on the I. The III, launched at the same time, was a II with a built-in meter. The IIa (1950) and IIIa (1952) were lighter, more modern versions of the II and III. They ceased production in 1961.

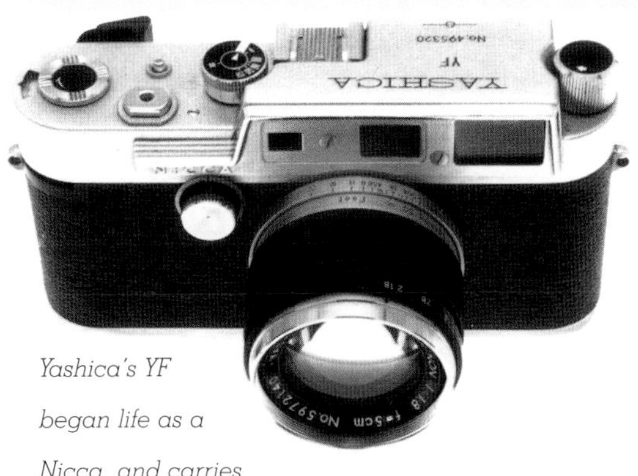

Yashica's YF began life as a Nicca, and carries both names

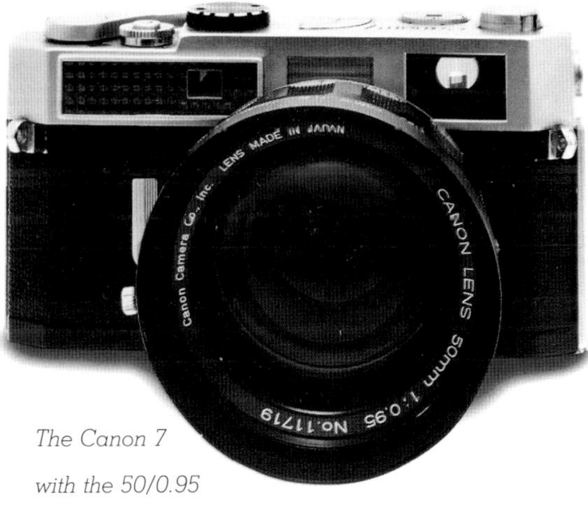

The Canon 7 with the 50/0.95 was often known as the 'Canon Dream'

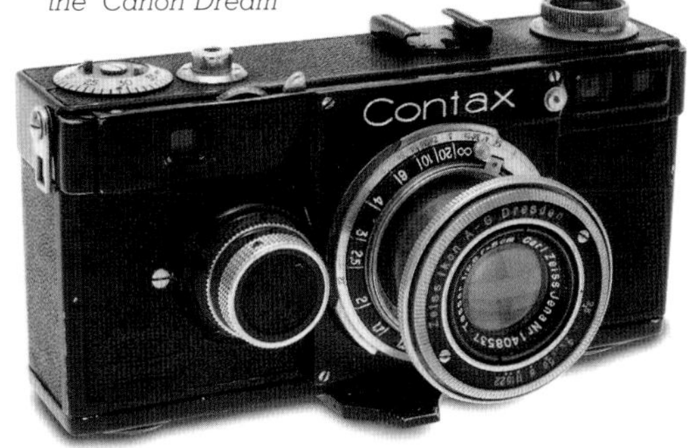

The Contax I was a blocky, black beast with appalling ergonomics

The trouble is that classic Contaxes are wilfully complicated. There are two lens mounts; focusing controls for the standard lens are incorporated in the body; the linkages are fantastically complex, compared with the simple Leica arrangement; and the shutter resembles nothing so much as a roll-top desk made of brass slats.

Only 50mm lenses go in the inner bayonet: all others go on the outer bayonet. The lens throat is a mere 34mm; this limits the range of lens designs, though less than you might expect. If classic Contaxes go wrong, they can be difficult or impossible to repair, so they are best left to collectors. Also, although the lenses were great in their day, few can stand comparison with modern lenses.

Contax derivatives

Two major systems shared the Contax lens mount and some or all of its other features: Nikon and Kiev. A third, from Voigtländer, was launched when this book was at proof stage, but details came out too late for the camera to be incorporated. Because these are all usable cameras they are covered in the next chapter.

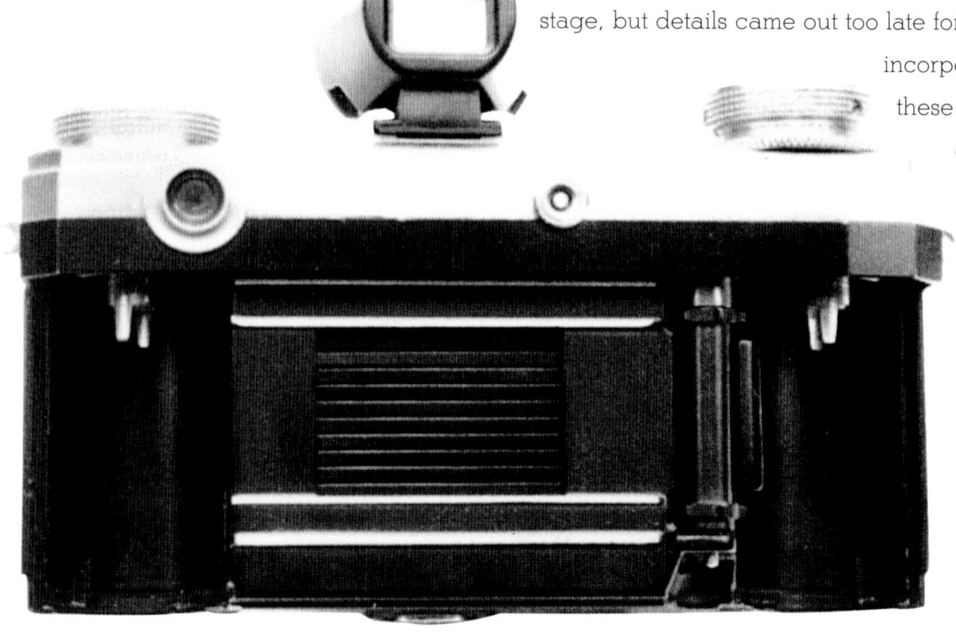

The famous (or infamous) 'roll-top desk' that was the Contax shutter

OTHER 'SYSTEM' 35MM CAMERAS

Most other 'system' CRF 35mm cameras from the past are
either staggeringly rare (and often equally
staggeringly expensive) or are simply not very good.
The principal exceptions are covered below or in
the next chapter.

Among the rare-but-great cameras, the Swiss-
made Alpa is wondrous as a combination SLR
and CRF. Prototypes were built in about 1942,
but the first production cameras seem to have
appeared in 1946 (the Alpax), followed by three more models
in 1949: Alitax, Alpa 3 Prisma Reflex, Alpa Primitax. The Alpa
7 (1951) and 8 (1957) were rangefinder equipped; the 8b,
with lever wind and instant-return mirror (1959) seems to have
been the last combination CRF-SLR.

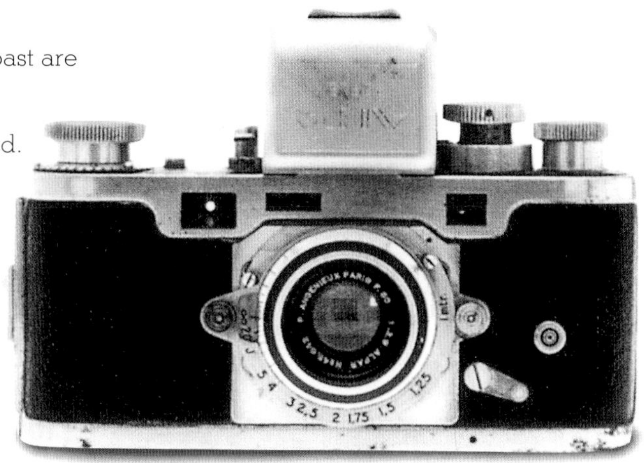

*Early Alpas were
remarkable for
offering both CRF
and reflex focusing*

Kodak's Ektra and Bell and Howell's Foton were beautiful, but
extremely rare. The former was killed by appearing at an
inauspicious time (1941), as well as by price, the latter mainly
by costing $475 (about £307) on its appearance in 1948,
maybe $100 (around £65) more than a Leica IIIf. The Munich-
built Steinheil Casca, circa1949, was very good, with its own
unique bayonet lens fitting, but fewer than 2000 were made.

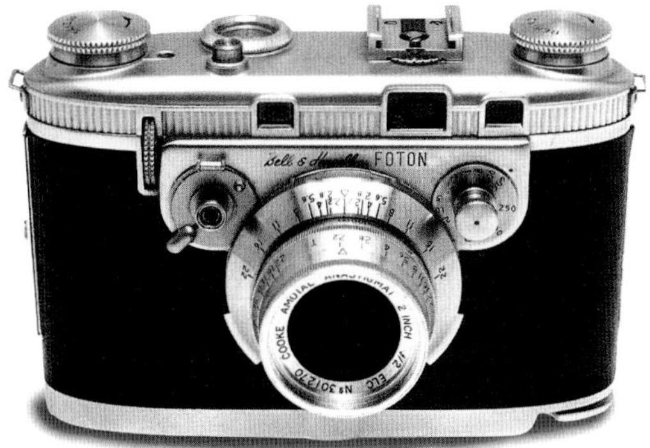

*The Bell and Howell
Foton was too
expensive to sell well*

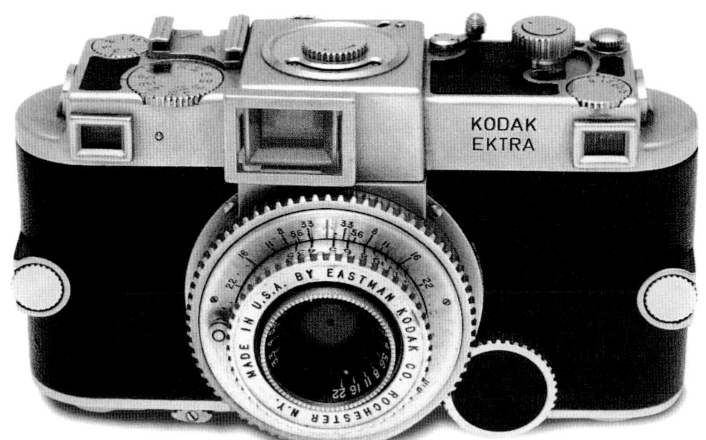

*Introducing the Kodak
Ektra early in WWII
did nothing for the
marketing plan*

Xaghra Mill, Gozo

In the 1930s, 28mm was ultra-wide. In the '50s, 21mm was ultra-wide. In the early '70s, the 16mm Hologon was greeted with amazement. This was taken at the beginning of the twenty-first century with a 12/5.6 Ultra-Wide-Heliar, which is close to the theoretical limit for wide-angle lenses. Leica M4-P, Fuji Acros at 50 in DD-X, on MG IV

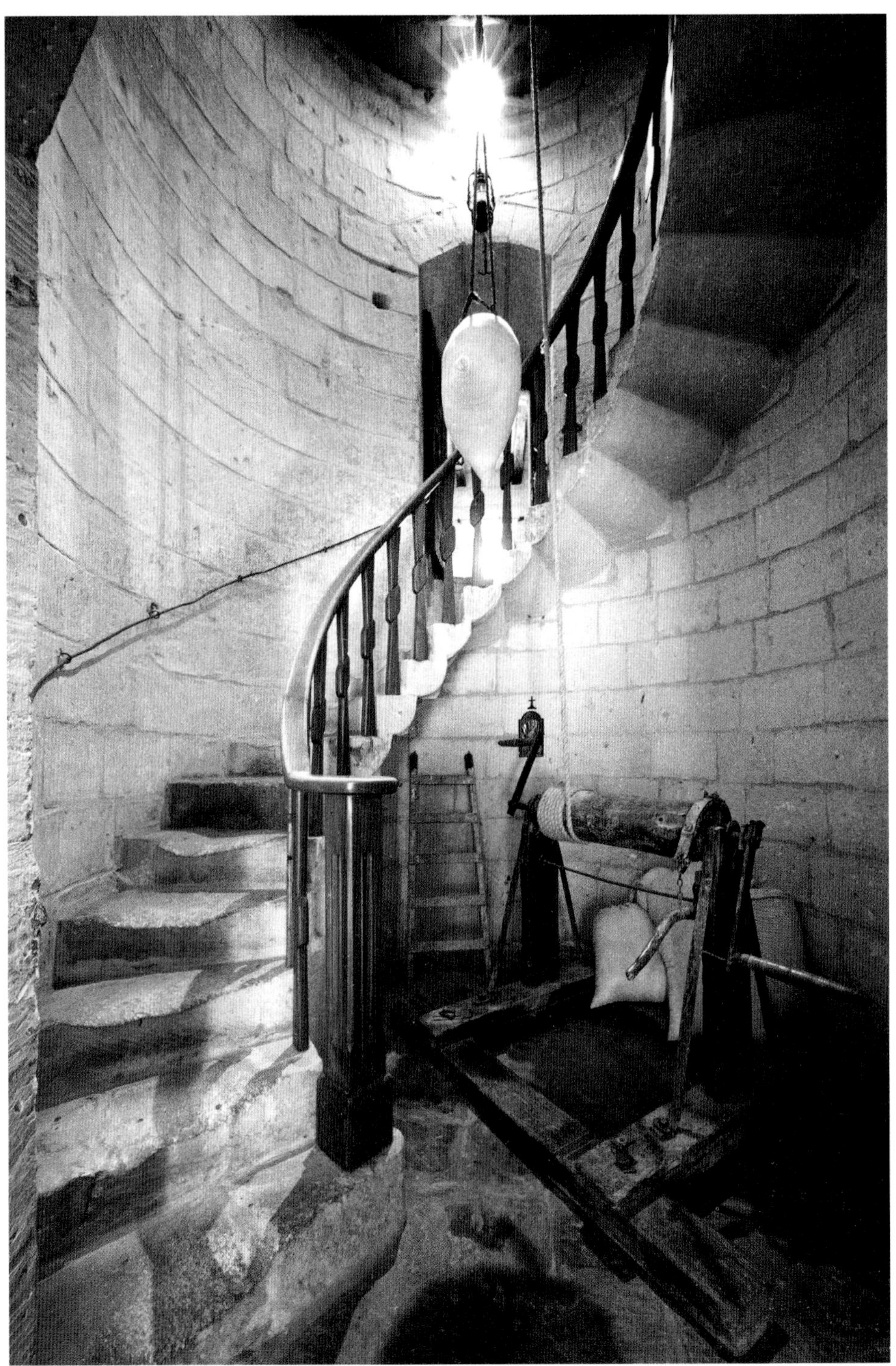

Zeiss's Nettax (mid-1930s) had a rotating wedge for
the rangefinder built into each interchangeable lens,
while the leaf-shutter German Akarex from the early
1950s had separate range/viewfinders built into each
of its three lenses. The Voigtländer Vitessa T was a
rigid-bodied derivative of the original 1952 'bomb
doors' Vitessa (see page 169) with good but slow lenses; the
'bomb doors' was obtainable with the much more desirable
Ultron f/2 and is more compact to boot.

Kodak's interchangeable-lens Retinas were, likewise, derived
from fixed-lens cameras, and again are better in fixed-lens
form, but they are more usefully covered in
the next chapter.

The lenses for the late-1950s Agfa Ambi Silette were good but
slow, and the parallax-compensated bright-line finder was
very good, so this is a fairly affordable classic. Some
Werras from East Germany had interchangeable lenses,
but they are rare. And although interchangeable lenses
were promised for the rather eccentric American-
made Mercury half-frame, we have never seen one.
Finettas were just plain nasty and Paxettes were only
slightly less so.

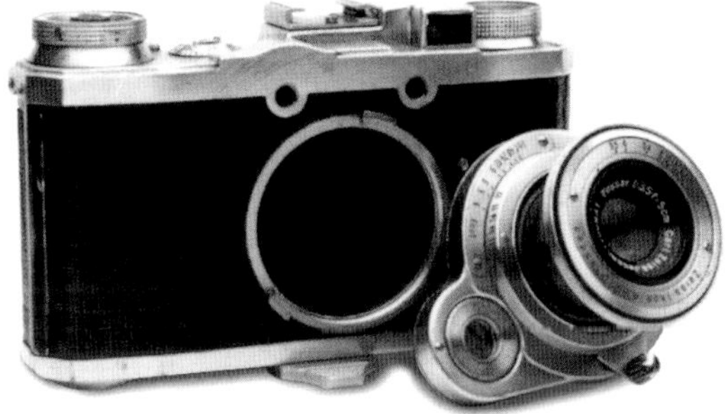

*In the 1930s, Zeiss
made a bewildering
range of 35mm RF
cameras: this is a
Nettax*

*The front rangefinder
element of the Nettax
was incorporated in
the interchangeable
lenses*

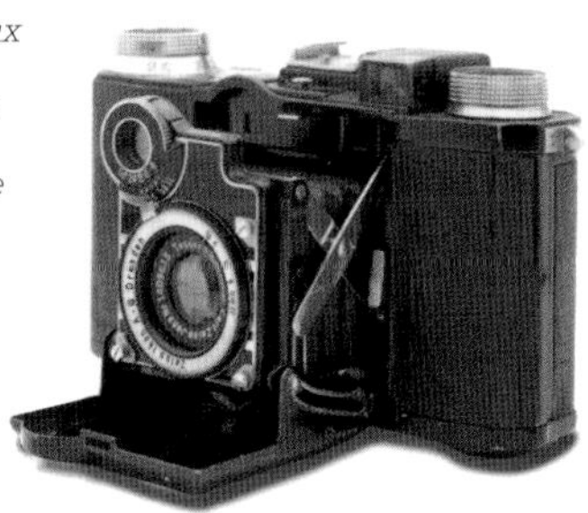

*That the Super Nettel
is related to the
Nettax is clear*

*The American-built
half-frame Mercury
had an improbable
rotary shutter*

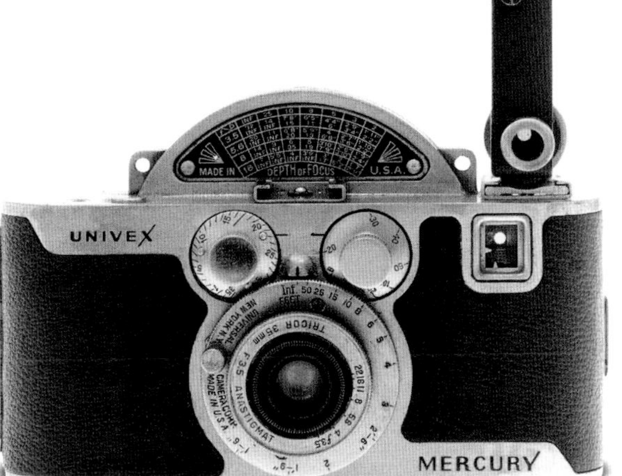

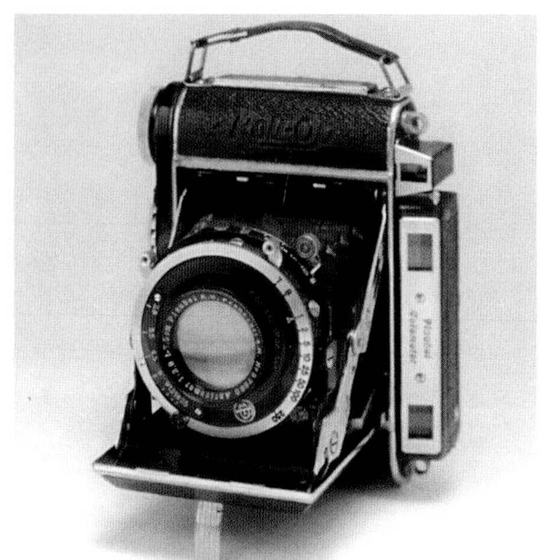

FIXED-LENS 35MM

A convenient breakpoint between 'ancient' and 'modern' fixed-lens cameras is the adoption of lens coating – and this is pretty much the breakpoint between collectable cameras (mostly pre-WWII) and usable cameras. To be sure, you can use older cameras with uncoated lenses, and in black and white you can get good results; but the cameras are likely to be worth a great deal more to a collector than to a user, so for our money there is not a lot of point except to satisfy your curiosity. We confess to putting films through several of the 'collector' cameras featured in these pages, such as the Krauss Peggy. But we would not pretend that even so excellent a camera as the Peggy could seriously compete with a post-war camera costing perhaps a tenth as much.

ROLL FILM

We are great believers in old roll-film RF and DV cameras, though not, perhaps, in the ones that most people expect. Roll-film folders were often distinctly rickety when they were new, with poor lens/film alignment, and the passage of a few decades will not have improved them. Also, many have been haphazardly repaired, often to the further detriment of alignment, and in many cases to the point where the lens is grievously mis-spaced. In our experience, even such legends as the Zeiss Super Ikonta are trouble more often than not, and lesser cameras can be a lot worse.

The uncoated lens on this Roll-Op from Plaubel means it is best left to collectors

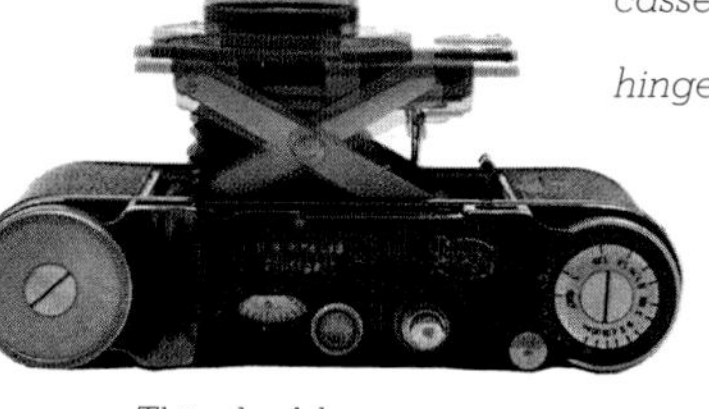

The Krauss Peggy was killed by incompatibility with Kodak cassettes

Inside the Peggy you can see the unusual cassettes and the hinged pressure plate

This double exposure shows how the focusing works on a 'doppel-klapp' camera

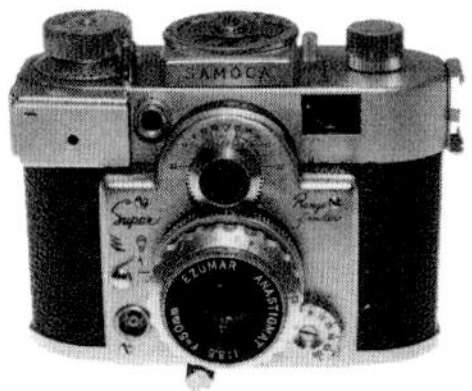

Small and light, but hardly uncomplicated: the Samoca

Zeiss's Super Ikonta is a legend, but in our opinion, overrated

Paradoxically, the best results often come from more modest folding cameras, because they have been less heavily used and are less likely to have been (badly) repaired. We would rather have a plain (non-rangefinder, that is, non-Super) 6 x 6cm Ikonta than a top-of-the-line 6 x 9cm Super Ikonta for this very reason. And we have never yet had a Plaubel Makina (the original Frankfurt model, not the Japanese version) that we would trust.

Once again, there are plenty of cameras from the 1950s onwards that we are happy to use, and these are covered at greater length in Chapter 4.

LARGE FORMAT

Most handholdable 4 x 5in and 9 x 12cm cameras from the past were made in relatively small numbers (such as the British-built Dawe) or used single-sheet 9 x 12cm plate-holders that were only semi-standardized and are both hard to find and inconvenient to use today: the VN 9 x 12 is a good example. There were also some lovely quarter-plate (3¼ x 4¼in, 83 x 108mm) press cameras, mostly in the United States, but quarter-plate film is hard to find today.

There are plenty of very old 'hand and stand' cameras (so-called because they could be used handheld or on a tripod), but most use non-standard or semi-standardized film holders. They are not really common enough or easily usable enough to be worth bothering with here. Many, too, are quarter-plate. But yet again, from the 1950s onwards there are several cameras that are readily available at an affordable price and readily usable. Some of these are covered in Chapter 4.

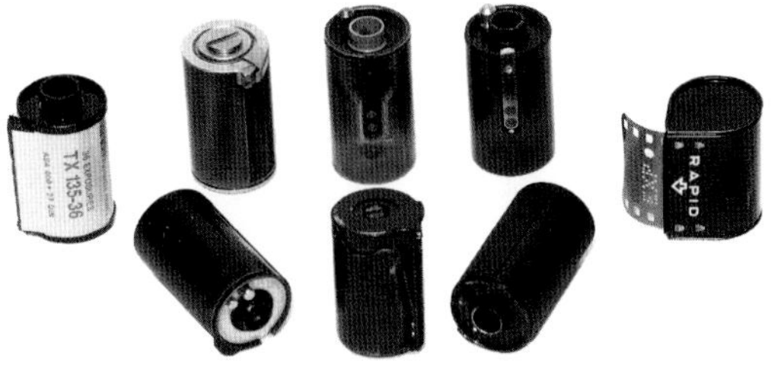

Cassettes, top L to R: Kodak, Shirley Wellard, early Leica, late Leica, Agfa Rapid. Bottom: Kiev (Contax type), Robot, Nikon

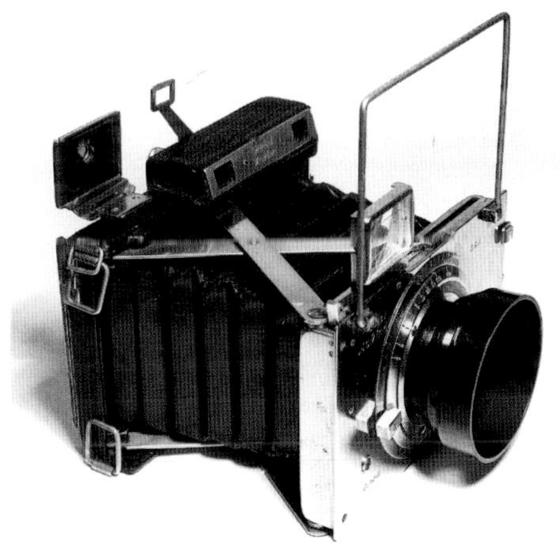

Plaubel's original Makina ran from the 1930s to the early 1960s but has not worn well

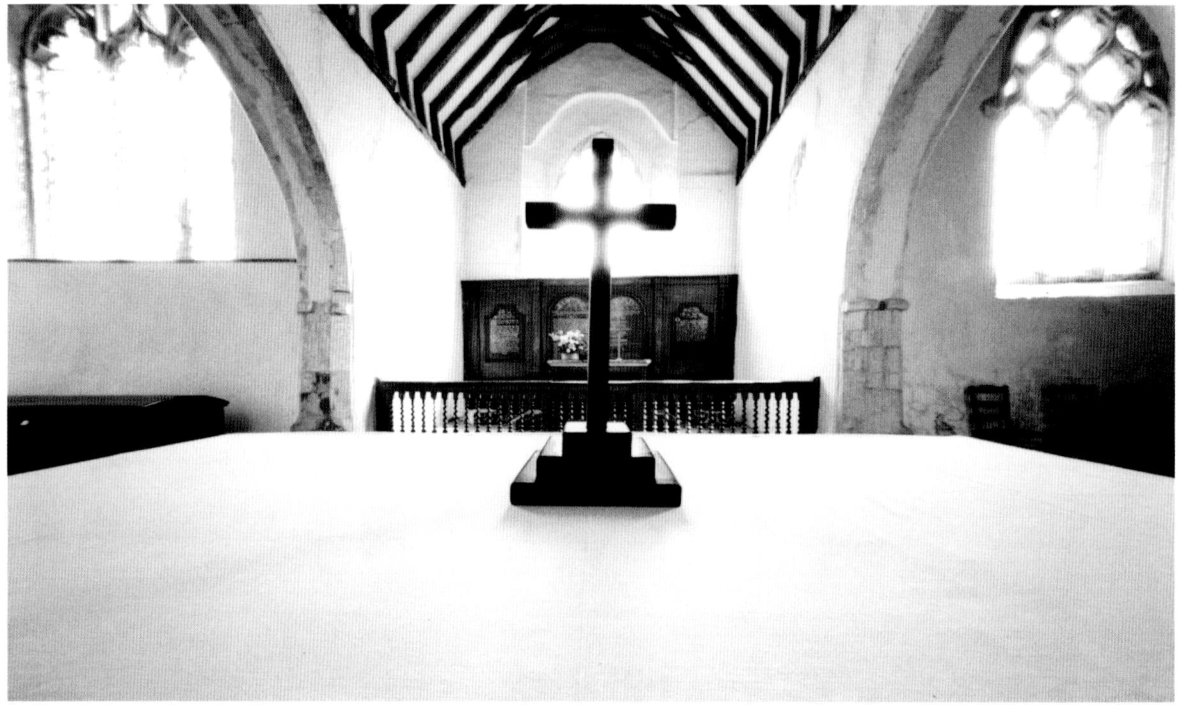

Cross, St Clement's

Because I shot this with a 12mm Ultra-Wide-Heliar, the camera was about 30cm (12in) from the cross. I composed carefully in the viewfinder, then raised the centre column of the tripod by the precise amount necessary to compensate for the parallax difference. XP2 on MG IV

SUB-MINIATURE

In the 1920s and early 1930s, anything smaller than quarter-plate was commonly referred to as 'miniature': Super Ikontas and Rolleiflexes were lumped together with Leicas and Contaxes, and with Robots with their 24 x 24mm format on 35mm. The 18 x 24mm format was sometimes treated as 'miniature' (which is what we have done here) and sometimes as 'sub-miniature' – an odd term when you think about it. Anything smaller than 18 x 24mm was 'sub-miniature'.

Probably the best-known sub-miniature is the 9.5mm Minox, which has an entry of its own at the end of this chapter; not the very best place logically, seeing that it is still in production (along with a number of other cameras using the same film, but even more basic), but it didn't really fit anywhere else either. Besides, sub-miniaturists tend to impinge on the mainstream of RF and DV cameras only tangentially.

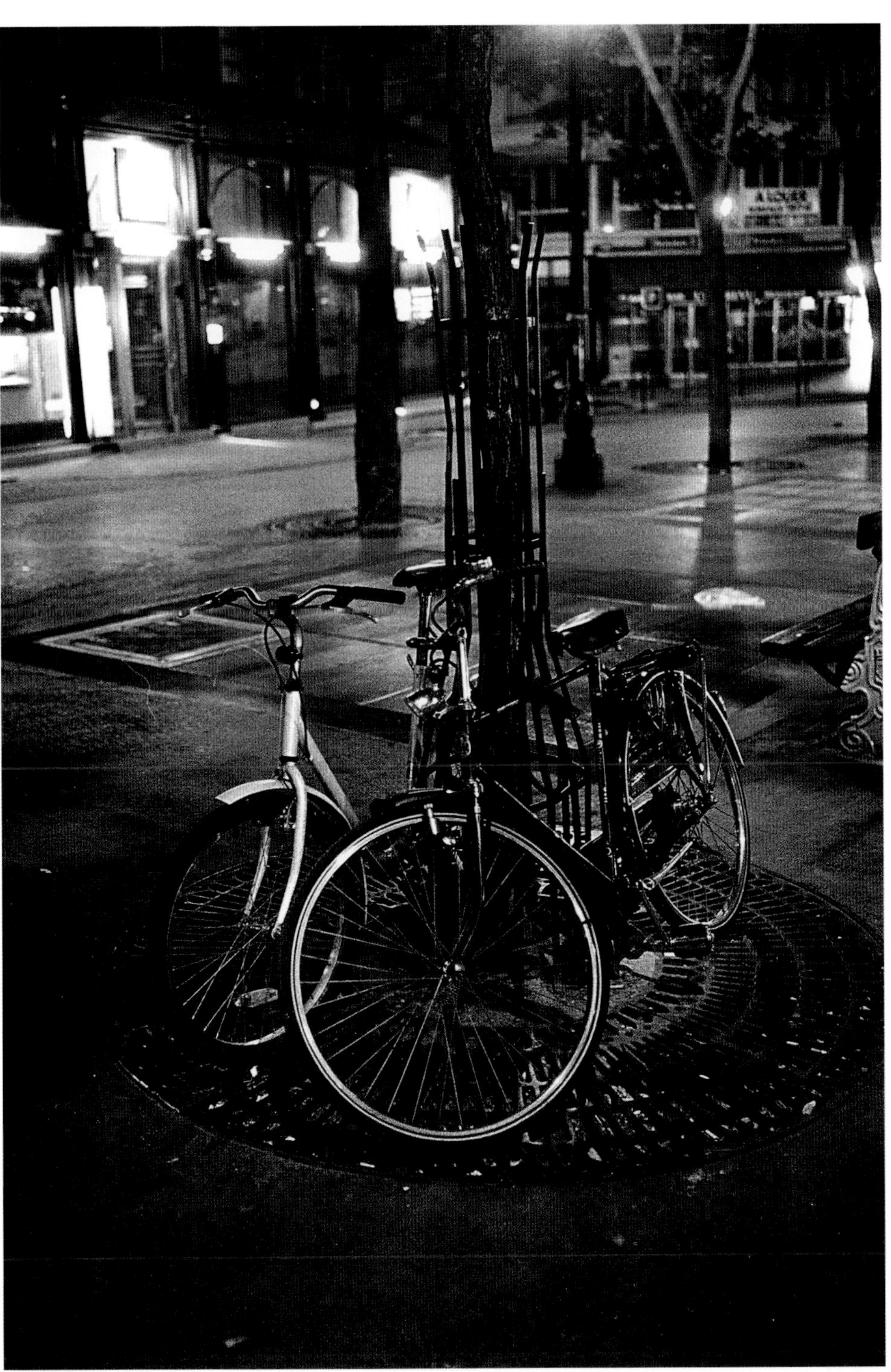

Bicycles, Paris

Today, I use a fast 35mm lens for shots like this, but in the late 1960s and early 1970s, when classic Leica lenses were a lot cheaper and I was at University, I used a 50/1.5 Xenon to take very similar pictures. I've always had a weakness for photographing bicycles, and I've never really liked flash very much. Bessa-R, 35/1.7, HP5 at 500 in DD-X, MG Warmtone

The sub-miniature that delivered the highest quality images of all, the one that really was favoured by spies, was actually a twin-lens reflex, the Swiss-made Tessina with its 14 x 21mm image on 35mm in special cassettes, so there is no need to cover it here.

There have been many very good 16mm cameras, from such luminous names as Rolleiflex, Minolta and Mamiya, quite apart from Central and Eastern European models. Unfortunately, they have used a wild profusion of different cassettes, which range from difficult to impossible to obtain today; with many, the only hope is to reload existing cassettes. Some used the full width of imperforate 16mm film; some had a smaller image to permit the use of single-perforated; and some even allow the use of double-perf. A common format is 10 x 14mm, just one-sixth of the area of full-frame 35mm, and a postcard-sized enlargement is pushing your luck with a negative this small.

Although we have owned and used a number of sub-miniature cameras (and still had a Minolta 16 somewhere at the time of writing), we have to admit that they are too much like hard work. If we want a really small snapshot camera, we use either a fully manual Olympus Pen W half-frame, or a fully-auto Kodak Advantix Advanced Photo System camera.

Minox

The seemingly immortal Minox is the only well-known product of the Latvian photo industry. The original Riga-built stainless

The current Minox TLX is very similar to the first metered model, and only a little bigger than the Riga original

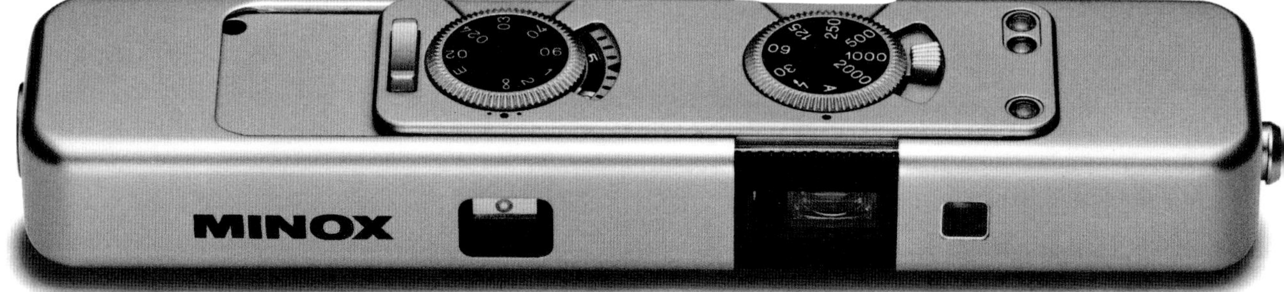

steel model was introduced in about 1937, though production was interrupted shortly thereafter and resumed in about 1947 in Wetzlar in Germany, also home to Leica. The newer model, the A, used a lot more light alloy, the later B sported a built-in exposure meter (which quite spoiled the fun for purists) and the C was fully automatic. The snake-chain that attaches to the camera is beaded to mark set focusing distances down to about 20cm (8in).

All shared (and continue to share) an 8 x 11mm format on imperforate 9.5mm film: about a tenth of the area of full-frame 35mm. They also share a fully focusing 15/3.5 fixed-aperture lens: exposure control is via a shutter speeded 1/2 to 1/1000 of a second in the early models, though later models vary, with (for example) 1/30 to 1/2000. Commercial developing and printing delivers surprisingly good pictures rather below postcard size, and devotees use Minox developing tanks and Minox enlargers to produce still better results.

The DV finder is housed in the sliding outer shell and can be used only when the camera is extended, which also winds on the film and cocks the guillotine shutter. Minoxes are tremendous fun for about half a film: after that, the imminence of the hassle of getting the watch-spring film developed and printed (or worse still, doing it yourself) tends to put off all but the dedicated.

Several other cameras have used the Minox format. Some are still in production today, though many are little more than novelties. Minox themselves make miniatures of several famous cameras, including Leicas, Rollei TLRs and Contaxes.

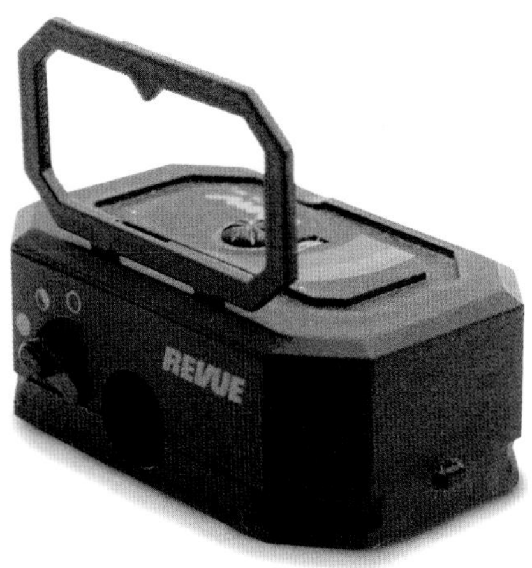

The German-made CamWatch was reputedly the smallest Minox-format camera ever made

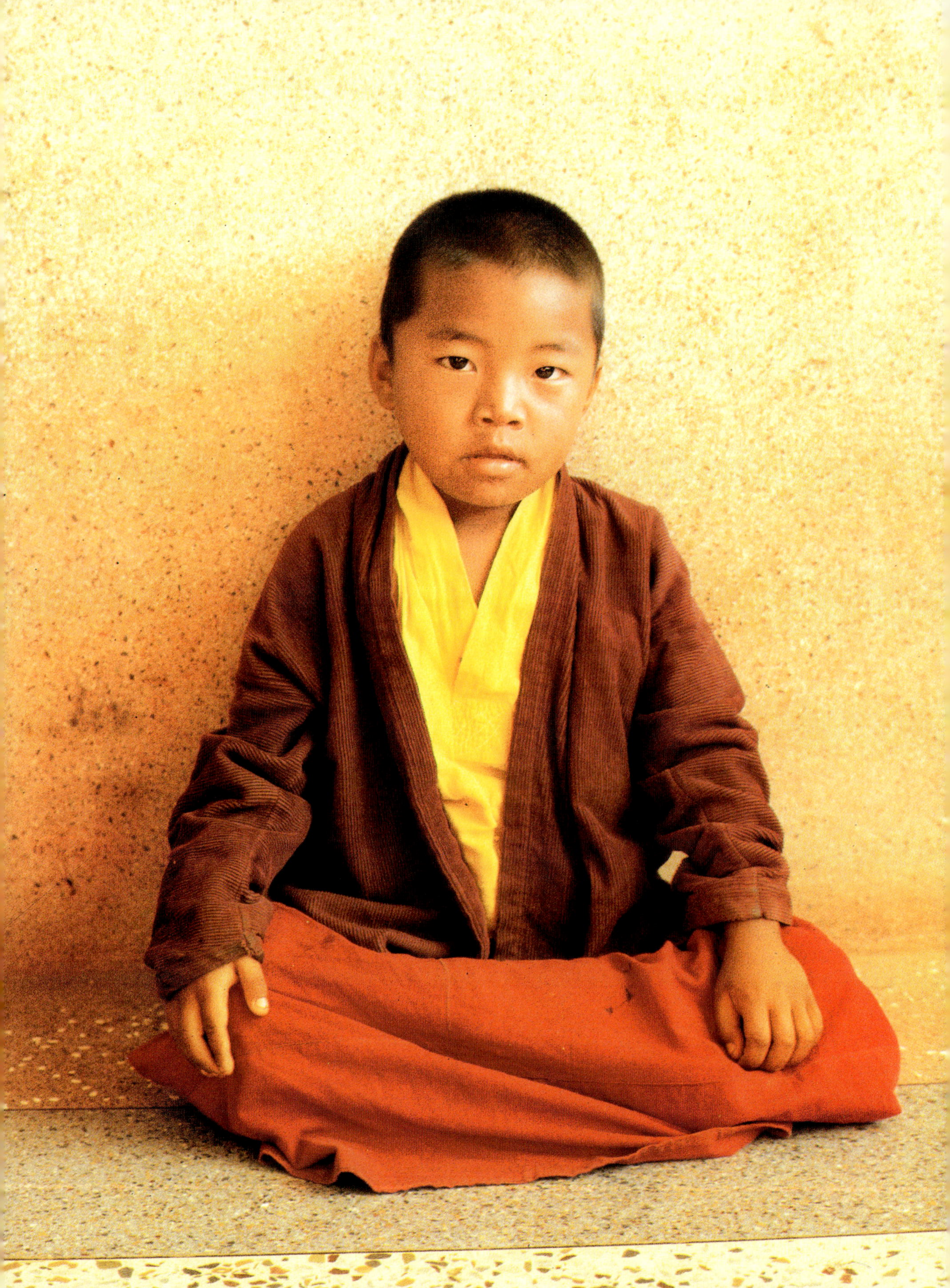

3 CLASSIC 'USER' CAMERAS

In the previous chapter, we looked at cameras which appeal
more to the collector than to the user. In this chapter, we
reverse these priorities, though here we cover only 35mm:
roll film and cut film are in Chapter 5.

There's obviously a tremendous crossover. Almost any camera
is usable and almost any camera is collectable, quite apart
from the fact that many eminently usable cameras belong to a
'family' that may have extremely collectable members. Then
there are current cameras that descend from earlier models,
which may be either collectable or usable. There's a good
degree of subjectivity in our classification, so please feel free
to disagree.

Young Tibetan monk

R *As soon as you buy it, a camera is
second-hand; keep it long enough, and it
becomes a classic. I shot this in the early 1980s
with my then-new M4-P and 35/1.4 Summilux –
and I'm still using both. I no longer use
Kodachrome, though: today's E6 films are as
sharp and very nearly as stable*

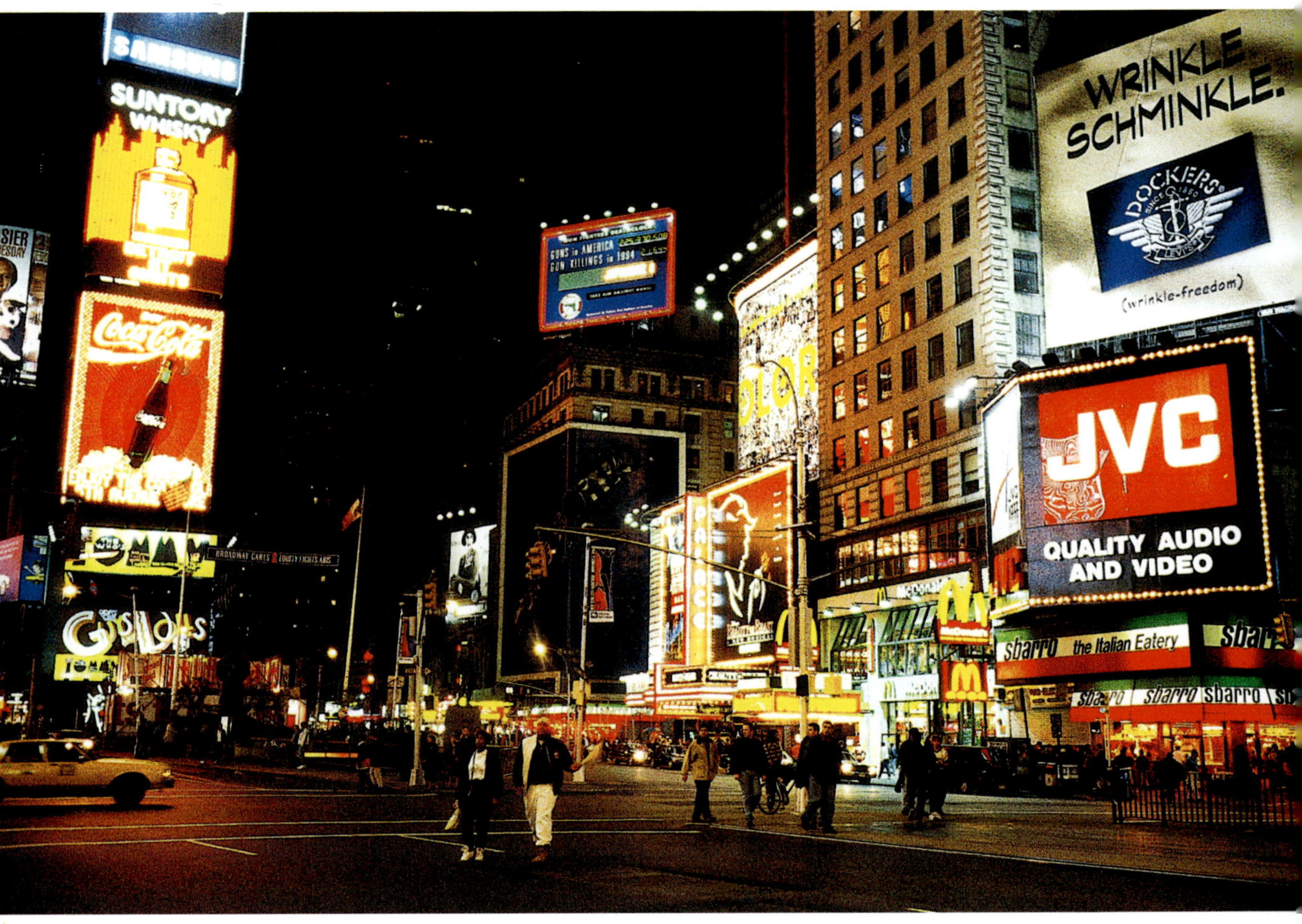

Times Square

With a shot like this, considerations of image quality are largely academic. What matters is lens speed and film speed: this was Fuji RSP at 2000. The non-aspheric 35/1.4 that I used on my M2 for this shot is demonstrably inferior to the current model – but would a 35/1.4 ASPH give me a better picture? I somehow doubt it

FIXED-LENS CAMERAS

The biggest bargains, without question, are among fixed-lens cameras from the 1950s onwards, and we therefore make no apology for starting with these; we'll move on to the 'system' cameras afterwards.

From the early 1950s to the mid-1970s, very high numbers of very high-quality cameras were made with fixed lenses, leaf shutters and coupled rangefinders. Indeed, plenty of excellent fixed-lens RF/DV cameras were made as early as the 1930s, and some were made after the 1970s. But the late 1950s, the whole of the 1960s and the early 1970s were the heyday. So what do you look for?

Manual control

As well as manual-control cameras, an awful lot of fully-auto RF cameras were made during this period – and, one might add, a lot of awful fully-auto cameras. But because DX coding had not yet been invented and film-speed setting was manual, the right film at the right speed allows superb results: Ilford XP2 at EI 250 or 320, or a colour-print film similarly down-rated by 1/3 to 2/3 of a stop may astonish you. Do, however, check carefully that the film-speed scale goes high enough if you plan on using modern ultra-speed films (EI 800 and above).

The biggest argument for manual control in old cameras is reliability. Later cameras with CdS cells are much more reliable than selenium, where the cells quite often die merely from over exposure to sunlight, but you are always dealing with a relatively fragile electro/mechanical interface. By contrast, complex though mechanical leaf shutters are, they were made in huge numbers and refined to a staggering level of reliability. And in most cases, they can be cleaned or repaired (assuming it is economical to do so) by any reasonably skilled specialist in old cameras.

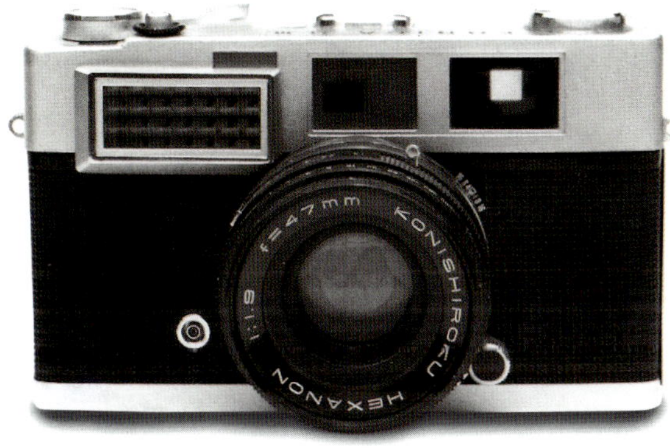

This old Konica III is typical of the surprisingly good fixed-lens RF cameras of the 1960s

Cheap cameras normally offered a more limited range of speeds than expensive ones, so a camera with a shutter running from 1 second to 1/500 is likely to be a more expensive (and higher quality) model than one with only 1/30 to 1/250. This is not an invariable guide – the Olympus Pen W, one of the best half-frame cameras ever made, offered only 1/8 to 1/250 – but it is a useful indicator.

If a shutter doesn't stick at 1 second, the chances are that the other speeds are OK too, though 'OK' is a relative term. Typical results with our ZTS Tester PRO show that speeds on leaf shutters are as marked or 1/3 of a stop slow at 1 second or 1/2 a second (i.e. 1 1/3 of a second and 2/3 of a second); as marked from 1/2 or 1/4 to 1/30 or so; 1/3 stop slow at 1/60 and 1/125 and maybe 1/250 (i.e. a true 1/50, 1/100, 1/200); and at least 2/3 of a stop slow at 1/500 (a true 1/320 if you're lucky). For what it's worth, focal plane shutters are generally better at the slow speeds (up to 1/125 or even 1/250), but a marked 1/1000 is doing well if it is 1/640 and very well indeed if it is 1/800.

Good lenses

The lenses fitted to CRF cameras ranged from simple triplets to 6-glass and even 7-glass designs. By and large, speed is a good guide. Lenses of f/3.5 and slower are likely to be triplets or at most Tessar-type (4-glass, 3-group). At f/2.8, the better cameras will mostly be Tessar-type (though a few triplets may survive); there may be a few 5-glass and even 6-glass designs, though they are very rare. At f/2, f/1.9 and f/1.8, they are likely to be 5-glass and 6-glass, often delivering excellent quality even by modern SLR standards, and these, by and large, are the cameras to go for. Few cameras had faster lenses, though some went to f/1.7 and the Yashica Lynx 14 had an f/1.4 lens.

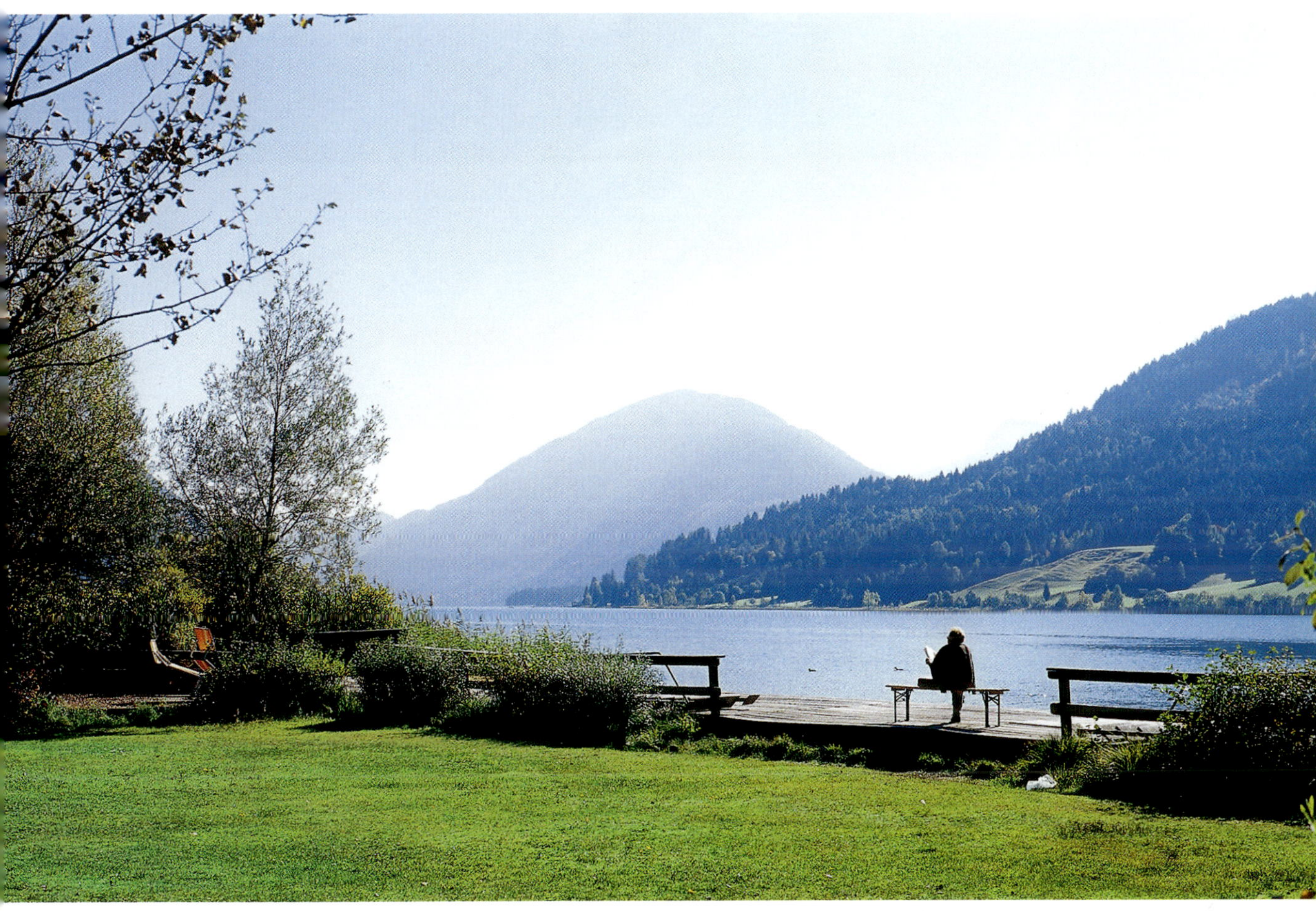

For a 'quick and dirty' assessment of how many glasses a lens has, check the number of reflections you can see from a bright point source. Either open the shutter or (which is probably easier) count the reflections on each side of the shutter. Bright reflections are air/glass interfaces; dimmer reflections are glass/glass (cemented) interfaces, so if you see three reflections, bright-dim-bright, you are looking at a cemented doublet.

Good range/viewfinders

The biggest dangers with an elderly rangefinder are twofold. Firstly, it may be out of alignment. In general, if it is properly aligned at infinity it will be all right – assuming, of course, that it isn't stuck at infinity, which does not take long to check. Secondly, the mirror or prism may have dimmed, which makes the rangefinder much harder to use. It is rarely worth the expense of having the rangefinder cleaned, let alone re-silvered. And, of course, some rangefinders weren't too bright when they were new. It was a dim rangefinder that prompted us to get rid of our Yashica Lynx 14. Always try a range/viewfinder in the poorest light you can find: one that works well in bright sunlight may not be anything like as handy in a gloomy room.

As for the viewfinder, it's a matter of personal preference. Parallax-compensated moving bright-lines are good (and Konica's are among the best), but what ain't there can't go wrong. Dim or exceptionally squinty viewfinders can be inconvenient enough to justify rejecting a camera, though. Accessory finders are a possibility, but remember that 50mm finders are relatively rare or expensive, or both, because most cameras had them built in.

Other considerations

Erratic or non-functioning meters are a constant hazard with ancient cameras, but the purist will not give this a thought: guessing the exposure (surprisingly easy after a while) is morally superior even to a separate handheld meter. Alternatively, consider a tiny shoe-mounted exposure meter: Voigtländer's shoe-mount meter (see page 141) has reintroduced this option.

After handling a relatively small number of cameras you can acquire a 'feel' for quality and general soundness, and in most cases you are not risking a fortune anyway. If you don't already own a rangefinder camera, something like our Konica III will cost about the same as a second-hand standard lens for your SLR and expand your horizons a lot wider.

There are so many possibilities, some from big names such as Konica, others from long (and deservedly) forgotten manufacturers, that we have narrowed our comments to just a couple of common cameras.

Wrecked Peugeot

What appealed to me here was the contrast of textures, plus of course the casual treatment of an outstandingly beautiful part of the world: this is the island of Gozo. In so far as one can have a cheap, knockabout Leica, this was taken with one: an M2 with my old 35/1.4 Summilux, loaded with XP2. MG Cooltone

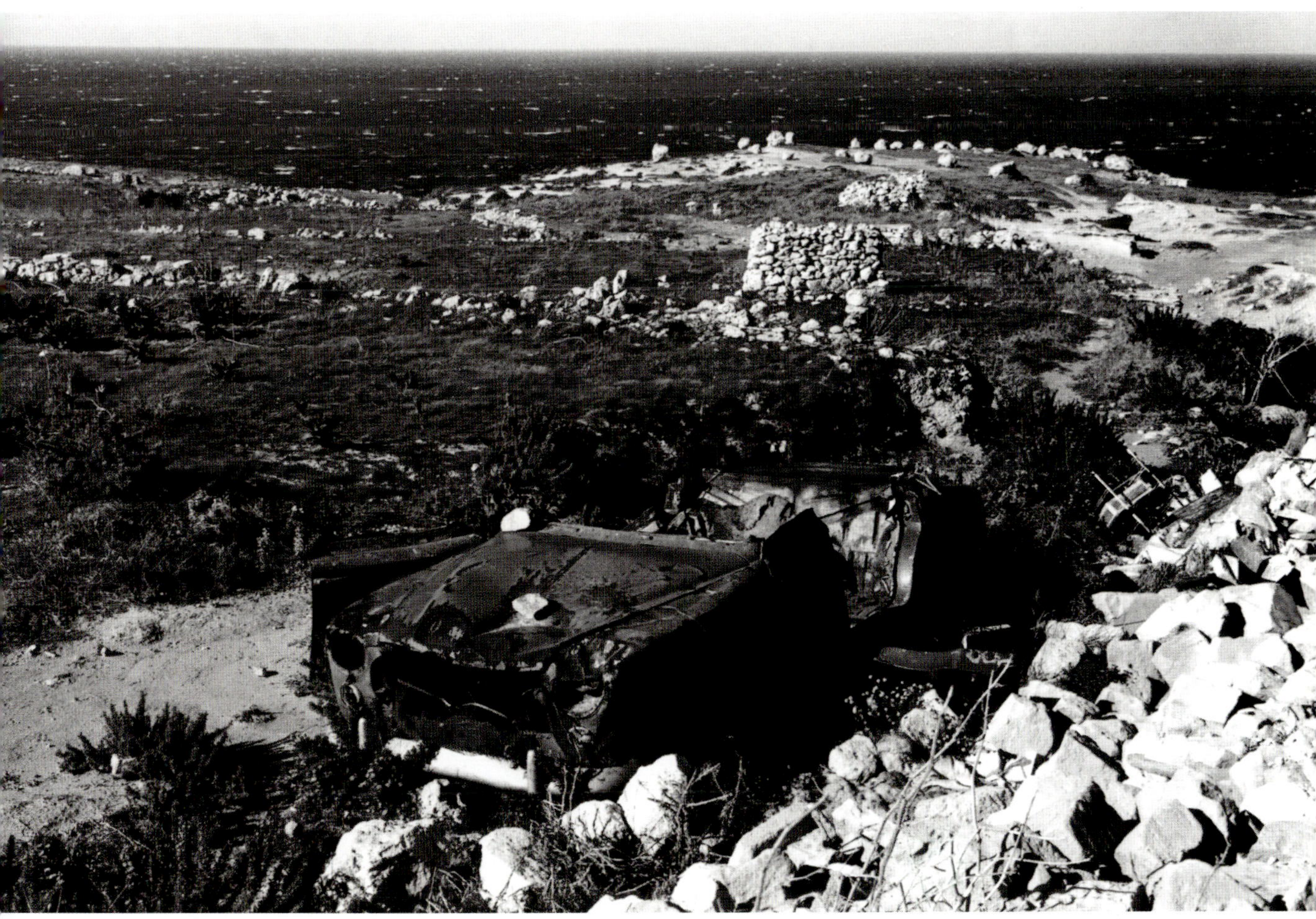

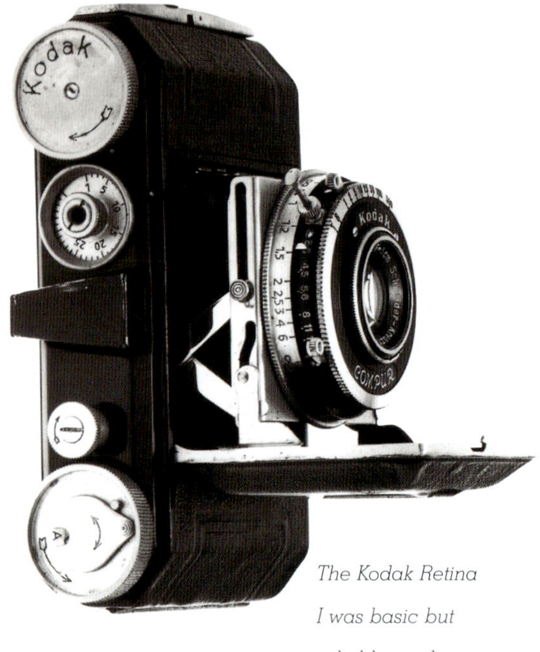

The Kodak Retina I was basic but reliable, and introduced 35mm to thousands

Retina

Kodak introduced their first 35mm camera in 1933, the Retina I (Type 117). It was pretty basic, with separate shutter cocking and film wind, but it delivered excellent results – not least because it was unusually rigid for a folder. All Retinas are delightfully compact and very strong when folded. They also deserve note because Kodak's 35mm cartridge was designed to fit in Retinas, Leicas, Contaxes and most other 35mm cameras of the period. The Krauss Peggy, which couldn't accept it and was not modified, soon died.

The Retina I grew a rangefinder in 1936 to become the Retina II (Type 122); in 1939, the rangefinder and viewfinder were combined in the IIa (Type 150). The first modern Retina, still very usable today, was the lever-wind IIa of 1951 (Type 016). It featured coupled film wind and shutter cocking (first seen in the knob-wind Type 011 in 1946), and coated lenses including the 50/2 Schneider Xenon; the Ia was the rangefinderless version. The IIc and IIIc introduced interchangeable lenses, and are therefore considered below.

In parallel with the Retinas were the Retinettes, basically similar folding cameras but with cheaper lenses or shutters (or both). As snapshot cameras, loaded with colour-print film, they still have a great deal to commend them today. Later rigid-bodied Retinas and Retinettes deliver perfectly adequate quality, but are very dull next to the folders.

Olympus

We surprised ourselves by deciding to give Olympus a section to themselves, not least because they were half-frames; but there were countless models ranging from the highly desirable to the all but useless, beginning with the original Pen (1959) and ending some time in the 1980s.

Thousands were made. The most desirable are the Pen, Pen S, Pen W and Pen D-series, all manual and (with the exception of the D-series) unmetered. Lenses ranged from 25/2.8 (the rare and desirable Pen W of 1964–65) through 28/3.5 (Pen and Pen S), 30/2.8 (Pen S), 32/1.9 (Pen D, D2) and 32/1.7 (Pen D3), while shutters varied from 1/8 to 1/500 (D-series) through 1/8 to 1/250 (Pen S and W) down to 1/25-200 (Pen). Most lenses were scale-focused, though a few were fixed-focus; none had a rangefinder.

The EE-series were all automatic, and are best avoided unless you are prepared to put up with distinctly rough exposure algorithms or can find an EE-D, which had the 32/1.7 lens and speeds from 1/15 to 1/500 – though still no manual override. There were also versions of the EE that used the Agfa Rapid system, which is not compatible with standard 35mm cassettes; these are still more to be avoided. The motorized EM had a nice 35/2 lens, but, again, no manual override.

Few labs offer half-frame printing, and those that do are expensive. But if you order 5 x 7in or 13 x 18cm prints from a conventional full-frame lab, you can cut them in half to get two postcard-sized pictures.

'SYSTEM' CAMERAS

As in the previous chapter, the Leica defines the market, so it makes sense to begin there. Most others – which are covered in alphabetical order – are somewhere between collectibility and usability. Financially, it may make more sense to buy something newer, but often there is a charm to the older cameras that is akin to the difference between driving a modern car and a classic. Either you see the appeal or you don't. Roger does; Frances is not so sure.

Leica

The origins of the undisputed doyen of 35mm rangefinder cameras have already been discussed in Chapter 2. Here we are concerned with the later M-series bayonet-mount cameras, even though the screw-mount models still remain eminently usable.

Evolution has been gradual; and the latest M-series (the M7 and M6 ttl, at the time of writing) bear a very strong resemblance to the original 1954 M3. Because of the evolution, it is easiest to run through them in chronological order.

The M3 was probably the finest Leica ever made, from the point of view of quality: silky smooth, quiet, the epitome of mechanical precision. Early models (pre-1959) have a two-stroke lever wind, which some people can live with, but others find all but unusable; they are normally advertised as DS (double-stroke). Later models, 1959–1968, were single-stroke. Very early models have a glass pressure plate and old-fashioned shutter speeds (1/5, 1/10, 1/25, etc.) instead of 1/4, 1/8, 1/15, 1/30. Viewfinder magnification in all models is 0.91x.

Despite its sublime quality, the disadvantage of the M3 is that its parallax-corrected, projected viewfinder frames, automatically selected by the appropriate lens (or the appropriate screw-to-bayonet adapter), are for 50–90–135mm only, so you need a separate viewfinder for 35mm, or a special 'spectacles' version of the 35mm lenses that corrects the field of view of the 50mm frame.

The M2 (1957–1969) is somewhat simpler – in particular, the film counter is manually reset, not automatic as on the M3 – but it has the great advantage of frames for 35–50–90, again

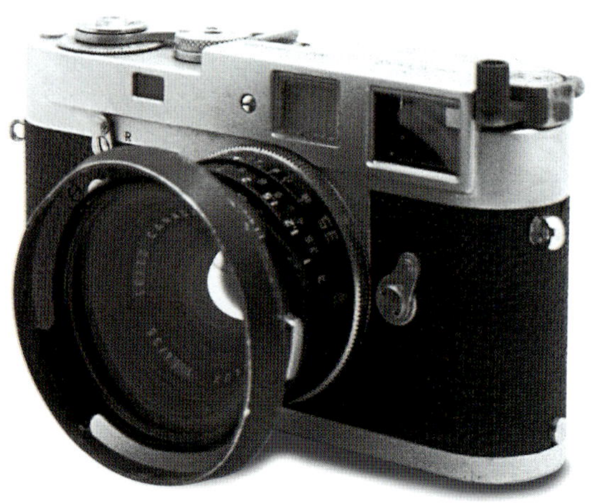

Roger's workhorse Leica for 25 years has been an M2 from the early 1960s

parallax-corrected projected-frame, again automatically set by fitting a lens. To accommodate the 35mm lenses, viewfinder magnification is 0.75x. Roger has used M2 Leicas for years.

The M1 (1959) is essentially a rangefinderless M2, with 50mm and 35mm frames permanently displayed. The MD (1965) omits even the viewfinder, as do the MDa (1966, based on the M4, below), the MD-2 (1977, based on the M4-2, below) and the rare half-frame MD-22.

The M4 (1967) has all four frames of the classical canon: 35/135 simultaneously, 50, 90. It also has a much more convenient canted rewind crank in place of the old pull-up knob, and a self-resetting frame counter. Unlike the M3, where you have to remove the take-up spool to reset the counter, removing the base plate will do it.

The M5 (1971) is a much bigger, heavier camera than other M-series, and the first to incorporate through-lens metering. Some lenses foul the pop-up meter arm: always check (with the back off and the shutter open) before trying to use them – and remember that collapsible lenses may foul when collapsed, even if they are all right when erected.

The M4-2 (1976) was introduced when it became clear that the M5 was not widely popular. It is essentially an M4, allegedly with better dust sealing and 'winterized' to allow use at very low temperatures; traditionally, 'winterized' Leicas were cleaned and re-lubricated with special low-temperature oils, permitting unduly rapid wear at more usual temperatures.

The M4-P (1980) is pretty much an M4-2 with additional frames, now displayed in pairs: 28–90, 35–135, 50–75. Many find these pairs distracting, and besides, compared with the

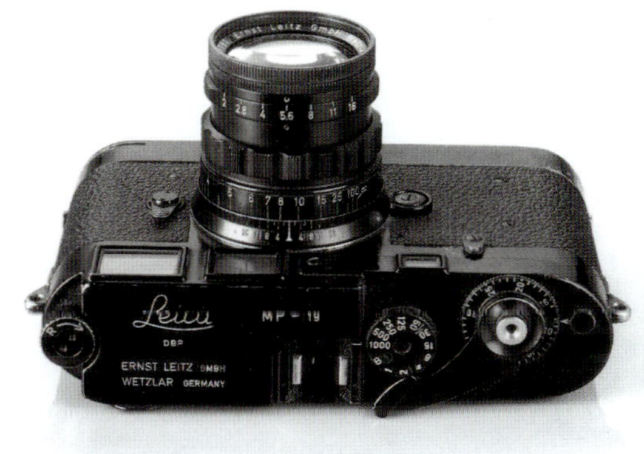

The Leica MP with the trigger wind is one of the most collectable of Leicas

M2 and M3 it is a pretty rough camera. There is a distressing tendency (also found in the M6) for the central rangefinder patch to flare out when you are shooting at night and there are bright light sources in the picture.

Many bemoan the way that Leica switched to 'black chrome' instead of black paint, which wears much more gracefully

The M6 (1984) is essentially an M4-P with through-lens metering – a very good, very simple null system, with three LEDs arranged >o< – and the M6 ttl adds through-lens flash metering. This and the M7 are the current Leicas, and as such are discussed in the next chapter, which is also where we talk about using Leicas.

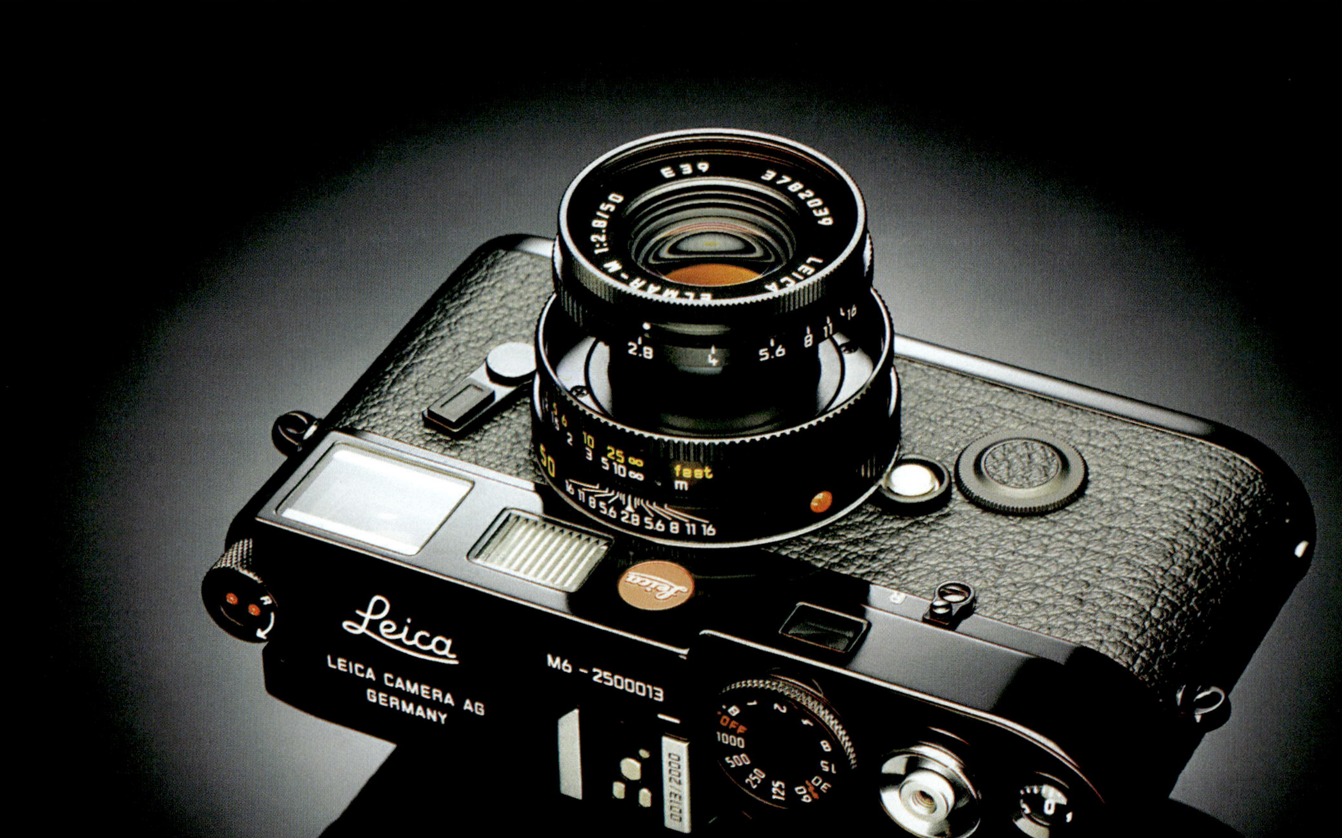

Off to one side, there is the Minolta-built Leica CL (1973). This is significantly smaller than a conventional M-series, with which it shares the M-bayonet, but it still has a through-lens meter, concerning which the same reservations apply as to the M5, above. Because of the short rangefinder base, the use of fast lenses such as the 90/2 is not recommended. A special series of lenses was made for the CL: 28/2.8, 40/2 (there is no 50mm frame in the camera) and 90/4.

Fed

The earliest Feds, still commonly found in camera stores today, were pretty close Leica copies, and indeed form the basis of many unconvincing (but often entertaining) fake Nazi Leicas: the sort that has a *Reichsadler* clutching a swastika in its claws, and is gold-plated.

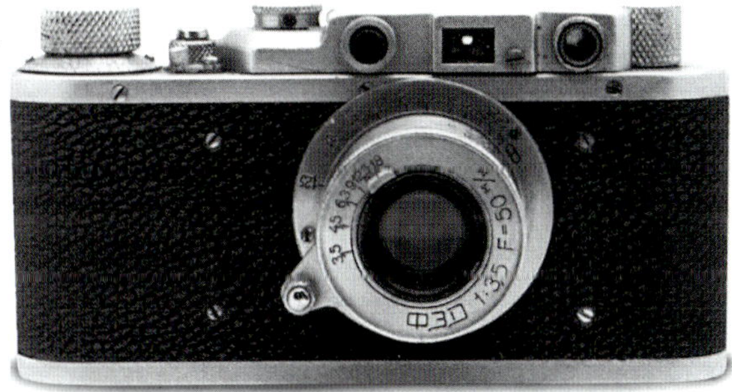

The resemblance between an early Fed and an old Leica is clear

More modern Feds (still intermittently available new) have come some way from their roots, though they still retain the Leica screw thread. They are quite bulky cameras, with typically tractor-like Russian handling, and in our experience the meters are hopelessly unreliable: unmetered models are preferable. The only finder built in is 50/55mm; the usual lens is a 55/2.8 Tessar-type of indifferent quality.

The 5C has a meter and a hot shoe, with a shutter from 1 to 1/500 of a second; the 5B is a meterless version; and the plain 5 has dioptre adjustment for the eyepiece.

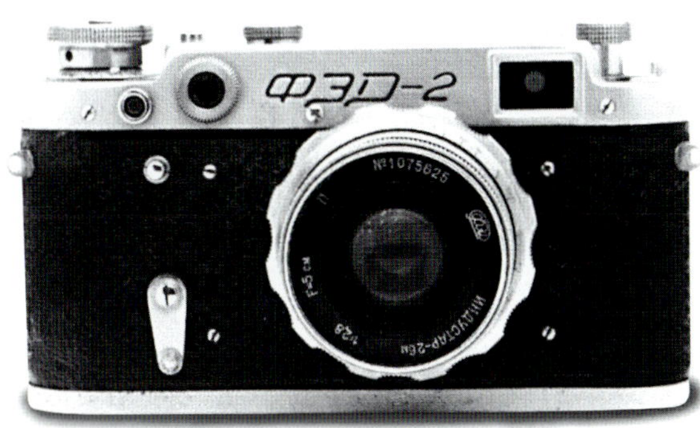

Later Feds like this 2 drifted further and further from their Leica-copy roots

As a very cheap way into traditional RF/DV cameras, Feds have their uses. Though as the lenses are pre-war Zeiss designs, you may do better to fit Voigtländer or indeed pretty much any other lenses instead. All Feds have a rather crude rangefinder follower – a cam, not a roller – and they may not always mate properly with lenses from other manufacturers.

In extreme cases, you can damage the camera, or the lens, or both if you try to force things, though this would be unusual.

There is also a stereo Fed, with fixed f/2.8 lenses, which again is intermittently available new. But it is auto-exposure and so far from the mainstream that we mention it only for completeness.

Kiev

The Ukrainian-built Kiev is essentially a pre-World War Two Contax with rather poorer quality control but with added flash synch (at least in the later models). It is a big and heavy camera (about 790g, almost 28oz), and it even has the 'roll-top desk' shutter with speeds from 1/2 second to 1/1250 (marked as a less dishonest 1/1000 on later models), along with a fiercely serrated (and rather stiff) focusing wheel on the body for the standard lens.

The relationship between Contax and Kiev should be pretty clear from this picture: Kiev-Contax-Kiev

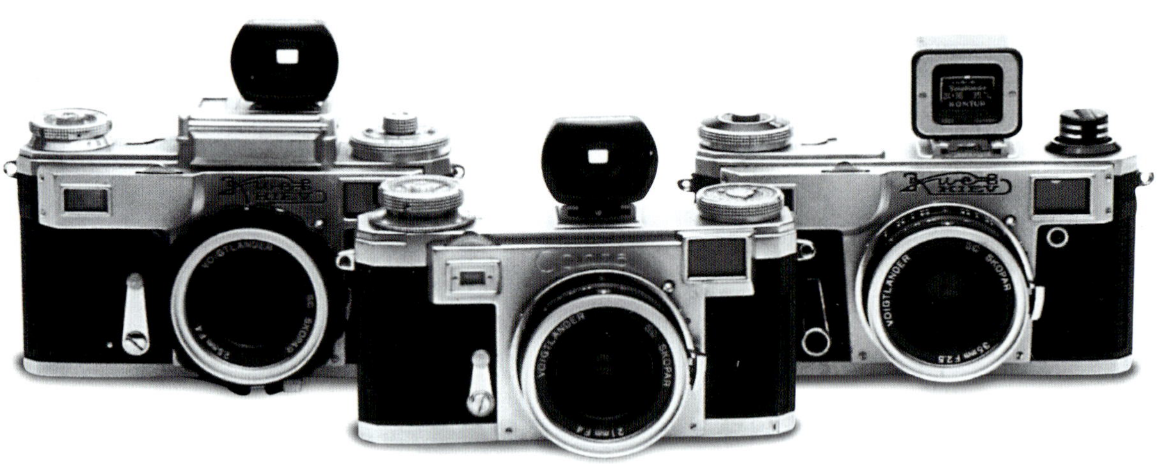

The only built-in finder is for 50mm. Both metered (selenium-cell) and non-metered versions were made. Thanks to its hinge-down lid, the meter cell on the (reasonably accurate) meter is likely to have survived better than most.

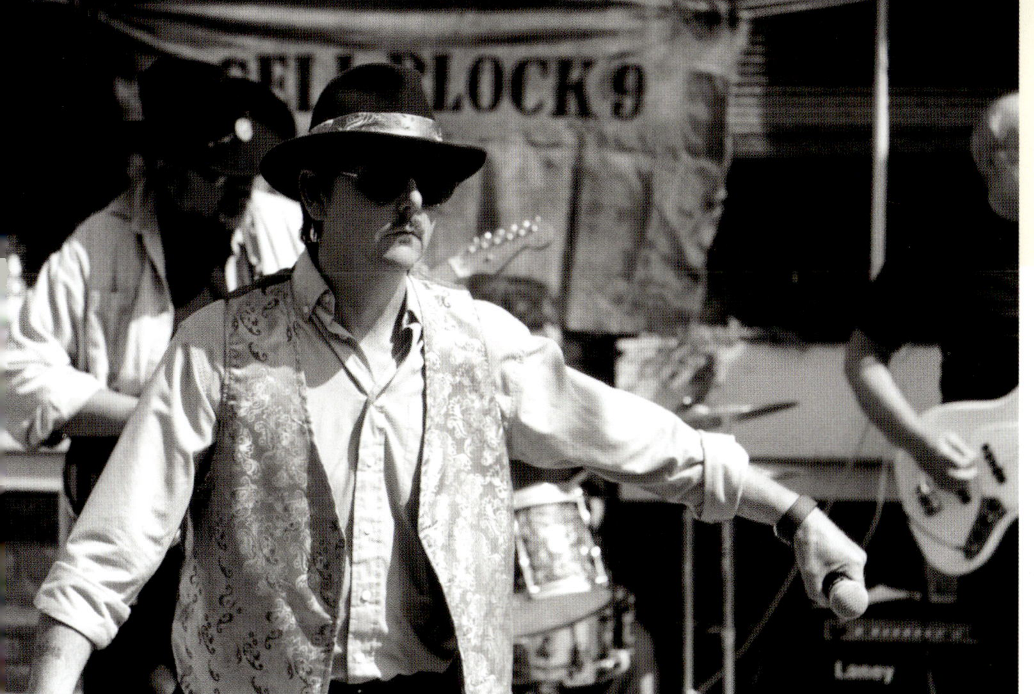

Kievs were made in very large numbers (over a million) at the Arsenal works from about 1947 to the mid-to-late 1980s; production ceased in about 1987 at the latest. They have a certain charm, but as the lenses are the same as for the Fed and Zorkii, you should not expect too much from them. Fortunately, Nikon-fit Voigtländer lenses are available, transforming the performance of the camera: 21/4, 25/4, 35/2.5, 50/1.5, 50/2.5 and 85/3.5

Minolta

The Leica CL also appeared as a Minolta, with Rokkor lenses in the same focal lengths and speeds as the Leica's. These are very usable little cameras, but the collector market is increasingly driving prices up to the point where something more modern (and with more useful viewfinder frames) is a better buy.

Clockwise from top left, these Nikon S3 cameras are fitted with 35/1.8, 50/1.1, 50/1.4 and 35/2.8 lenses

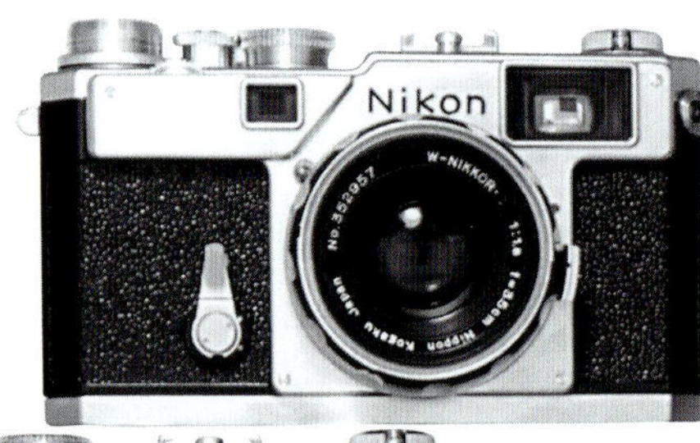
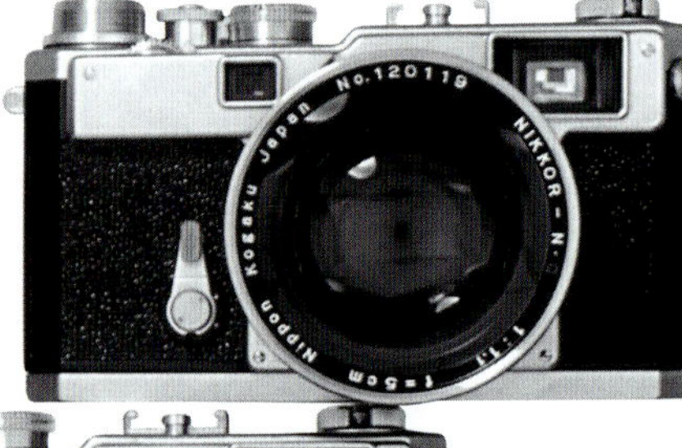
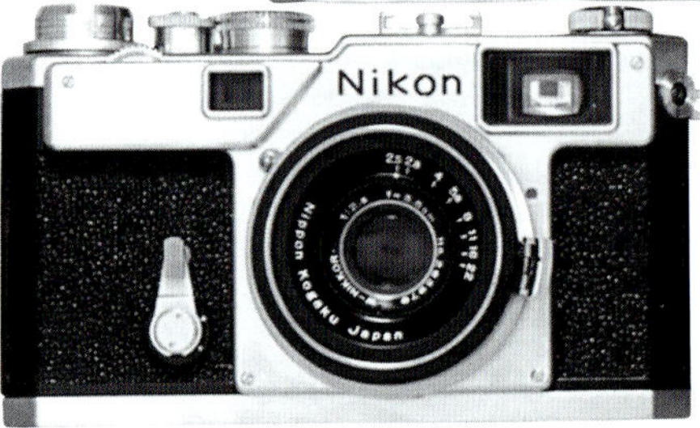
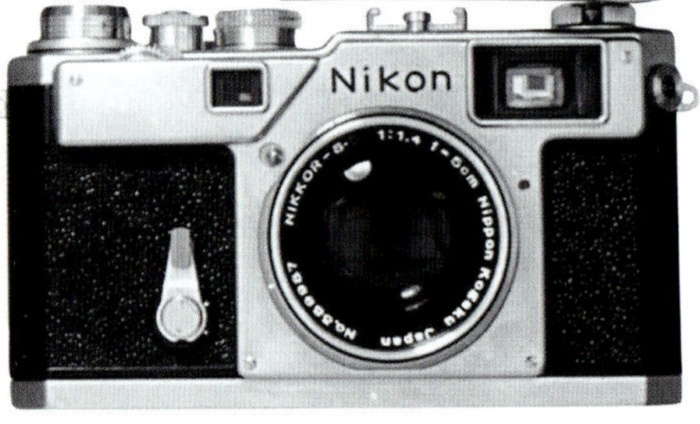

Nikon

The original Nikon rangefinders were derived from the Contax, but with numerous changes, including (at first) the format: the 24 x 32mm I of 1948, the 24 x 34mm M of 1950. In 1951 the S succumbed to 24 x 36mm, and the S2 of 1954 was an S with lever-wind. The greatest of them all was the 1957 SP, but later came the simplified S3 (1958) and S4 (1959). The S3M is a half-frame version from 1960. Production finished sometime in the early 1960s, though the S3 was reintroduced in 2000 and is briefly noted on page 73.

Given the range of built-in finders in a Nikon SP, there seems little need for an auxiliary finder

Not only did Nikon abandon the roll-top desk shutter in favour of a much better Leica-type shutter, they also had significantly cleverer viewfinders. The SP range/viewfinder had a permanent 50mm frame, with manually selected 85, 105 and 135mm frames, all parallax-compensated, plus a subsidiary non-corrected finder for 28mm and 35mm.

Nikons are not too hard to find, but they are so sought-after by collectors that they are hardly cost-effective: a good SP will cost more than a new M6 or M7 Leica, and even an S2 or S3 is comparable with an older M-series.

Nikonos

These direct-vision underwater cameras started life in about 1950 as the French-made Spirotechnique, then later became the Calypso/Nikkor. They exhibit typical Gallic ingenuity, not least in the combined wind-on lever and shutter release, which tends to provoke camera shake. The last model, the Nikonos V, was discontinued in 2001, though stocks of new models ran into 2002: the V was almost as huge and expensive as the early ones were compact. All are heavy and next to indestructible. Early lenses other than the 35/2.5 standard are suitable only for underwater use, but a Nikonos with a standard lens is ideal for use in humid, wet, or hazardous conditions. Later lenses in a variety of focal lengths could be used both underwater and on dry land.

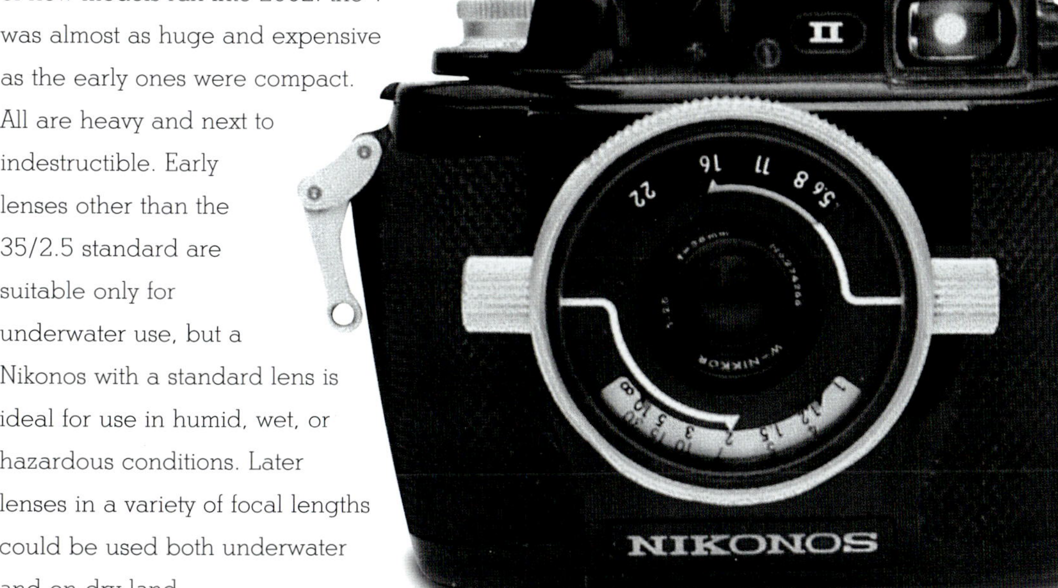

The Nikonos II is not only waterproof: it is enormously strong as well

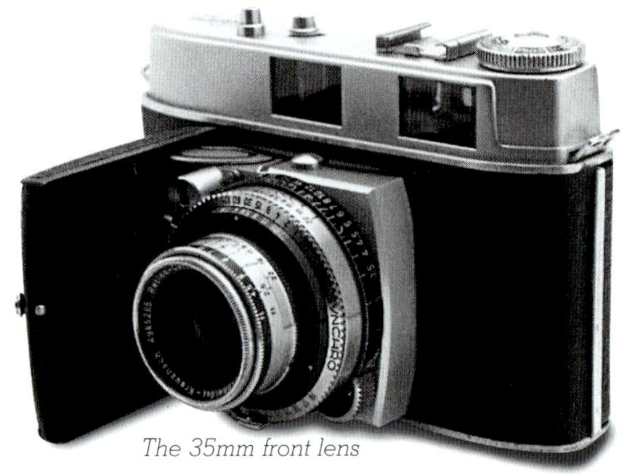

The 35mm front lens group for the Retina IIC was compact, but this was its only merit

Retina

The 1954 Retina IIc (Type 020) and IIIc (Type 021, with meter) grafted an ingenious system of interchangeable front elements onto the folding-camera design described above, to give 35mm and 80mm as well as the standard 50mm. But the camera would not close with the other lenses in place and the rangefinder was coupled only to the 50mm lens: the reading had to be transferred to the focusing scale of the other lenses. The IIC/IIIC ('big C') models, Types 028 and 029, had bright-line finders with all three frames showing: the finder sometimes seemed to be more bright-line than finder.

Without the interchangeable lenses – which were made in two series by Schneider and Rodenstock – the 'System' Retinas are very good, and there are some wonderful accessories for (among other things) close-ups and stereo, but the extra lenses are more trouble than they are worth.

The original Robot featured a swing-in filter and a non-sequential frame-counter dial

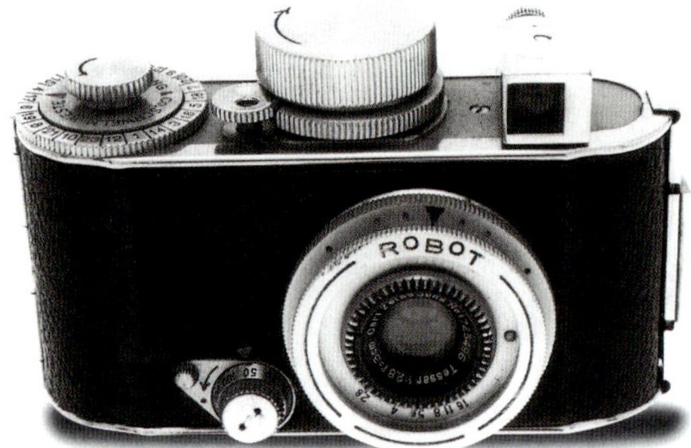

Robot

Robots are like nothing else. The classic models are machined from a block of stainless steel (and weigh accordingly); use a 24 x 24mm format; have a unique body-mounted rotary shutter (which explains the format – the shutter aperture is just 16mm square); and are powered by a big clockwork spring. A wide range of first-class lenses has always been available, including f/1.9, in a tiny 25mm screw mount.

The Robot Star is unusual for having the winder set into the top plate instead of sticking up

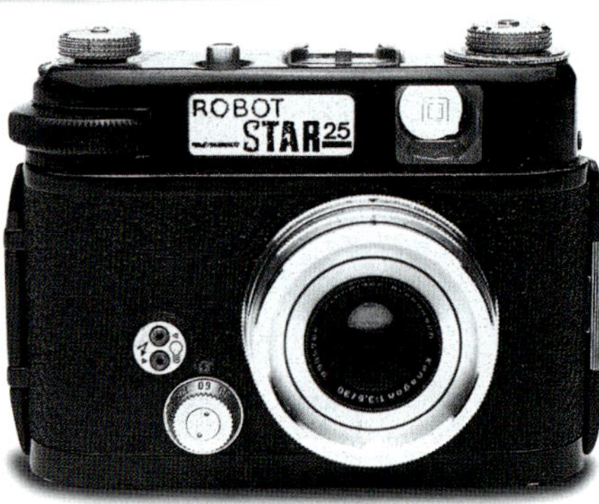

The earliest Robots (I, 1935, II, 1939) used unique feed and take-up cassettes, which even differed between feed and take-up, but the 1951 IIa allows standard feed cassettes (you still need a Robot take-up cassette) and the Star (1952) allows rewinding. The Junior resembles a Star but will not accept Robot feed cassettes. All can

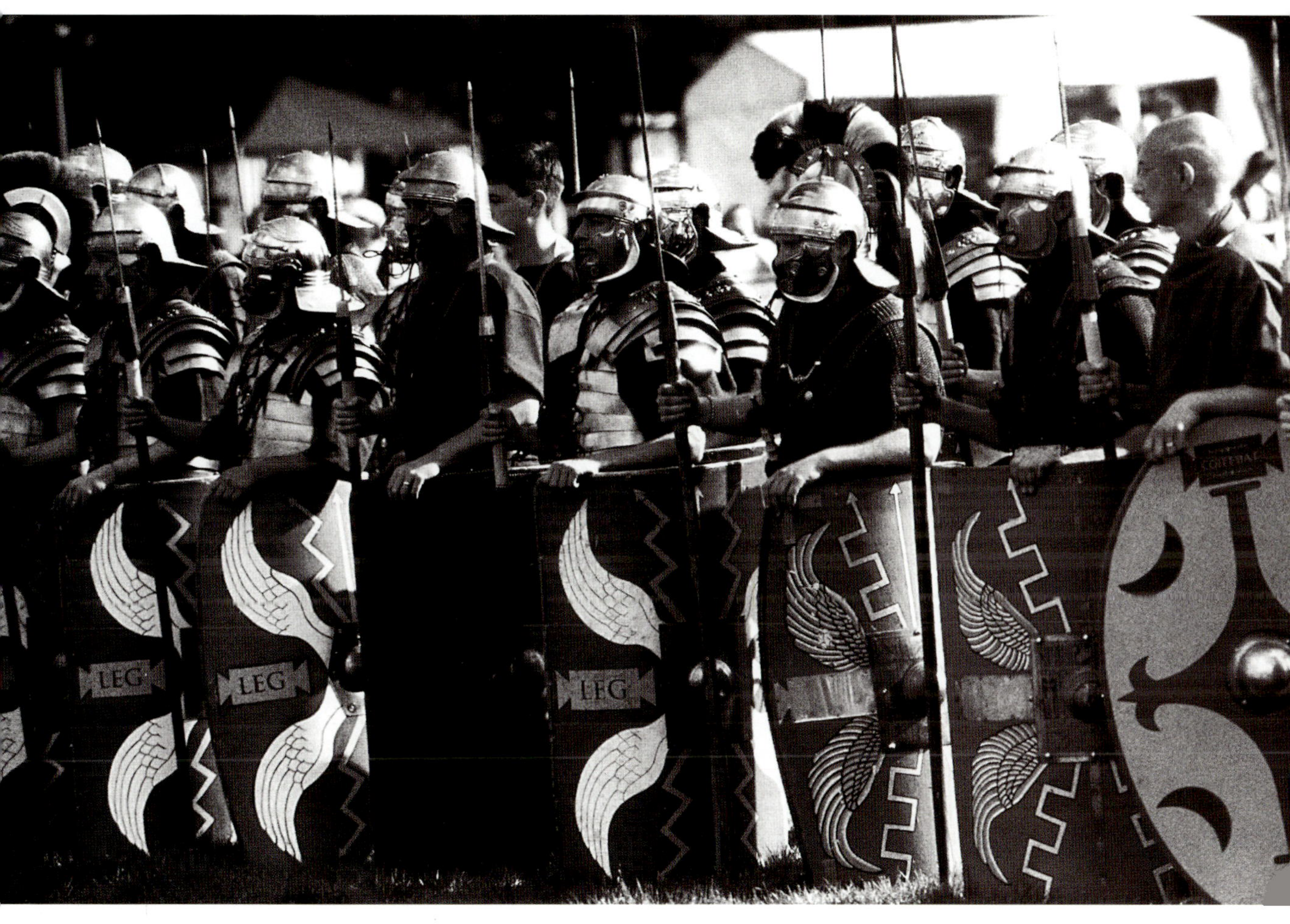

be surprisingly affordable, even the ones engraved 'Luftwaffen Eigentum' (Luftwaffe property) and all remain usable – though you do need the trick cassettes for the early ones.

In 1955 came the highly desirable Royal 24 (24 x 24mm) and Royal 36 (24 x 36mm) CRF models (all others are scale-focus), but these are much rarer and have mostly been snapped up by collectors. They have conventional shutters and a different lens mount; lenses are harder to find too. The Royal II (1954 to 1956) is a rangefinderless Royal 24. Robots are still available new and are mentioned briefly in Chapter 4.

Roman soldiers

When I first started in photography, my favourite lens was a 90mm. Then I slowly drifted towards wider and wider lenses, including eventually a 15/2.8 Sigma fish-eye and the 35/5.6 Apo-Grandagon on 6 x 9cm on my Alpa, the equivalent of about 15mm on 35mm. But when we got the 90/3.5 Apo-Lanthar, I rediscovered my liking for 90mm. Bessa-T, XP2 on MG warmtone in selenium

Voigtländer Prominent

The 1950s Prominent was probably the finest interchangeable-lens leaf-shutter CRF camera of all time. The standard (50mm) lenses included the 50/1.5 Nokton, 50/2 Ultron and 50/3.5 Skopar; the others were 35mm and 100mm and (via a dedicated mirror box) 100mm and 150mm. A particularly interesting feature of the Prominent is that lenses other than 50mm (which was unit-focusing) were focused by moving the back groups; they may thus have been the first internal-focus lenses for 35mm cameras.

The 50/1.5 Nokton for the Prominent was the first new-generation rare earth fast lens after WW2

If you don't mind the knob wind and the fairly slow wide-angle, Prominents are very usable cameras that deliver excellent results and are still relatively affordable: you should be able to find one slightly cheaper than a new Voigtländer Bessa-T.

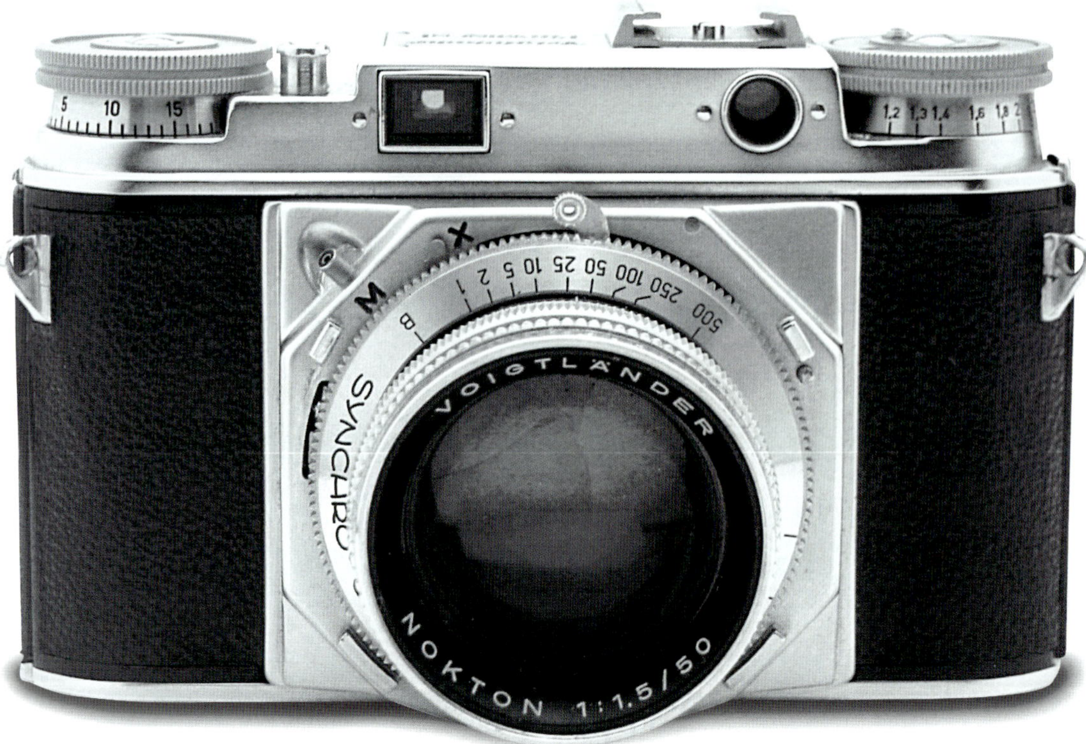

Zorkii

The Zorkii or Zorki is a Leica derivative, somewhat resembling the Fed but rather smaller and more attractive. Once again, it is Leica screw mount; once again, the shutter is the lift-twist-and-drop variety, though fully speeded from 1 second to 1/1000. The speed can only be set after winding on and must not be moved between the markings for the out-of-sequence 1/30 second and 1 second; go to 1/30 via 1/1000 and B (!). As usual, the Russian/Ukrainian lenses are best replaced with something newer; and once again, not all lenses couple properly.

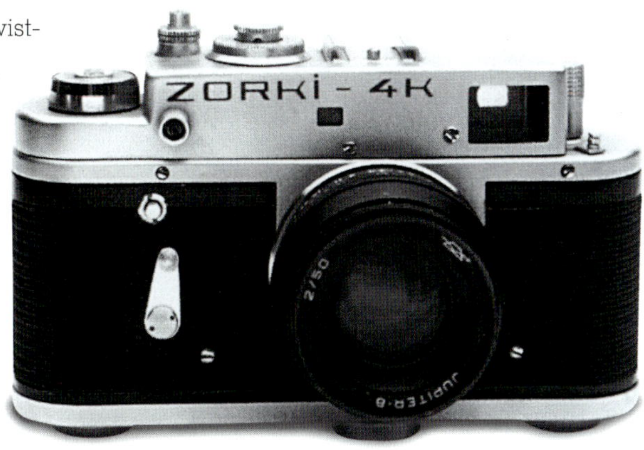

The lever-wind Zorkii 4K is one of the cheapest routes into 'system' rangefinder cameras

The very earliest models were similar to Feds, but overwhelmingly the most common and usable models are the knob-wind 4 and the (much preferable) lever-wind 4K, made from 1973 to the late 1970s or early 1980s in very large numbers. Most came with the 50/2 Jupiter (a copy of the pre-war Zeiss Sonnar), though you can occasionally find the rare and awful 50/1.5, and some have the 55/2.8 or 50/3.5 more usually associated with Feds. The only built-in finder is for 50mm, but there is an excellent dioptric adjustment for the combined range/viewfinder. The back and base come off, Contax-style, for loading. It's crude and it's noisy, but with a good lens on the front, it behaves very well.

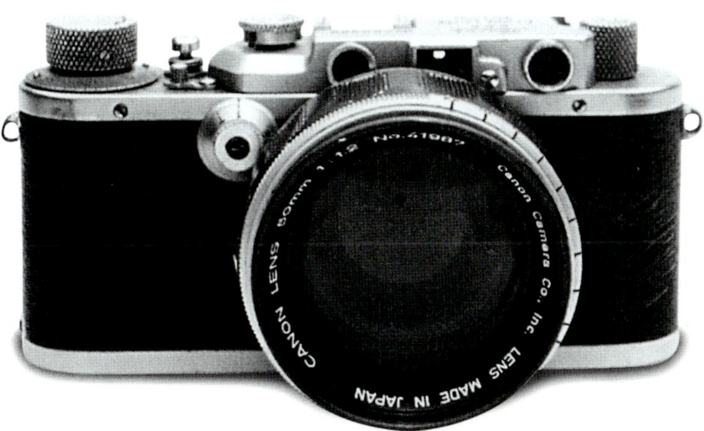

The dubious precision of lens/film alignment on a Leica IIIa makes it unwise to use this Canon f/1.2 lens

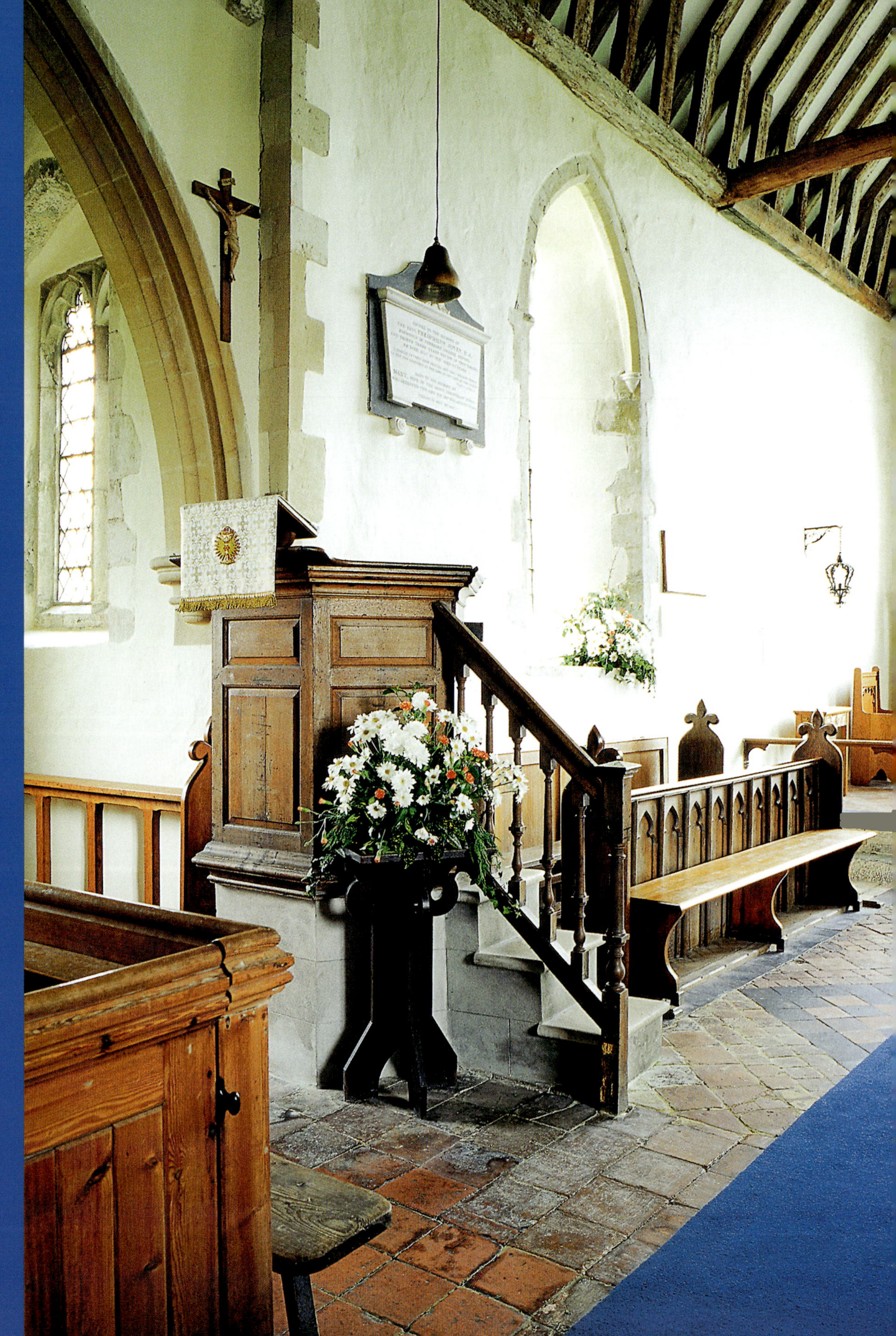

Just as Leica dominated the previous two chapters, Voigtländer dominates this one and demands pride of place. It is not that the Cosina-built RF cameras are superior to Leicas – perish the thought – but they are vastly more affordable, and as an introduction to RF photography with new cameras, they may well be unbeatable. There are, therefore, two long entries in this chapter – Voigtländer and Leica – and then several more in alphabetical order.

Paradoxically, availability of some of the newer and even current models may not be as great as for some older models. The revived Nikon S3 'Millennium Edition' seems to have been aimed mainly at collectors; modern Robots are more rarely encountered than older ones; and Yasuharas are very thin on the ground, their thunder having been somewhat stolen by Voigtländer Bessas.

Although we have concentrated on interchangeable-lens cameras, a few of the most important fixed-lens cameras have also been included. It is important to emphasize that our intention was not to provide a model-by-model analysis – the book would date too quickly if we did that – but rather to highlight the design philosophies adopted by the different manufacturers, and the strengths and weaknesses of particular families of cameras.

Church interior, Romney Marsh

Although (like most RF users) I use my cameras mostly handheld, I'm not a purist about it: I'll use a tripod wherever I can. This was shot on a Velbon MAXi343E tripod, using my Bessa-T and 28/1.9 Ultron, on Kodak EBX

VOIGTLÄNDER

The Bessa series of cameras came from nowhere, and were more responsible than any others for both the rangefinder revival and this book.

The Japanese firm of Cosina is run by Mr. Kobayashi and his two sons, one of whom, Hirofumi, became a Leica aficionado when still in his teens. He was responsible for licensing the Voigtländer name (from Ring Photo, of Germany) and for introducing, initially, one camera and two lenses, all with the Leica 39mm x 26tpi screw mount.

The camera, the Bessa-L, was based on an SLR chassis that Cosina made for another well-known manufacturer. Stripped-down, rangefinderless, viewfinderless but nonetheless equipped with through-lens-metering, it was offered to accompany an astonishing 15/4.5 and a bargain-priced 25/4. Both lenses were praised for contrast, sharpness and overall quality, though the camera was regarded as a bargain-priced but rather basic body. Unlike the original Yasuhara, Voigtländers have double shutters that are fully light-tight.

Then, in dazzling succession, came three more bodies and twelve more lenses, from 12mm to 90mm. The lenses are covered in Chapter 6; here we are concerned with the bodies.

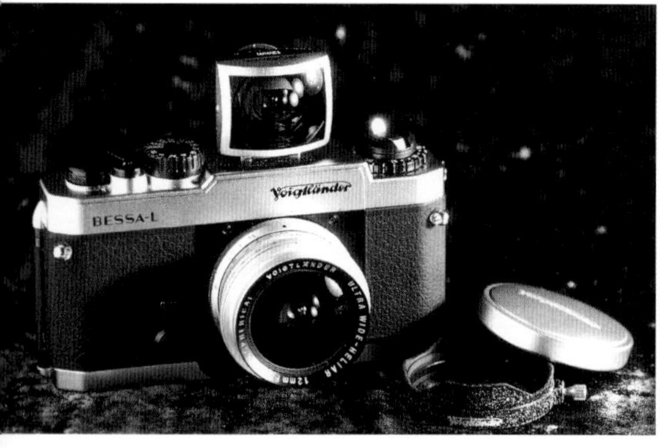

The Bessa-L is the base model, with no RF or viewfinder – here with the 12/5.6 Ultra-Wide-Heliar

Tree in landscape, Slovenia

I find my Bessa-T and 90/3.5 Apo Lanthar an ideal combination for landscapes. The lens is very contrasty, which can be useful when there is haze in the air, and both together are small and light. This is an unusually symmetrical composition, but I wanted to draw attention to the colour contrasts. Bessa-T, Kodak EBX

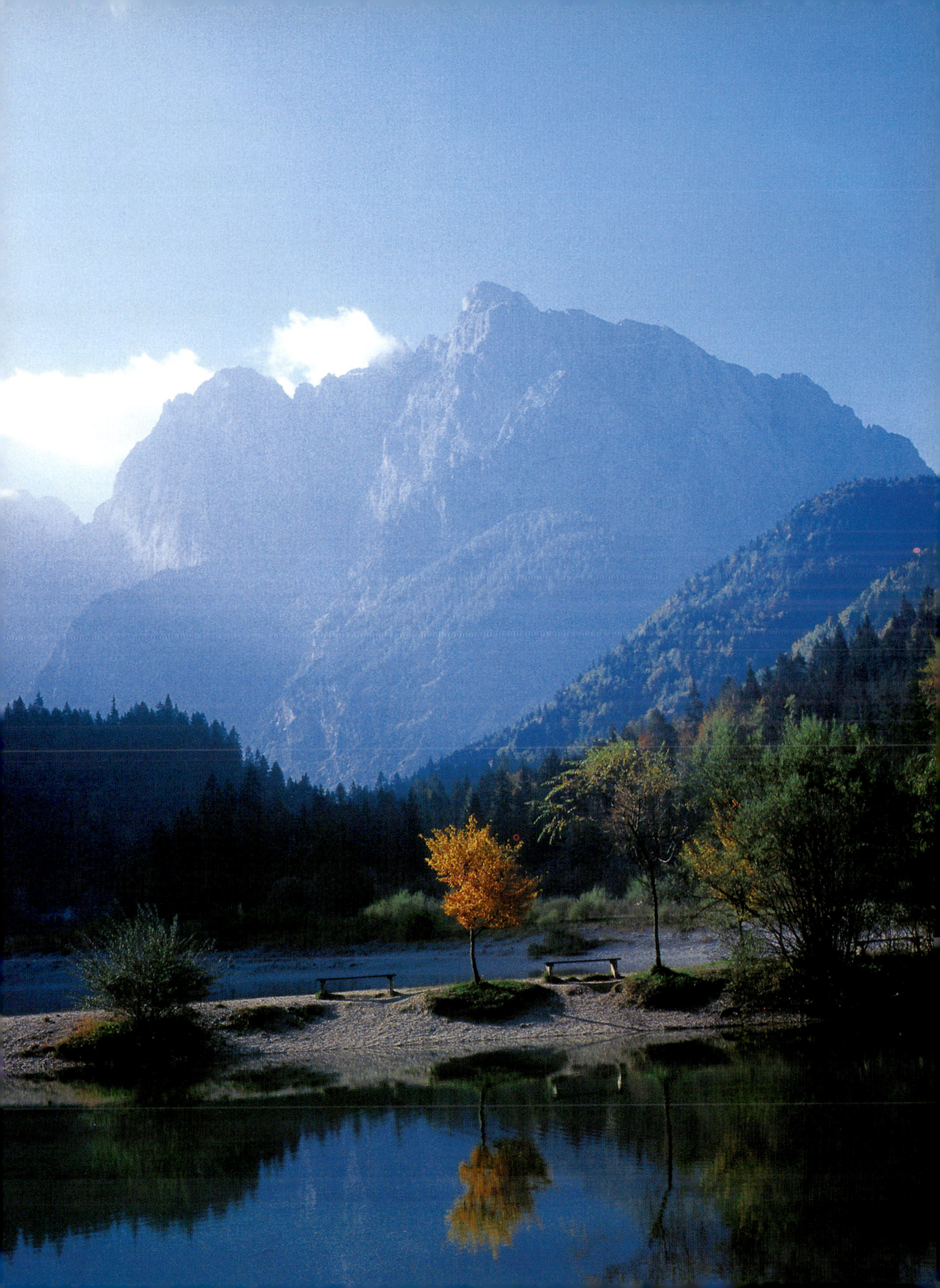

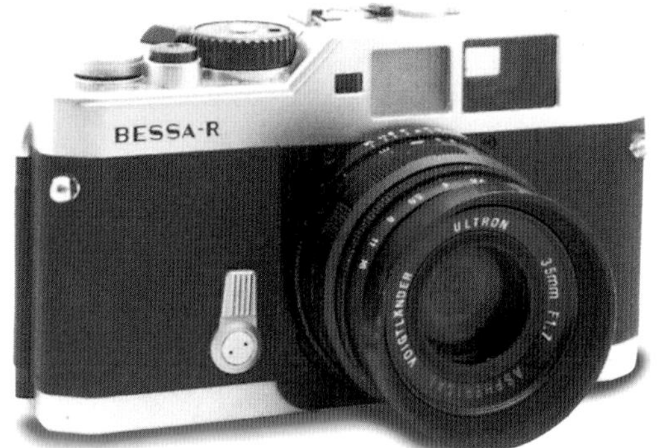

The Bessa-R can stand proudly alongside Canons and other top-flight 39mm x 26tpi cameras

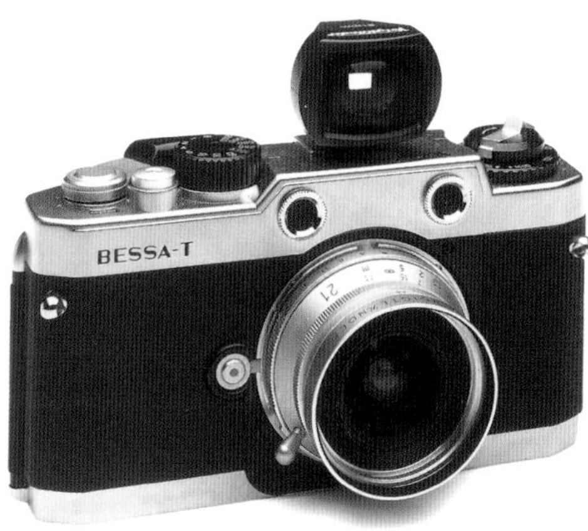

The Bessa-T is unique among 35mm RF cameras in having no built-in viewfinder

At the time of writing, the Bessa R2 was the top of the Voigtländer line

The Bessa-R was based on the Bessa-L, but with the addition of a coupled range/viewfinder and manually-selected, parallax-compensated bright-line frames for 35/90mm (as a pair), 50mm and 75mm. Next came the Bessa-T, unique among RF cameras in offering a CRF but no built-in viewfinder and featuring a four-claw bayonet Leica M-mount, as well as the option of a rapid wind trigger (see page 139). The newest at the time of writing was the Bessa-R2 (early 2002) which was a Bessa-R with the M-mount and trigger-wind option of the Bessa-T, plus refinements such as more metal and less plastic in the construction and a better rewind crank. In price order, from the cheapest to the most expensive, they run L-T-R-R2. The top-of-the-line R2 is still well under half the price of a current Leica M6 ttl, while a basic L is rather under a fifth of the price of the Leica.

The L, T and R have all been made in both black and chrome and, presumably with an eye to the collector market, there has also been a short run of Bessa-T models in colours: grey, blue, brown and olive drab. The R2 is made in olive drab and black. Although the appeal of the T is hard to explain, it is Frances's favourite in the line-up: because the rangefinder is separate from the viewfinders (which slot into the accessory shoe), it can be magnified, which makes for greater ease and accuracy of focusing, and it has an eyesight correction lens which makes it still easier to use.

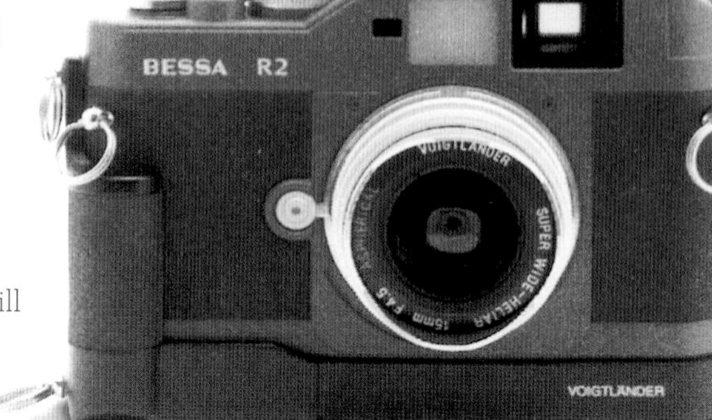

Meter and battery-independence

The meter is a simple centre-weighted type, reading off the grey front shutter blind, and is far better than it has any right to be. Film-speed range is modest (25–1600 on the L and T, 25–3200 on the R and R2) but adequate for most purposes: if you want to use Ilford Delta 3200 at 3200 and beyond, you should know enough to be able to make the necessary corrections to exposure.

The meter is battery dependent, obviously, but the rest of the camera is totally mechanical, and purists have even been known to remove the batteries in order to extinguish the 'traffic light' read-out. On the L and T, there are three lights on the outside of the body, red-green-red, while on the R and R2 they are all red.

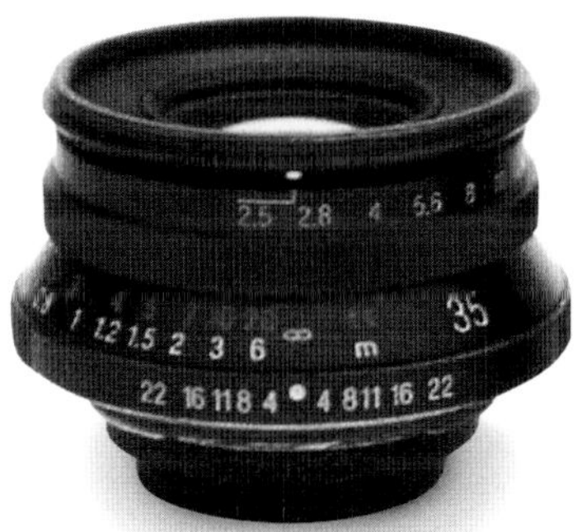
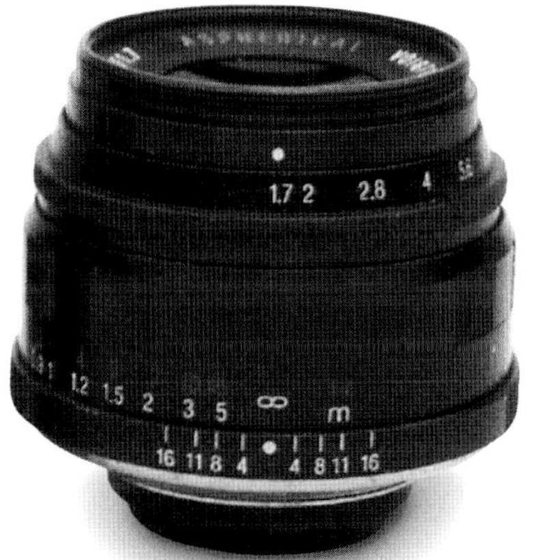

Voigtländers really joined the mainstream when they started to offer both 35/1.7 and 35/2.5 lenses, and a 35/1.2 was added in early 2003

Those who refuse to believe that such relatively modestly priced cameras can be any good have concerns about the longevity and build quality of Bessas, but we have been using them since they first came out and have had no problems: they receive no more cossetting than Roger's Leicas.

The only problems we have ever heard of are rangefinders going out of alignment (or, worse still, being out of alignment when new), but in the few cases this has happened, the fault has been easily rectified. And Roger's Leicas have needed rangefinder adjustments and other repairs from time to time, too.

Nikon- and Contax-compatible Voigtländers

These were introduced after this book was delivered, and shortly before it went to press, so there is very little that can be said about them. Both use a Nikon/Contax-style focusing wheel and accept Nikon S-fit lenses (R2S) or Contax-fit (R2C). They are, arguably, up-market of the Bessa series and better built, but they are also more expensive, and not everyone finds them as convenient to use.

LEICA

The current M-series Leicas are the M6 ttl and the M7. The former is to a large extent an M6 with through-lens flash metering (just as the M6 is an M4-P with through-lens metering); the latter closely resembles the M6 ttl and still uses a horizontal-run cloth shutter based on the M3, but now has electronic governance, optional aperture-priority auto-exposure (with exposure compensation) and DX-coding. The only mechanical speeds in the event of battery failure are 1/60 and 1/125 of a second.

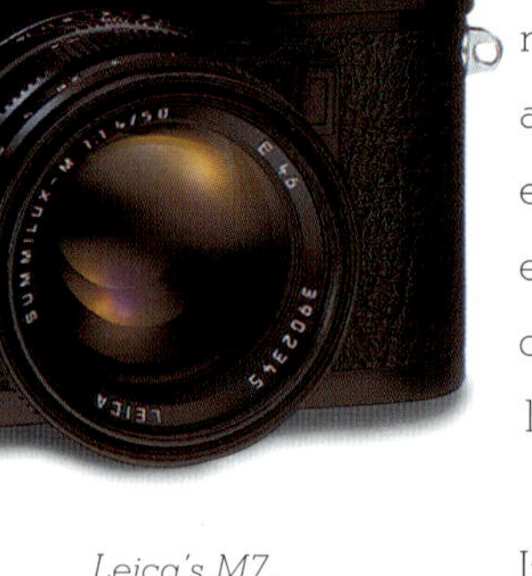

Leica's M7,

introduced in spring

2002, was the first

classic M with

automation

If you have never owned a Leica and want a new one and can afford an M6 ttl or M7, do not let us discourage you. They are still sublimely quiet, beautifully built, and designed to last forever – though there are inevitable question marks over the very long-term availability of spares for the M7, where a mechanical camera can normally have parts made up by a sufficiently skilled machinist. We are talking about substantial fractions of a century here, but this is what Leicas are about: Roger's M2s date from 1959 and 1961, and his IIIa was made in 1936.

If you already use Leicas, however, there is a discontinuity between the older cameras and the present generation that is all but unforgivable: the shutter-speed dial goes the wrong way. All previous Leicas have gone clockwise for higher speeds, but the M6 ttl and M7 go anticlockwise. Long-term Leica users, used to setting shutter speeds by touch, will switch from (say) 1/125 to 1/60 and find that they are at 1/250. This only matters to established Leica users, but as Roger bought his first Leica in 1971, his first M-series in 1974, and his first new Leica in 1983, he finds the M6 ttl and M7 unusable.

There are several variants of the M6, M6 ttl and M7, with different viewfinder magnifications from up to 0.85x; the 28mm frame is not visible in the 0.85x models.

Choosing an M-series

If you can live without through-lens metering, a 'classic' Leica is a wonderful camera – though M2 and M3 models are now getting very old (the most recent models date from 1967/68), and they do require repair or servicing from time to time.

As noted, the M3 is the best made, but the absence of a 35mm frame rules it out for many; a good M2 remains Roger's favourite to this day. The single viewfinder frames are very simple, and this is arguably the camera for the purist.

The M4 series are very usable, but not as elegant as the earlier cameras, while the earliest M6 cameras were not always that reliable, although after the first year or so, that problem was solved. The reversed shutter-speed dial of the M6 ttl has already been mentioned. Both the M5 and (increasingly) the CL command such high prices that you might as well buy a 'real' M-series.

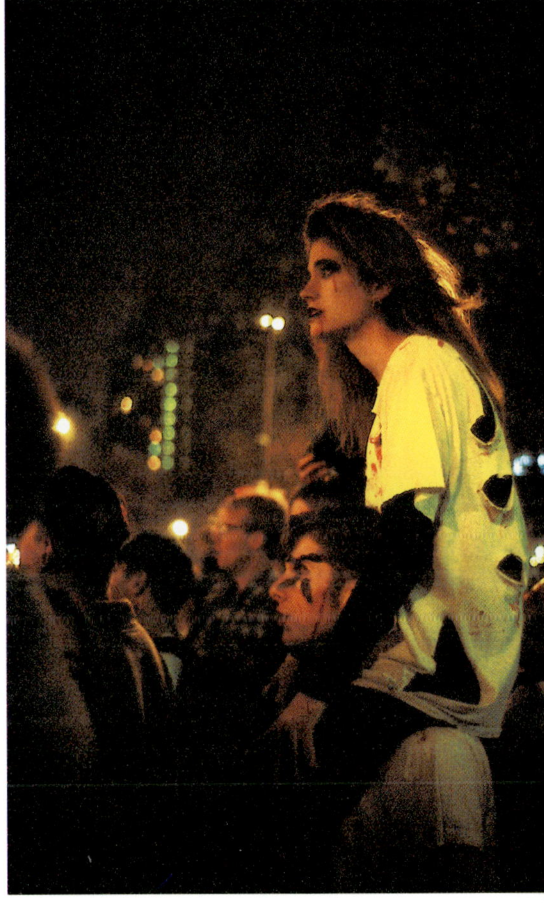

Hallowe'en parade, New York City

If you are into people-watching, there's nothing like an RF camera, a fast lens and fast film – and besides, it's rude to interrupt others' enjoyment by constantly firing a flash. I used my M4P and 35/1.4 Summilux with Fuji RSP at EI 2000 for this picture

Using an M-series

The only things that are worth remarking are a few omissions and old-fashioned features that may strike some photographers today as odd. For example, some classic M-series have self-timers (usually represented as DA, delayed action, in advertisements) and others don't, while some models were made in both versions.

The horizontal-run cloth shutter of a classic M is very leisurely by modern standards. This accounts for both its quietness and its longevity, and also for the very modest flash-synch speed, even on the M7: an unexpected 1/50 of a second, click-stopped between the 1/30 and 1/60 settings.

Accessory meters are available for non-metered models. And there have been various kinds of ancillary rewind crank for the knob-rewind M2 and M3; these are covered in Chapter 7.

CONTAX

One of the proudest names in RF/DV cameras and, after Leica, the second oldest of the Great Names, Contax came back into the RF/DV market with the G-series in 1994.

The Contax is easily the most highly automated of all current 35mm non-reflex 'system' cameras

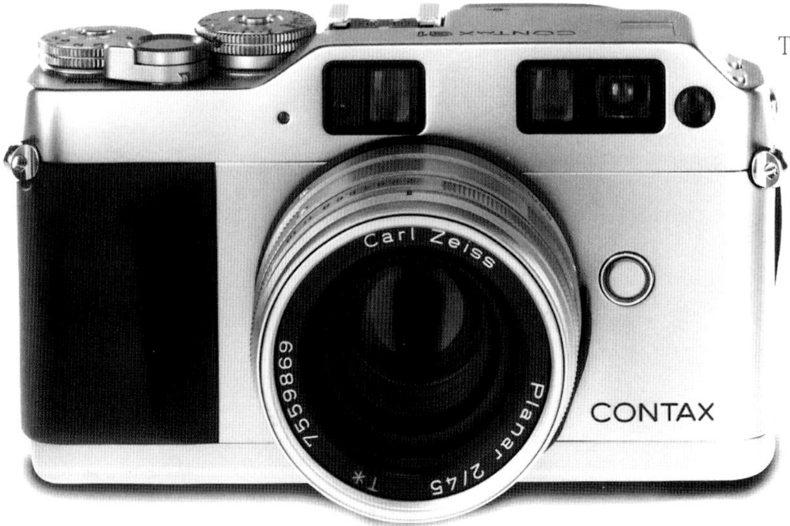

These are as far as one can reasonably get from the all-mechanical, fully-manual, battery-independent RF/DV cameras of yore, as they incorporate autofocus (except for the 16mm lens), optional auto-exposure (along with full manual control), 4 fps motorized film advance, and a motorized zoom viewfinder.

If you are firmly wedded to automation, but still want an interchangeable-lens RF/DV camera of the very highest quality, the G-series is the only choice. The Zeiss lenses are second to none: 16/8, 21/2.8, 35/2, 50/2, 90/2.8 plus a mid-range zoom. Unfortunately, the mount is unique to the G-series and (with the exception of the 16mm) these superb lenses can't be adapted to anything else.

The electronic shutter allows a very wide range of shutter speeds (1/4000 to 16 full seconds on the G2) with a correspondingly high flash-synch speed (1/200). The later G2 is reckoned to be a significantly better camera in every way than the G1, so this is the one to go for. Only the 16mm and 21mm lenses require additional finders.

If, on the other hand, you are averse to 'all-singing, all-dancing' cameras, you will do well to avoid the G-series. This is a matter of personal taste, but (for example) the 'manual' focus actually operates via a dial on the camera body and an electronic linkage, rather than by twisting a focusing collar.

The optical adjustment on the eyepieces is very welcome, but a small disadvantage is that the eyepiece glass is very deep-set. When it steams up under hot, sweaty working conditions (as all eyepiece glasses can) it is quite hard to wipe off.

FUJI

The Hasselblad XPan, below, is sold as a Fuji in Japan and possibly in some other markets. The body finish is different and (dare we say it) more attractive than the Hasselblad version, though this may simply be the lure of the exotic.

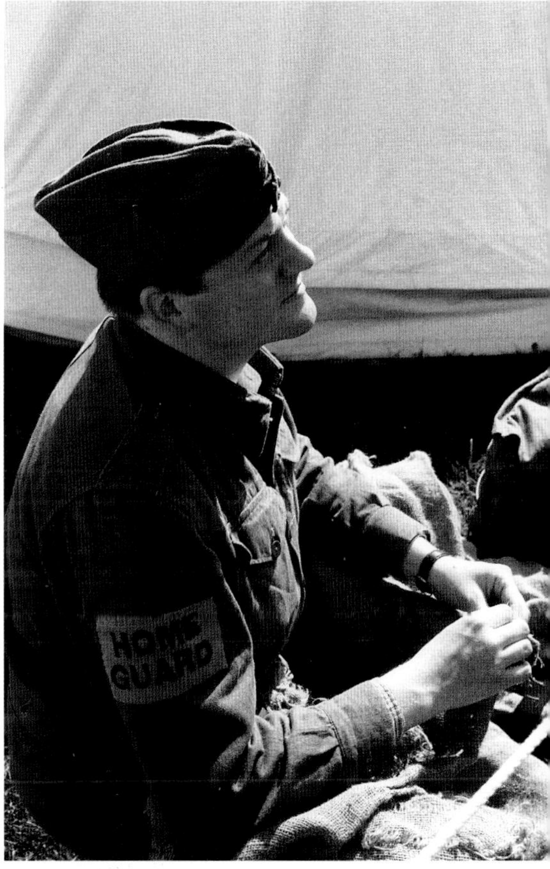

Home Guard

I've always been fascinated by the way that some people look as if they belong in a particular decade: Frances's mother, for example, was a child of the '60s who had the misfortune to be born in 1911. This man has a 1940s face; he doesn't look like a twenty-first century man in a 60-year-old uniform. Bessa-R, 35/2.5 Color-Skopar, yellow filter, HP5 in DDX at 500, MG Warmtone

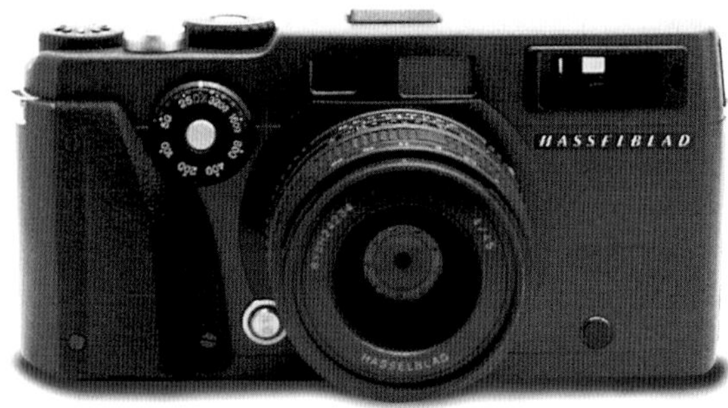

Hasselblad's Xpan is a wonderfully versatile and easy to use camera

HASSELBLAD

The XPan, introduced at photokina 1998, was developed jointly with Fuji, and offers a unique choice of the conventional 24 x 36mm format and 24 x 65mm; the latter printable, of course, in 6 x 7cm enlargers.

It mixes a superb traditional mechanical range/viewfinder (with full parallax compensation) with through-lens metering and electric film advance (which, of course, renders it battery dependent), and a choice of either full manual operation or aperture-priority auto (with +/- 2EV compensation) and auto-bracketing. On loading, the film is wound out fully, then rewound frame by frame into the cassette, and panoramic or conventional formats can be selected at any time, with even spacing between frames, thanks to the ability to move the film in either direction.

The extremely wide format means that the lenses have to have unusually large coverage, which means they are rather slow by the standards of conventional 35mm cameras: 30/5.6 (with special centre-grad filter), 45/4 and 90/4. It also means that they have to have a unique fitting. And it means that the huge, horizontal-run shutter reaches only 1/1000 of a second.

Although its format options mean that it is somewhat off to the side of the mainstream, those who try the XPan tend to fall in love with it, and there are persistent rumours of a model for the 24 x 36mm format only. Depending on how this was made, it could prove a serious rival for the Konica Hexar or the Leica, or maybe both.

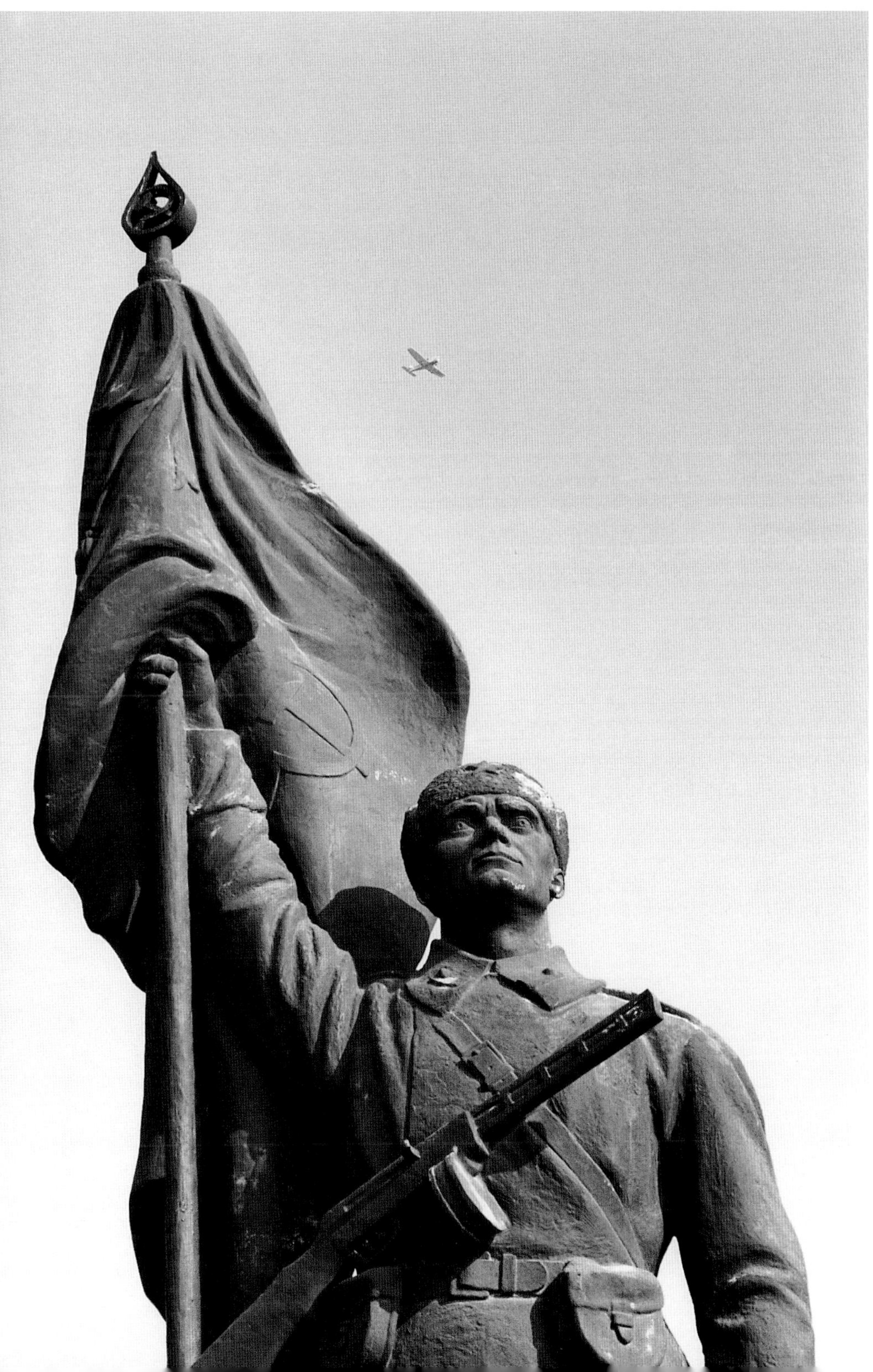

Soviet monument

During the Second Great Patriotic War, rangefinders were pretty much the only game in town for 35mm. This statue in the Monument Park outside Budapest reminded me of the propaganda pictures of that era. Thanks to continuous viewing, I could see exactly when this aircraft was in the best possible position. Bessa-R, 50/1.5 Nokton, yellow filter, XP2, MG Warmtone

KONICA

Arguably, the Konica Hexar-M paved the way for the M7: still a high-quality mechanical rangefinder, with manual focus and Leica M-fit lenses, but also with an electronic focal-plane shutter from 16 full seconds to 1/4000 of a second, optional auto-exposure (with full manual operation too) and 2.5 fps electric film advance (even the M7 relies on the thumb lever). Through-lens metering is, of course, taken for granted.

To others, the Hexar-M is exactly what the Leica should never have become, because of two words: battery dependence. Only you can decide which matters more to you: the convenience of a more modern design (the Konica) and the fact that you have to change batteries every 100–150 rolls, or the mechanical simplicity (a detractor might say primitiveness) of any Leica except an M7. The Konica can deliver results that are indistinguishable from the Leica, especially if you fit Leica lenses, so it really is a matter of those who decry the Leica as old-fashioned being ready to put their money where their mouth is.

The lens line-up is limited and rather slow: 28/2.8, 50/2 and 90/2.8. A 50/1.2 is available, but only with a special Millennium commemorative titanium-bodied version of the camera. There is also a slight question mark over cross-compatibility with Leica and other lenses: Konica were very evasive and said that the camera was designed only for their own Konica M-Hexanon lenses. Research by two American magazines in 2002 indicated that film-to-flange register sometimes required 'tweaking' by a skilled repairer.

The plain Hexar (not Hexar-M) has a fixed, manual-focus 35/2 lens of very high quality and is very well regarded.

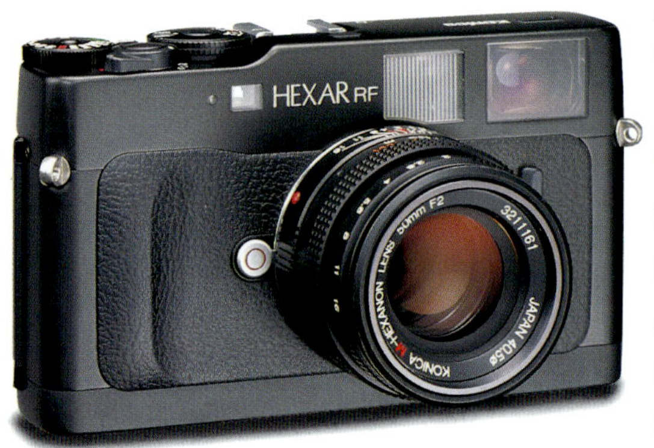

Konica's Hexar is ideal for those who want more automation than an M7, but not as much as a Contax

MINOX

As well as their famous range of sub-miniatures (see page 34), Minox has, since 1974, made an extremely fine and very compact folding 35mm camera fitted with a fixed 35/2.8 Minoxar. Some professionals carry these as 'back-ups', and we have known several who, for one reason or another (such as lost baggage, theft or breakdown of their main camera), have had to use them on assignment, when the cameras acquitted themselves very well indeed. Go for the ones with manual control (some are fully automatic) and be aware that their principal drawback is the tiny lettering on many of the controls: one good friend got rid of his when he could no longer see well enough without glasses to use it.

Although the original mercury cell is no longer available, a replacement Minox battery holder lets you use two readily available current cells instead. There was an autofocus version, but it is rare, made only from about 1988 to 1990. Aficionados prefer the much more readily available manual version.

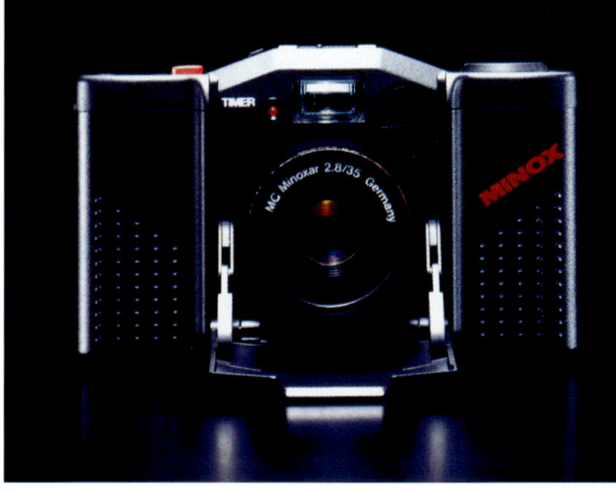

The Minox 35 has been through many iterations, but all are very compact folders

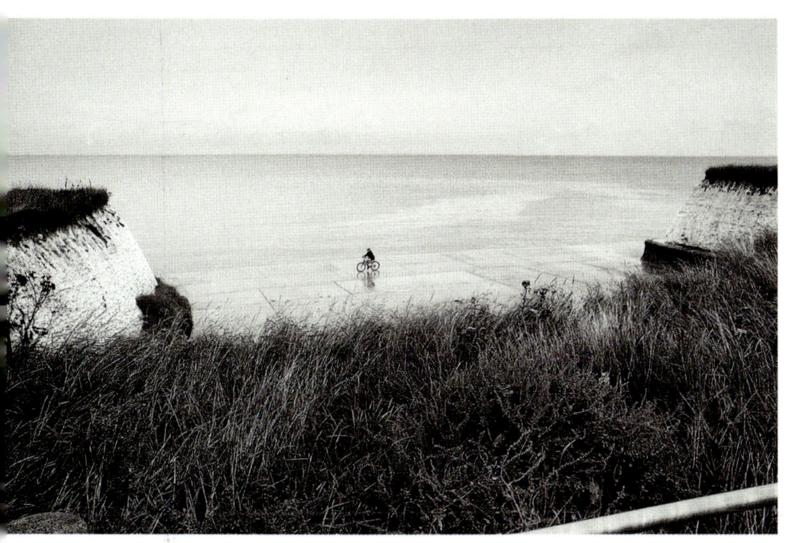

Bicyclist, Minnis Bay

One of the things I really like about RF cameras is that they are simple: operation soon becomes almost instinctive. I was focused on something 1m (3ft) away when this cyclist hove into view, going quite fast. It took a split second to re-focus and reduce the shutter speed by two steps. Bessa-R, 21/4 Color-Skopar, yellow filter, XP2, MG Warmtone

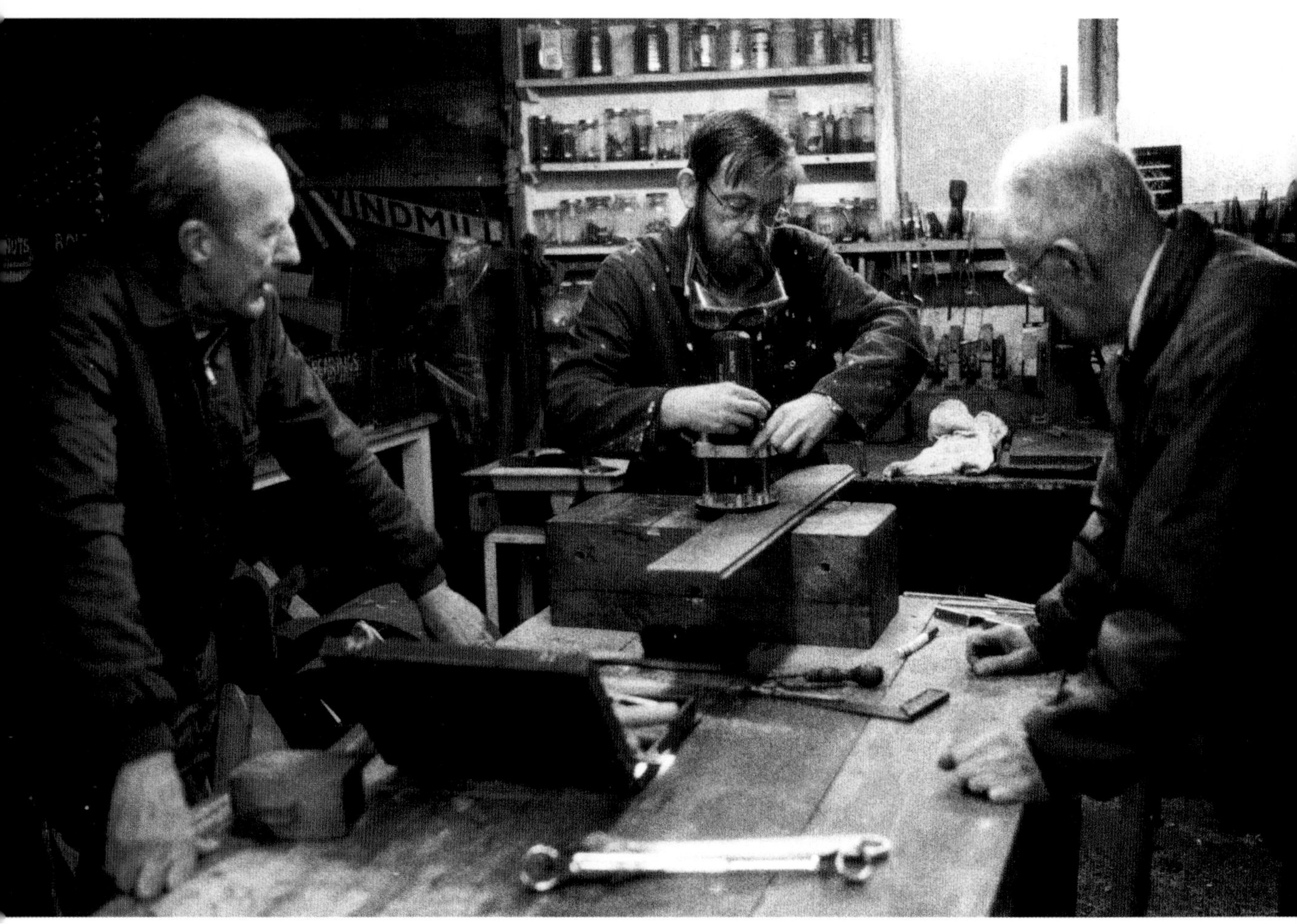

Draper's Mill

Ultra-fast lenses are much less necessary with today's high-speed films. When I started photography in the 1960s, the fastest film you could get was ISO 400, pushable to maybe EI 1000. Today, with Delta 3200 (at EI 3200, as here), I can stop down to f/4 and still use the same shutter speed as with ISO 400 and an f/1.4 lens. Bessa-R, 35/1.7 Ultron, MG Warmtone

NIKON

In 2000, Nikon announced a limited-edition 'Millennium' re-issue of the S3 rangefinder camera. Right down to the finger-rasping focusing wheel (with infinity lock) and the revolving 5cm lens, this is a late-1950s camera, and it is more about nostalgia and collectability than usability. Also, Nikon offered just the 50/1.4 'Olympic' lens, though Voigtländer jumped in with the option of 21/4, 25/4 and 35/2.5 for those who wanted a more usable camera. Price alone rules the S3 out for most users, though the determined (and rich) will find that it performs very well.

ROBOT

Robots are still available new, but they are astonishingly expensive and sell mostly for bank surveillance and other security applications: German speed cops use them (or used to) in their Porsches. Most do not even have viewfinders, and many have external electric drives and remote releases. By all means check the current line-up, but you will probably find that used ones are a better bet.

ROLLEI

Rollei makes a number of high-end auto-everything 35mm cameras, but the tiny (385g [12oz]), boxy, all-manual Rollei 35 is the camera that most serious photographers praise most highly. Arguably, this was the camera that killed half-frame: despite being full-frame 35mm, it is smaller than many half-frames. The lens is a non-interchangeable collapsible 40mm, scale-focusing, only down to 1m (3ft); there is no parallax compensation in the viewfinder.

Introduced in 1966, it has been through many iterations, and has been built in Germany and Singapore. Modern German-built Rollei 35 cameras are as good as any have ever been, but they tend to be positioned at the collector/wealthy amateur end of the market, so for the user, a second-hand example may be best. About two million have been made, so they're not uncommon.

German-built models command a higher price than Singaporean, and a great deal depends on the lens. The 40/2.8 Zeiss Sonnar is understandably the best, and is unit-focus rather than front-cell focus; late models are multi-coated ('HFT'). The 40/3.5 Zeiss Tessar is good, and the 40/3.5 Triotar is probably better than you expect, though clearly inferior to the Tessar. Tessars and Sonnars are in shutters speeded 1/2 to 1/500 of a second, Triotars just 1/30 to 1/500.

It's an eccentric little beast, with a left-hand lever wind; hot shoe on the bottom (and no PC connection); a hard-to-see film counter, also on the bottom; and a body shell that removes entirely to load the film, with a film pressure plate that is a sort of trapdoor hinged to the body. All have non-TTL metering, either match-needle or the LED system preferred by many Rollei aficionados. If the meter packs up or the battery dies, the fully mechanical camera remains entirely usable. Like Minox 35s, Rollei 35s are favoured by many professionals as back-ups; the Sonnar-lens models deliver even better results than the Minoxes.

YASUHARA

The first Yasuhara was the T981, of which about 4000 were made between 1998 and 2001. A startlingly ugly camera, it was further handicapped by the fact that the shutter was not fully light-tight: it was borrowed from an SLR, where the mirror acts as a subsidiary shutter. As a result, it was recommended that the lens be capped at all times, except when actually shooting, and lens changing needed to be done in very subdued light.

To be fair, the Yasuhara preceded the Voigtländers which really repopularized rangefinder cameras, and it has a number of attractive features: a 1:1 range/viewfinder, with auto-parallax compensation, and TTL metering. It was replaced in 2001/2002 with the T102, a more advanced version of the same thing. Both use the standard Leica screw mount, but no Yasuhara-branded lenses were offered.

Production of the Yasuhara was apparently shifted to China in the interests of reducing costs, but the price remained very high and only a few seem to have been sold under the Phoenix name.

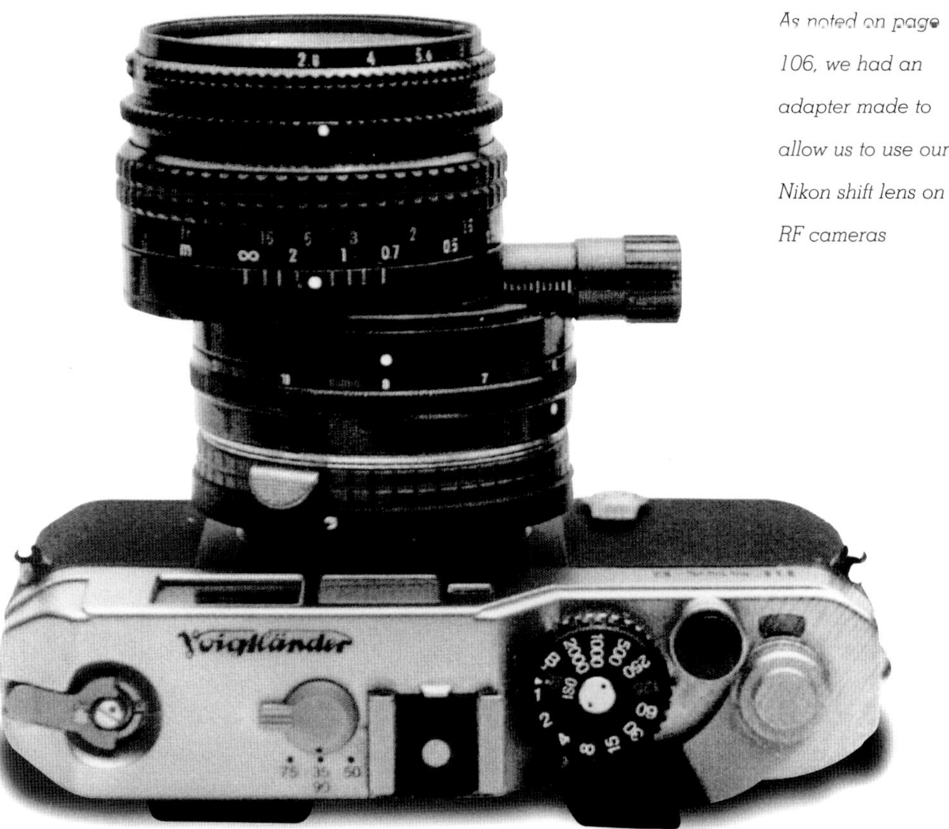

As noted on page 106, we had an adapter made to allow us to use our Nikon shift lens on RF cameras

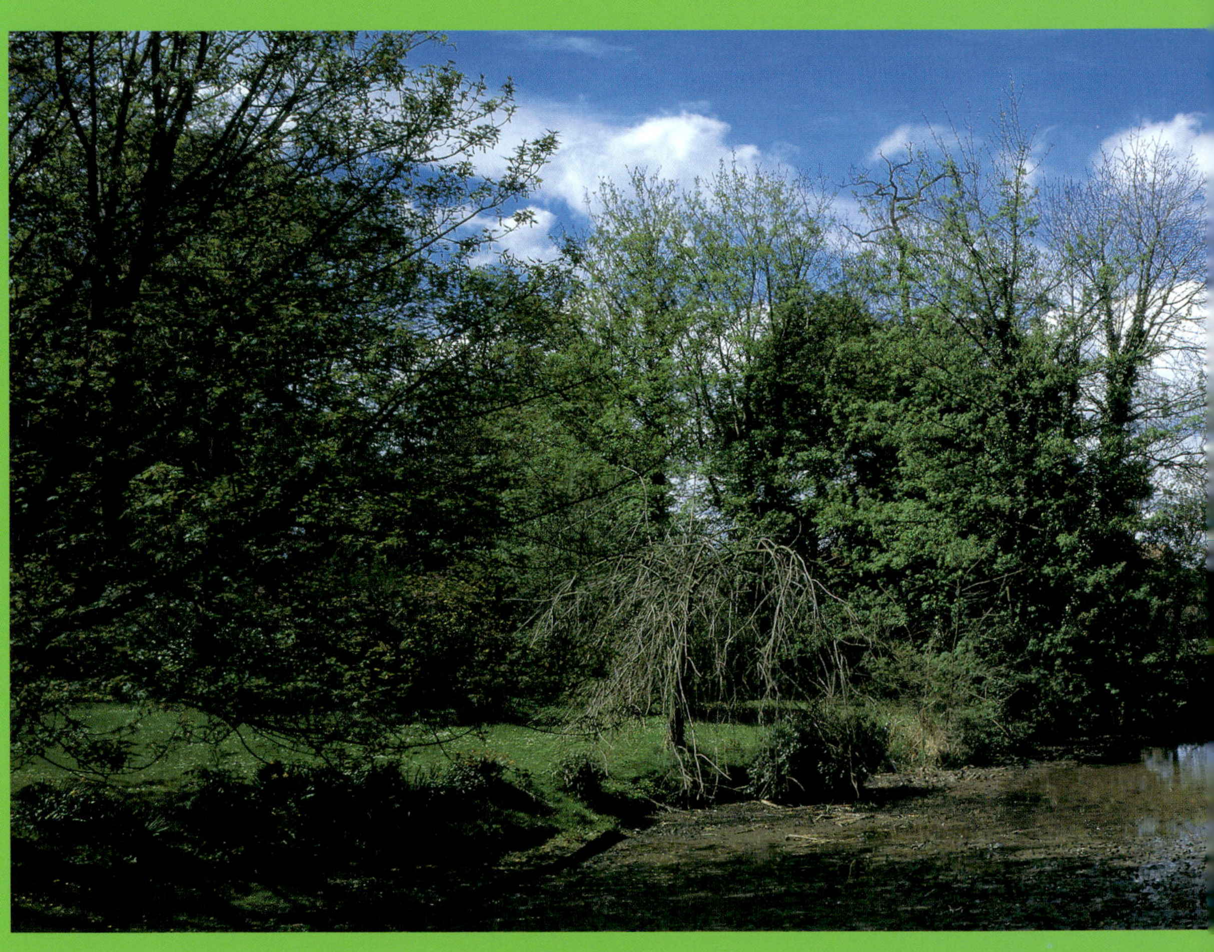

BUILD A BIGGER VIEWFINDER

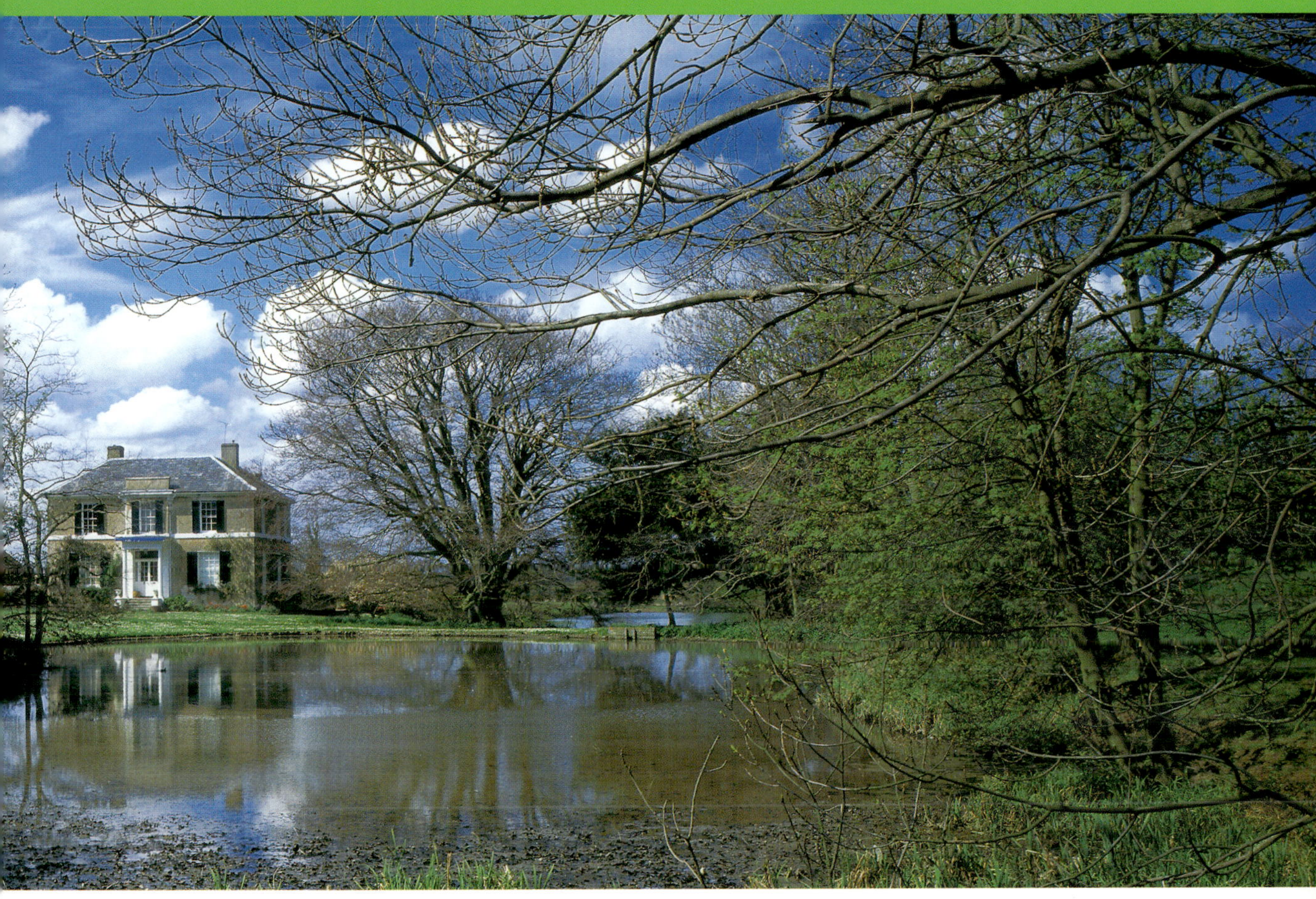

As the old saying goes: 'A good big 'un will always beat a good little 'un.' This was what kept 4 x 5in and 9 x 12cm cameras in use among the press for so long, and it is why to this day so many wedding photographers use roll film.

It also explains the appeal of medium-format (MF) and large-format (LF) cameras in many other fields, from landscape to portraiture. A first-class printer, under optimum conditions with the utmost care, can get a pretty good 12 x 16in or 30 x 40cm print from a 35mm negative; but just about any printer can do the same from a 645 or larger negative with a lot less effort.

Preston-next-Wingham

All right, I cheated for this shot: I put the Linhof 617 on a tripod. But I have used one handheld, plenty of times. If I could afford one, I'd buy it, despite the comments in the text about the merits of cropping 6 x 9cm. Just to reach the length of the 617, a 6 x 9 must be enlarged 2x. Fuji RDP

CHOOSING A FORMAT

With non-reflex cameras, bulk and weight increase far less
with larger formats than they do with reflexes. Although 645
and 6 x 6 SLRs tend to be similar in size, 6 x 7cm tends to be
a lot bigger; the 6 x 8cm Fuji is gigantic; and 6 x 9cm is so
vast that there have been very few since World War Two (the
Arca Swiss is the only one that is normally encountered). A 6 x 7
or 6 x 9 RF camera is inevitably bigger than a 645, but still not
hopelessly unwieldy. The same is true, a fortiori, of LF.

If you shoot colour negative, or chromogenic black and white
film such as Ilford XP2, the 645 format may be all you need.
Colour negative films are not particularly sharp, but they have
a tiny grain structure which reduces still further when they are
overexposed (though overexposure also reduces sharpness).

If you shoot conventional black and white, on the other hand,
you will (assuming you stick with the same film) get detectably
smaller grain, smoother tonality and better sharpness in big
enlargements from 6 x 7cm than you will from 645; we have
no hesitation in saying that, in this case, bigger is better.

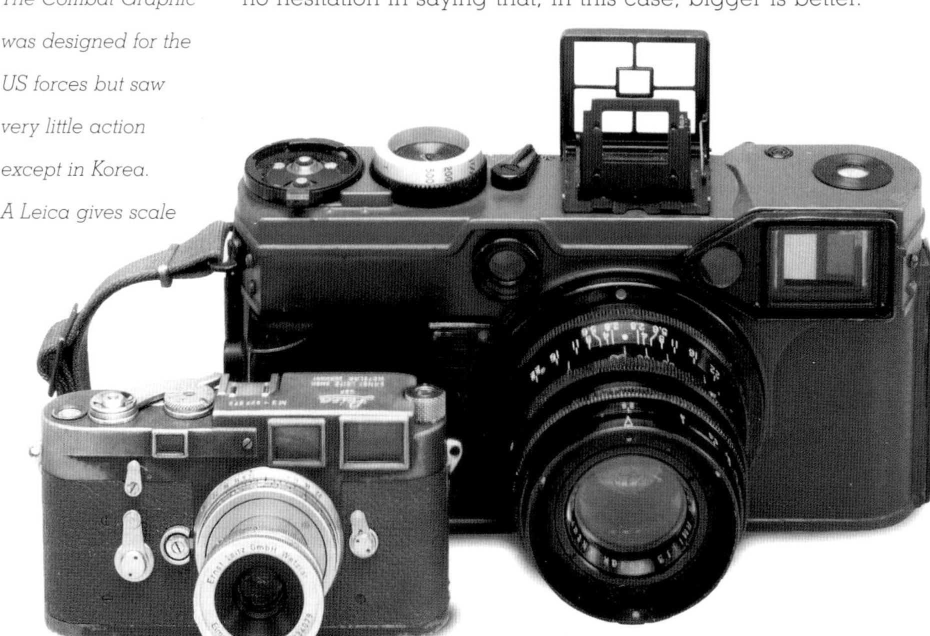

The Combat Graphic was designed for the US forces but saw very little action except in Korea. A Leica gives scale

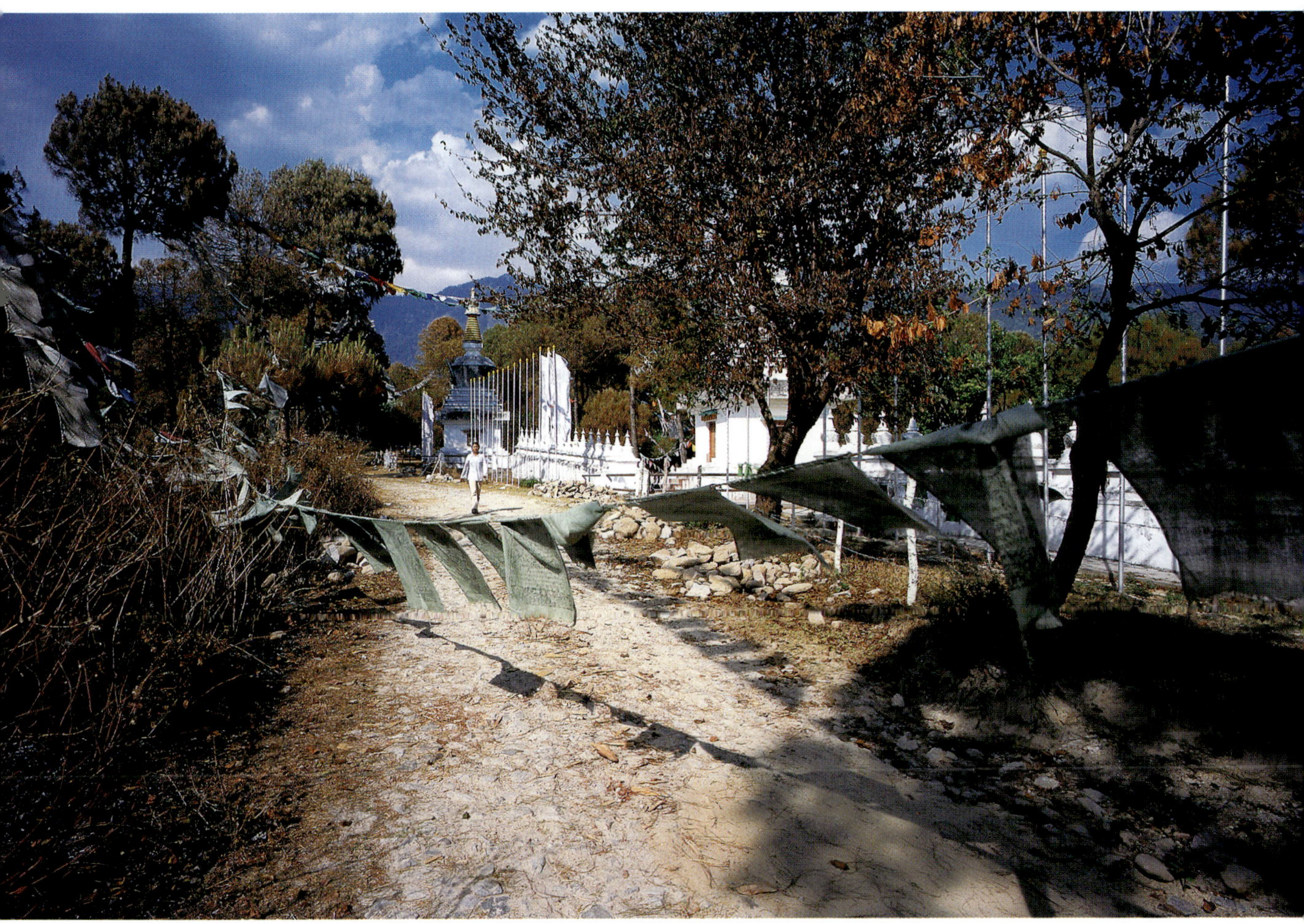

Lens speed and film speeds

Perhaps surprisingly, smaller-format roll-film cameras do not
have significantly faster lenses. Few, if any, can boast anything
faster than f/3.5, despite the fact that there have been a
number of f/2.8 lenses in the past, including 80 and 100mm
Rodenstock and Zeiss and 80mm Nikkors, to say nothing of the
pre-war 100/2.9 Anticomar.

The reason for this is that fast lenses are bulky, expensive, and
heavy, and depth of focus (rather than depth of field) is also a
consideration. Roll film does not lie particularly flat, and an

Youdon at Sherab Ling

*Sherab Ling, the 'Place of Wisdom', is a
massive Tibetan monastery in exile in the
foothills of the Himalayas. I asked Tsering
Youdon to walk towards me to provide a focal
point for the picture, which was taken with my
standard Alpa outfit: 38/4.5 Biogon on 66 x
44mm. Fuji Astia*

Pjazza Katedral, Citadella, Gozo

The delay between pressing the cable release and getting the picture is about 1/60 of a second with an RF/DV camera such as my Alpa or the 'baby' Linhof that I used for this shot – and about 1/10 of a second with a typical 6 x 7cm reflex. 100/5.6 Apo-Symmar, 6 x 7cm Fuji Astia

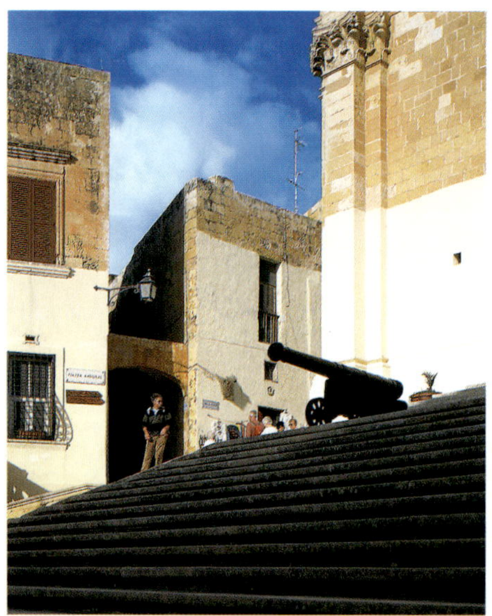

80/2.8 or (worse still) 100/2.8 can be in focus on some parts of a 120 image and out on others. Again, this is still more true with poorly located 4 x 5in or 9 x 12cm.

Also, there's not a lot of point in really fast lenses. For reportage, there is no way that roll film or cut film can compete with the f/2 and faster lenses of 35mm. On the other hand, you can use very, very fast films without worrying as much about grain and sharpness as you do with 35mm, and with a well-designed camera, smaller degrees of enlargement mean that you can get away with longer handheld speeds. Thus, a 90/3.5 on a Fuji 690 loaded with Ilford Delta 3200 at 3200 is roughly equivalent to a 50/1.2 on a 35mm camera loaded with Ilford HP5 Plus at 400 – quite apart from the fact that you will probably get less unsharpness due to camera shake with the Fuji at 1/30 of a second than with a 35mm camera at 1/60.

Although there aren't as many fast films available for 120 as there are for 35mm, there are enough to make this route feasible. In monochrome, Delta 3200 is easily the fastest; in colour slide, Kodak's E200 is the best bet, as it can be pushed to EI 1000; and if you want a colour negative, although the demise of Konica SRG 3200 is constantly rumoured, there are several films of ISO 800 or faster.

Comparing focal lengths

It is impossible to give absolute equivalents for focal lengths for different formats, unless those formats are identical in shape. The comparisons given in the text are based on diagonal coverage (from one corner of the negative to the other), which is the traditional focal length of a 'standard' lens. Obviously, vertical and horizontal coverage vary according to the shape of the image.

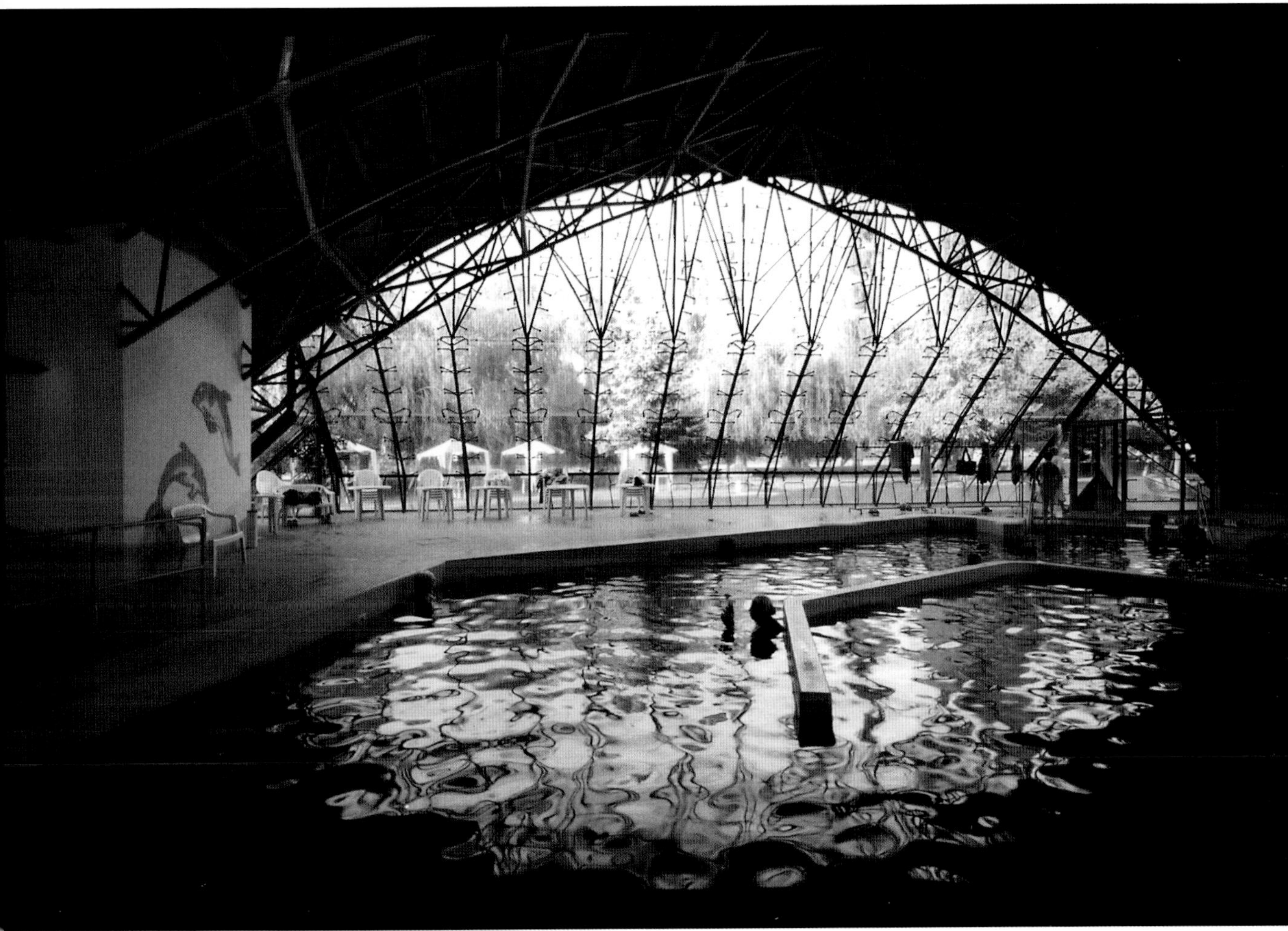

The diagonals of the various formats are approximately 43mm for 35mm (though a 'standard' lens was often 50mm); 70mm for 645 (where 80mm is quite common); 80mm for 6 x 6cm; 90mm for 6 x 7cm; and 100mm for 6 x 9cm. Moving up to cut film, they are 150mm for 4 x 5in (also used for 9 x 12cm), 210mm for 5 x 7in and 13 x 18cm (also used for half-plate, 4¾ x 6½in, 121 x 165mm) and 300mm for 8 x 10in (also used for 18 x 24cm).

Tomasi Baths

Hungary's spas are wonderfully democratic and affordable, but vary enormously in style and condition. Someday I'd like to do an extended photo essay on them – maybe even a book – using a Nikonos for shots in the baths, and my Alpa 12WA (as here) for more general pictures. 38/4.5 Biogon, 44 x 66mm HP5 in Perceptol at 250, MG Warmtone, selenium-toned

Film sizes

Overwhelmingly, the majority of roll-film cameras are used with 120 film, but inside Japan, and sometimes outside, you can buy a half-length 120 that gives 4-on 6 x 9cm, 5-on 6 x 7cm, 6-on 6 x 6cm and 8-on 645, though we have only ever seen this offered as colour negative. In the other direction, 220 is 120 without the paper backing (it has a paper leader and trailer instead): it gives 16-on 6 x 9cm, 20-on 6 x 7cm, 24-on 6 x 6cm and 30, 31 or 32-on 645. The choice of 220 films is limited, though, and often you can buy and process two rolls of 120 cheaper than one roll of 220, so unless you really need the long load, 220 doesn't make much sense. Some cameras have adjustable pressure plates and dual counters so that they can be used with both 120 and 220, while others are 120 only. The (long-discontinued) Linhof 220, confusingly, can be used with either.

One of the great missed opportunities of medium format is 70mm which, as its name suggests, is like double-width 35mm. It is normally encountered for 6 x 7cm only where, for example, the 56 x 72mm Linhof format is 50-on to 53-on for a standard 15ft (4.6m) load, which is loaded in a velvet-lipped cartridge like a giant 35mm cassette. The film runs cassette-to-cassette, so it can be unloaded at any time with the loss of a few frames, either to be reloaded later or to have the exposed film cut off and developed before putting the cassette with remaining film back into the camera.

Unfortunately, very few films are available in 70mm, and (it has to be said) the film is a swine to handle in the darkroom, so maybe it isn't that great a loss after all. Besides, how many applications demand 50 plus 6 x 7cm frames at a single loading? There have been a couple of 70mm cameras in the past (Combat Graphic, Komlosy), but today the only 70mm

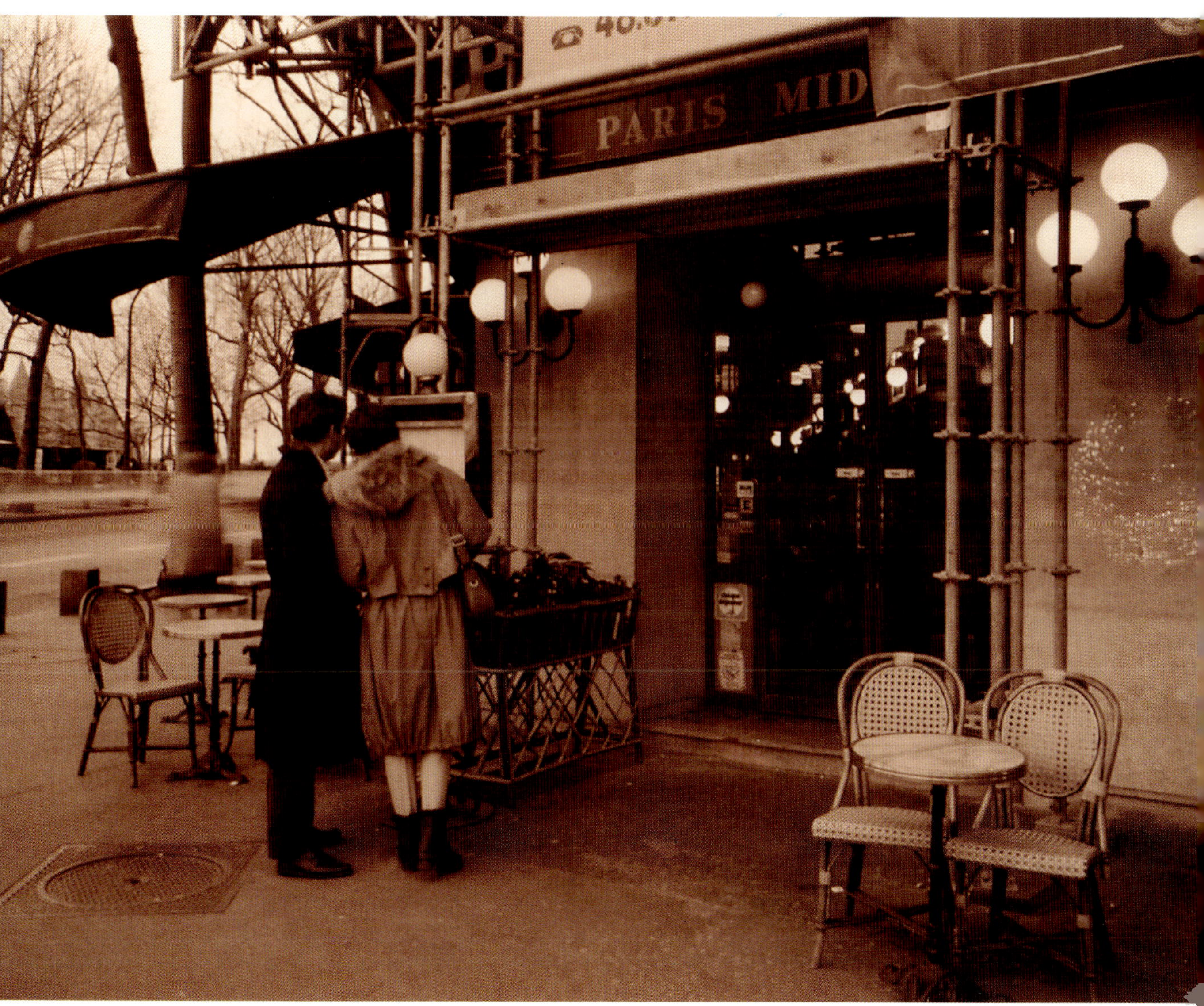

Bistro, Paris

This is the sort of picture that I like to shoot handheld, using a 5 x 4 MPP MK VII and a 90/6.8 Angulon. The Polaroid Sepia on which I took this is rather delicate: with all Polaroid prints, you can scan or copy them so that you have an unblemished copy, or you can let them take their chances. Here, the thumb print (courtesy of an origination house!) adds to the vintage quality of the image.

option is in interchangeable backs, principally from Linhof or (as modified Linhofs) for Alpa. We have a 70mm back for our Alpas, but we seldom use it.

Although the market for RF/DV roll-film cameras is small, and the market for RF/DV large-format cameras is even smaller, there is a surprisingly wide choice on the new market. And, if you are willing to use cameras that are a decade or two old, it is even bigger. The logical place to start is with the format that is closest in size to 35mm and work upwards.

645

Not only is 645 closest in size to 35mm, it also tends to be closest in features, with auto-exposure and even autofocus. Only two 645 RF/DV cameras were available new at the time of writing, from Fuji and Bronica.

Fuji's auto-everything cameras include auto-exposure, automatic reading of Fuji film speeds (via a barcode on the leader), auto-film advance and autofocus. They come with a range of fixed lenses: 45mm, 60mm and a 55–90mm zoom. In 35mm terms, these are roughly the equivalents of 28mm, 40mm and 35–55mm. They are nice little cameras with manual override, but they tend to be looked down upon as more suitable for 'happy snappers' than for serious photographers. In fact, loaded with something like Kodak Portra 400 film and the film speed set to about half the ISO speed, they deliver astonishing quality up to about 12 x 16in (30 x 40cm), though for the serious black and white user, a larger format is a good idea.

The predecessors of the auto-everything Fujis were somewhat simpler manual-focus machines, and included the GS645, a folding camera of unconventional appearance with a 75/3.5 lens, and two rigid-bodied models with fixed 45mm and 60mm lenses.

The Bronica, introduced at photokina 2000, is a 645 with (at least at the time of writing) a rather limited range of lenses: 55mm (35mm on 35mm), 65mm (40mm) and 135mm (90mm). The interchangeable lenses increase its versatility compared with the Fujis and, again, it's a good camera for colour.

6 x 6cm

There is not much excuse for this format in RF/DV cameras. The main reasons it existed were for economy in snapshot cameras – 12-on-120 is more economical than 8-on-120 – and for reflex cameras without prisms, which can't easily be tipped on their side to change from landscape to portrait. It's true that a few people compose square pictures all the time, and that most of us compose square pictures from time to time, but the vast majority of 6 x 6cm images are cropped for printing, and at that point you might as well use 645.

There are, however, two arguments for 6 x 6cm and one more against. The first argument for it is that if you crop out the bottom of the image, you get what amounts to a rising front for architectural shots. The second argument for it is that you can compose with either vertical or horizontal shots in mind, then crop at the printing stage. The argument against it is that you are not the only one who can crop at the printing stage: you let a square transparency out of your hands, for photomechanical reproduction, at your peril.

The only current RF/DV camera that we know of in this format is the Chinese-made Seagull RF folder. It is a very traditional camera, and reportedly the quality control is better than it used to be. Until recently, there was also the Mamiya 6, an interchangeable-lens camera that was, at least in its later versions, also multi-format: it could do 645 and 35mm as well. When the 6 x 7cm version appeared, logically called the Mamiya 7, the appeal of the 6 dropped rapidly.

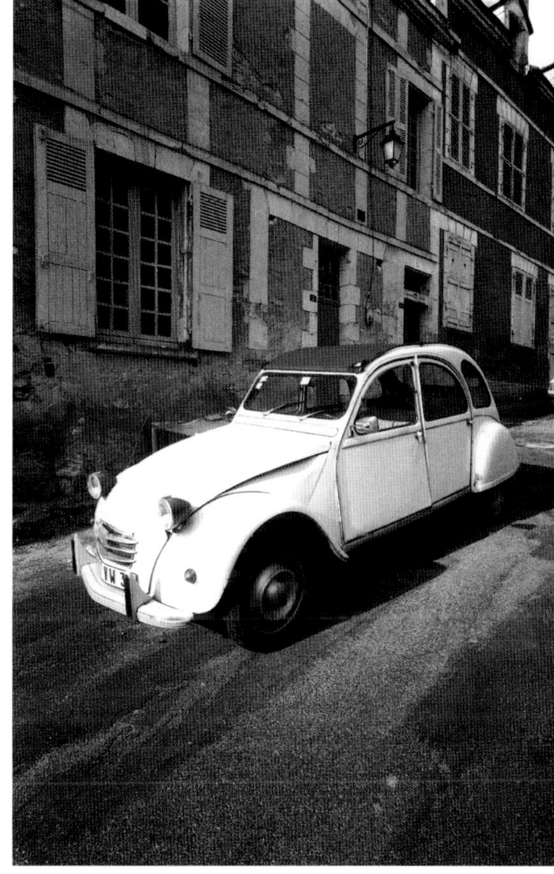

2CV, Preuilly-sur-Claise

I love the tonality of HP5, but there are times when I want finer grain than 35mm can offer. Developing in Perceptol helps, but the 44 x 66mm format of my Alpa means that an all-in print on 8 x 10in (20.3 x 25.4cm) paper is only a little over 4x instead of nearly 8x. 38/4.5 Biogon, MG IV

6 x 7 and 6 x 9cm

Although we generally subscribe to the view that bigger is better, the truth is that many people crop the long, thin 6 x 9cm format for printing, and will therefore cheerfully trade the extra few millimetres in length for two extra exposures per roll (10-on instead of 8-on). The great advantage of 6 x 7cm comes if you want to bracket colour (one on the button, one over, one under) because you can get three sets of three exposures on one film with one spare, while with 6 x 9 you can only get two sets of three.

Many (though far from all) RF/DV cameras can be switched between 120 and 220, however, and with 16-on-220 (6 x 9cm) you can get five sets of brackets on, plus one spare, while with 20-on-220 you can get only 6 sets plus two spares, unless, of course, you can get 21-on, which is apparently possible with some cameras.

The Mamiya 7 has already been described (at least by implication) and it is one of the most versatile RF medium-format cameras on the market, with lenses from 43mm to 150mm (roughly 21mm to 75mm in 35mm terms). We have long been astonished that it is not more popular as a wedding camera.

For knockabout strength, as well as superb quality, the other current choice in 6 x 7cm is the Fuji GW 670, often known as the 'Texas Leica'. This is a big, heavy 1460gm (51½oz) mechanical camera with a fixed 90/3.5 lens, and it is also available in 6 x 9cm guise with a choice of two fixed lenses: the same 90/3.5 or a 65mm. On 6 x 9cm these equate to 28mm and 40mm; on 6 x 7cm, 90mm is more like a 45mm in 35mm terms.

Among older cameras, the Graflex XL and the Omega/Koni-Omega are both attractive, both in the 6 x 7cm format. The former features separate film wind and shutter cocking, and the backs are the less than stellar Graphic versions, but there is a superb choice of lenses (including 80/2.8 and 100/2.8 Zeiss Planars) and a wide range of accessories including Polaroid backs, close-up extension backs, ground-glass backs, and more. The Omega is even bulkier and offers only 9-on-120, but has an (admittedly strange) combined push-pull film advance/shutter cocking. This can give trouble if it has been treated too brutally by a previous owner, but results can be excellent. The late models with the Konica lenses are probably better suited to users than the original Omegas, and not all have interchangeable backs (go for these if you can).

The Graflex XL was behind the times even when it was launched, but is a superb 'niche' camera

Slightly more fragile because of its doppel-klapp construction (front and back linked by x-struts), but commanding high prices because of its cult following, is the Japanese-built Plaubel Makina. Three versions were made: the standard with an 80/2.8 Nikkor, the wide with a somewhat slower 55mm, and a rangefinderless ultra-wide with movements and a 47mm Super Angulon. These are all considerably more usable than the original German Makinas.

Then there is the Mamiya Press, again with separate film wind and shutter cocking, but with a range of film sizes from 645 to 6 x 9cm in interchangeable masking backs. Avoid early lenses: later lenses are much sharper and offer greater contrast. Actually, the Mamiya Press brings us to our next category, namely:

MULTI-FORMAT CAMERAS

Any camera with interchangeable backs can use several formats, and then there is the astonishing DV Gilde that runs from 645 to 6 x 17cm via a complex system of masks and blinds, as well as stereo in a choice of formats. The Gilde is a wonderful camera, but even more blindingly expensive than Alpa – and Alpas make Hasselblads look economical. If you can afford a Gilde, buy one: you are unlikely to regret it, though it is more at home on a tripod than handheld.

We use Alpas, which again are terrifyingly expensive DV cameras, and which again are worth it. Roger uses the plain 12 WA ('Wide-Angle') while Frances uses the 12 S/WA ('Shift/Wide-Angle'). They deliver exquisite quality and are at least as much at home handheld as on a tripod. The usual lenses are wide-angles, from 35mm to 58mm, though longer lenses can be fitted to special order: 100mm is not too unusual, and 150mm has been known. Scale-focusing the longer lenses can, however, be demanding.

Frances mostly uses a 6 x 9cm back, with either a 35/5.6 Rodenstock Apo Grandagon (the equivalent of a 15mm shift lens on 35mm) or a 58/5.6 Schneider Super Angulon XL (the equivalent of a 25mm shift lens on 35mm), while Roger uses mostly a 38/4.5 Zeiss Biogon on the Alpa-unique 44 x 66mm format, which is simply masked down from 6 x 7cm: the Biogon's circle of coverage allows nothing with a diagonal of more than 80mm. On 66 x 44mm, 38mm equates to 21mm on 35mm. Roger also uses a 47/5.6 Schneider Super Angulon XL on 6 x 8cm and more rarely on 6 x 7cm; on these formats it equates roughly to 21mm in 35mm terms.

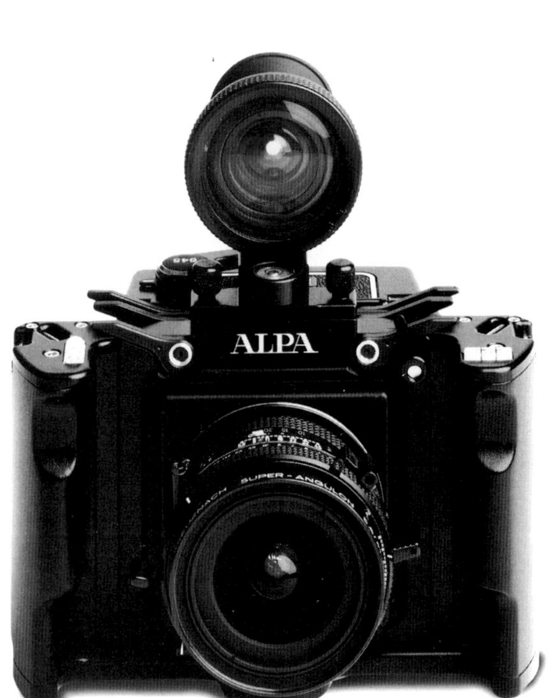

Few if any cameras are better made than the Alpa 12, though you pay for the privilege of owning one

PANORAMIC CAMERAS

These run from 6 x 12cm (6-on-120) through 6 x 17cm (4-on-120) to 6 x 24cm (3-on-120). All are DV; none has a rangefinder. The Art Panorama 6 x 24 is normally used on a tripod (as are the smaller Art Panorama cameras) but the other 6 x 17cm and 6 x 12cm cameras can be handheld with impunity. We have used Linhof and Horseman 6 x 12cm cameras, and Linhof and Fuji 6 x 17cm cameras (as well as the handbuilt Longfellow), and they are all fun and work well. The very long formats require inconveniently frequent reloading, however, as well as the use of large-format enlargers: 4 x 5in (9 x 12cm) for 6 x 12, and 5 x 7in (13 x 18cm) for 6 x 17.

Lack of film flatness over the big format also means that you may get at least equal quality by masking down smaller formats such as 6 x 9cm: at 42 x 84mm a cropped 6 x 9cm is still an impressive 21 x 42cm (8¼ x 16½in) at only a 5x enlargement.

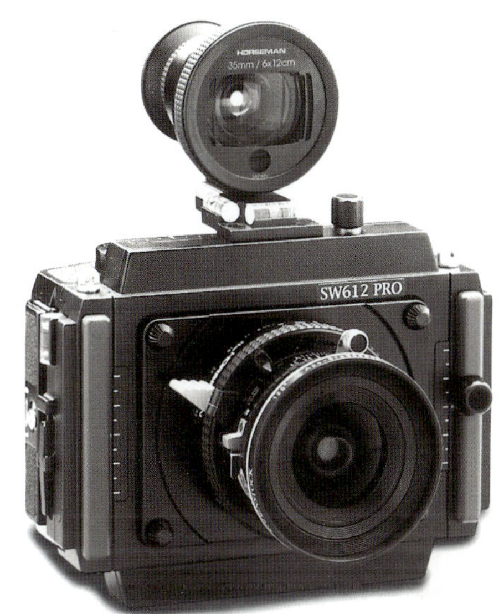

Although we find 6 x 12cm a somewhat stubby format, the Horseman SW12 is wonderfully easy to use

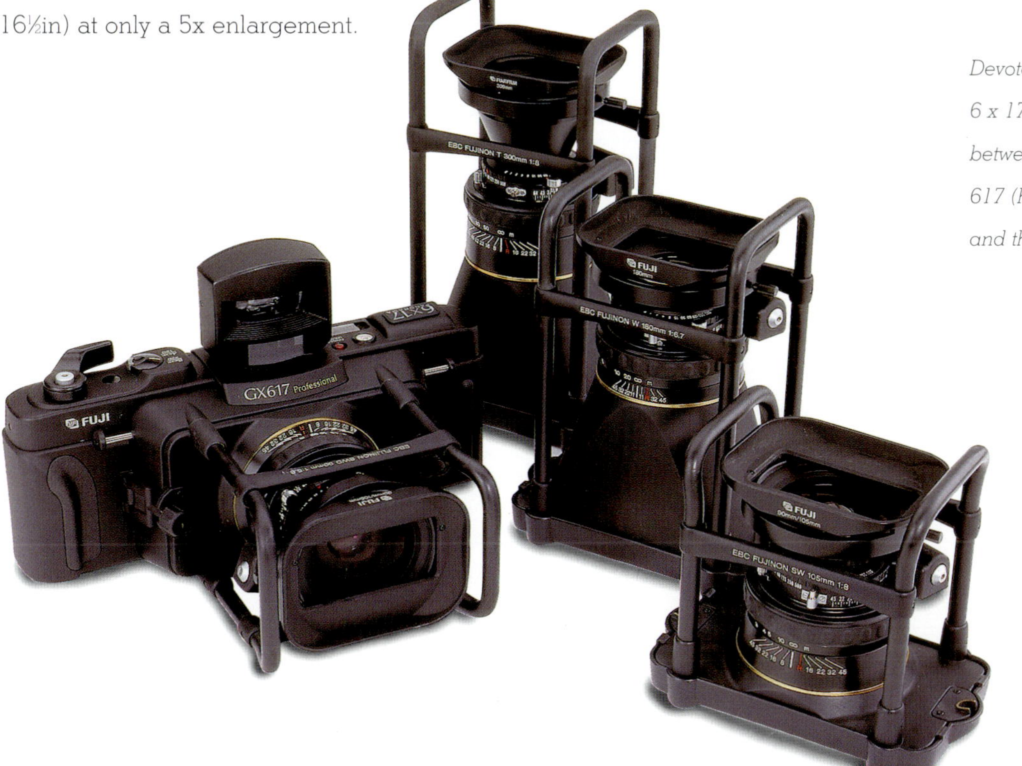

Devotees of handheld 6 x 17 can choose between the Fuji GX 617 (here), the Linhof and the Art Panorama

LARGE FORMAT

Actually, our first 'large-format' cameras are roll-film Linhof Technikas and Horsemans, neatly illustrating the difficulty of drawing hard-and-fast dividing lines between different kinds of camera. Though nominally 6 x 9cm, they are more often used with 6 x 7cm roll-film backs. We call them 'large format' simply because they are scaled-down versions of 4 x 5in cameras and it makes little sense to consider them separately from their larger brethren.

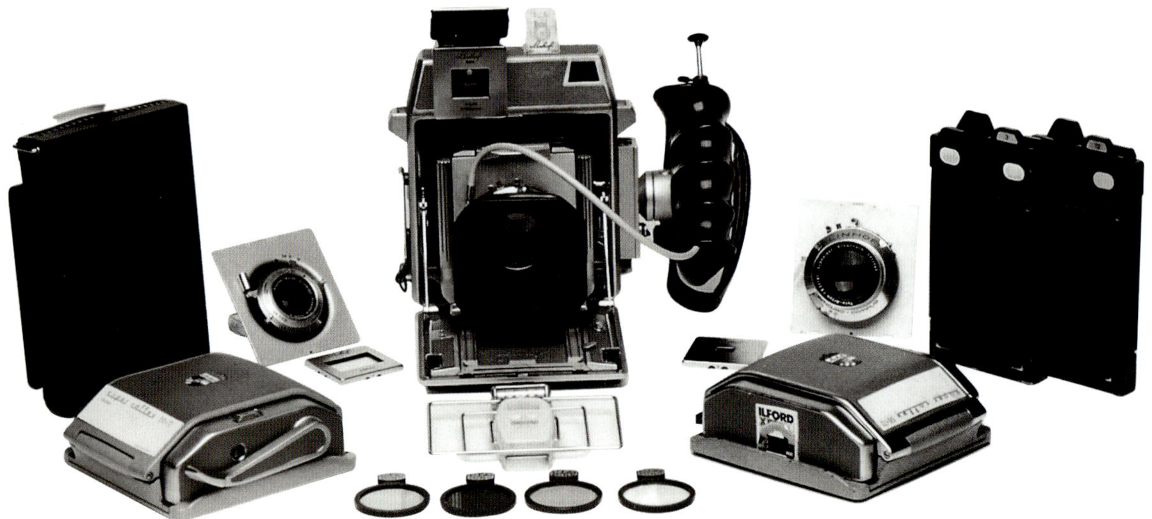

The 'baby' Linhof offers full Technika movements in a rather easier-to-hold package

We own, or have owned, both 'baby' Linhofs (Super Technika IV, Technika 70) and the mighty 13 x 18cm Technika V, all of which can be used handheld: they are 'baseboard' cameras which resemble the press cameras of old, from the days of snap-brim Fedoras with a press ticket tucked into the hat band. As well as handheld, they can be used on a tripod, when it is possible to use the view-camera movements with which they are equipped. There are current versions of both the Linhof and the Horseman, but expense and value for money will rule out the purchase of new cameras for most people; there are just too many good cameras on the used market.

Because they are of very limited appeal, the only thing worth saying about them is that the Technika 70 is the most versatile with the best viewfinder and the easiest to handhold, but it is also the bulkiest. Technika III and earlier models are best avoided because of the horrendously inconvenient arrangements for changing backs. 'Baby' Horsemans borrowed a good deal from Linhofs, but we have never used them, so we cannot comment on their comparability.

There have been a few other 'babies' too, such as the 23 (for 2 x 3in, or 6 x 9cm) Speed Graphic. Press cameras (like the Speed Graphic) have fewer movements than Linhofs or Horsemans and the movements they do have are more limited, but for handheld use this is hardly critical. Cameras that accept roll-film backs are a good deal more usable than those that accept only small cut-film holders.

4 x 5in technical and press cameras

Far more common than 'baby' cut-film cameras are those for 4 x 5in (102 x 127mm), the standard press format from the 1920s to the 1950s and even (among a few diehards) into the early 1960s. The Continental equivalent, 9 x 12cm (3½ x 4¾in), ran it a close second for years: modern, standardized cut-film holders for both 4 x 5in and 9 x 12cm have the same external dimensions and can be used in the same cameras, though the film cannot be exchanged in the same holders, as 4 x 5in film is too big for a 9 x 12cm holder and 9 x 12cm film will fall out of a 4 x 5in holder.

There are still several 4 x 5in CRF cameras available today: Linhof, Horseman, Wista and NPC. The first three are baseboard types, while the NPC is a doppel-klapp. Some baseboard types are available without rangefinders for those who want a tough, compact LF camera but don't really intend

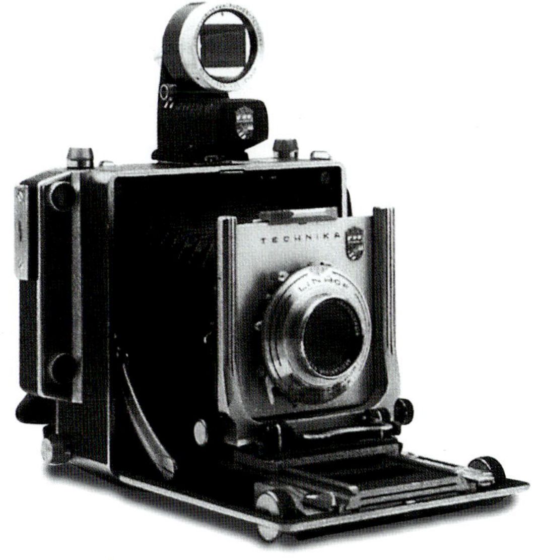

Linhof's Technika 45 has been steadily updated since its first appearance in 1936

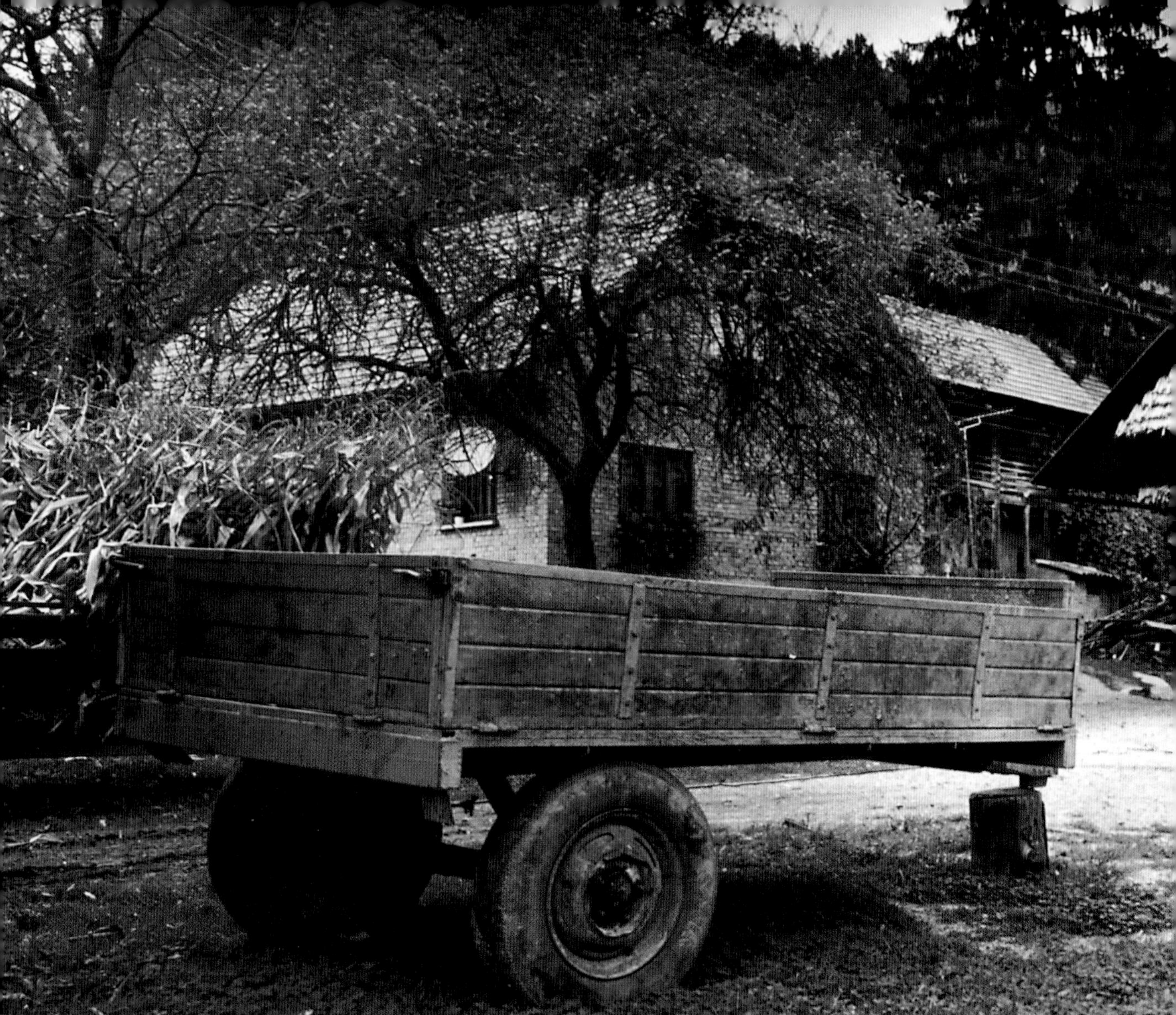

Trailer, Slovenia

to use it handheld (or who can live with scale-focusing).
All the baseboard cameras are 'technical' types, with good
ranges of movement for tripod use.

As already noted, new baseboard cameras are heavy and
expensive, and unless your personal vision demands
handheld 4 x 5in, they are a waste of money. If it does
demand handheld 4 x 5, you will generally do better with
an older camera or an NPC doppel-klapp or a Gran View.
There are quite a few old technical and press cameras on
the market, but in the US the Graphic/Speed Graphic is
overwhelmingly the most common; the Linhof is the most

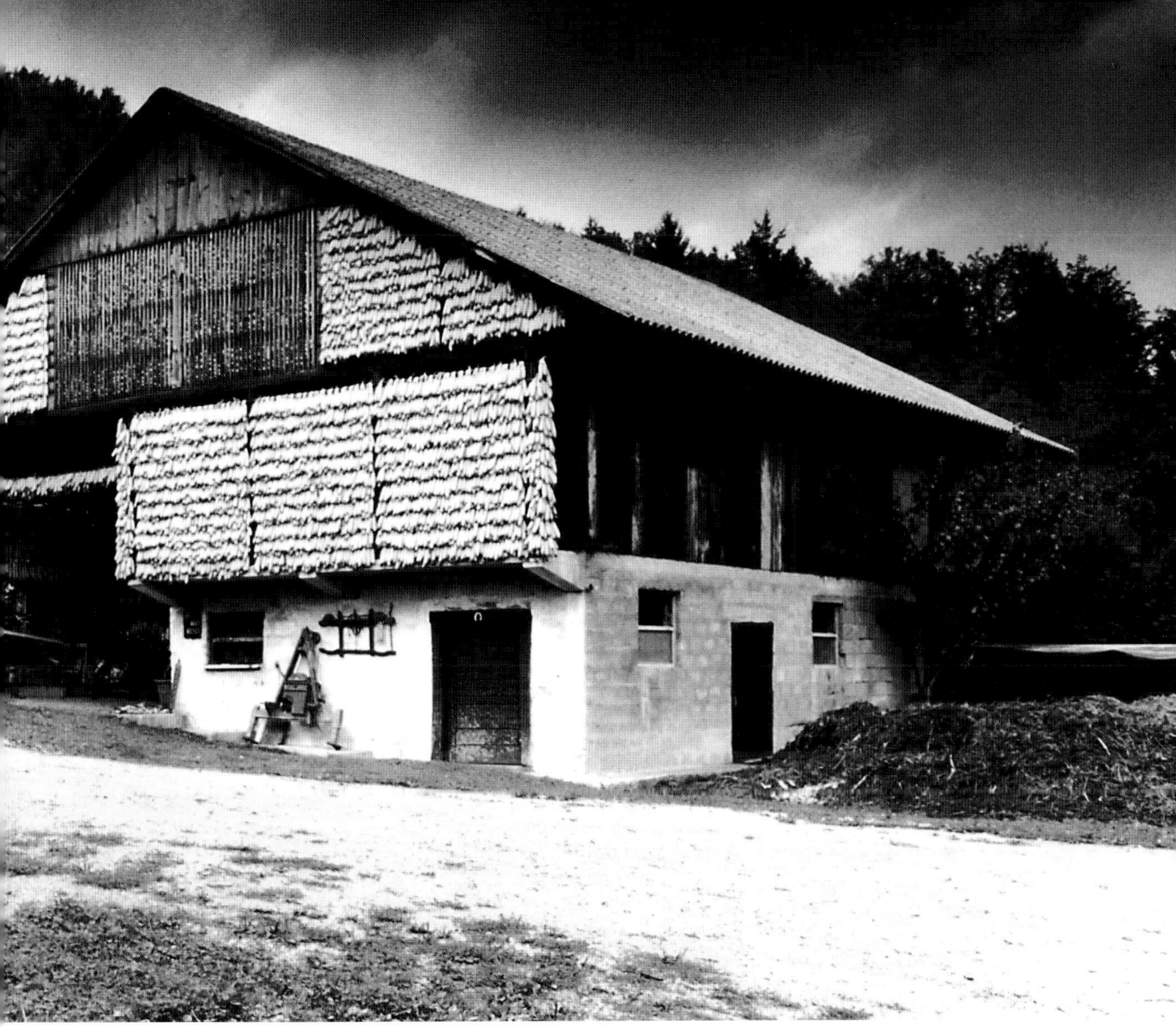

highly regarded worldwide; and in the UK (and much of
Europe) the MPP is a very worthy choice.

NPC

The NPC 45 is derived from the NPC 195 on page 96. Its main
attractions are its light weight and very compact size when
collapsed, along with the fact that it can (like almost all other
4 x 5in cameras) be used with roll-film backs up to 6 x 12cm.
On the other hand, the lack of movements mean that it cannot
compete with baseboard cameras for (say) architectural work,
and the fixed lens is another drawback.

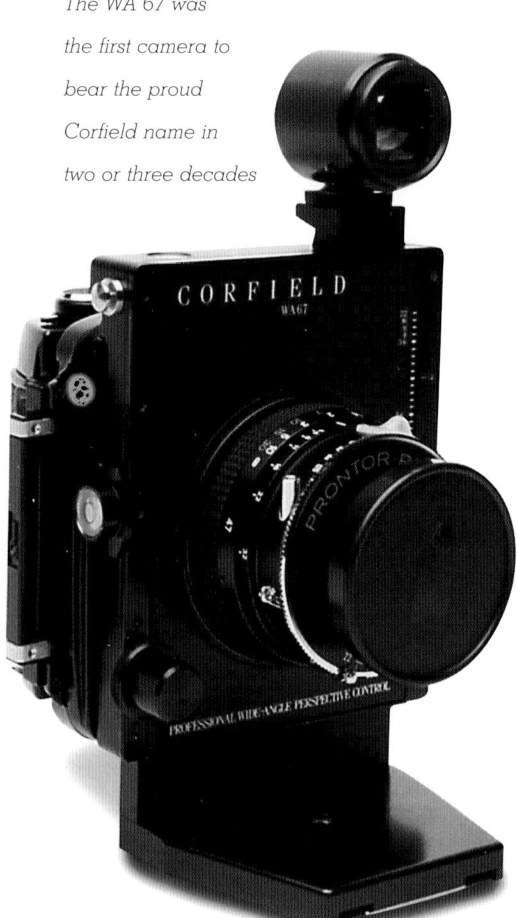

The WA 67 was the first camera to bear the proud Corfield name in two or three decades

The shutter on this 'baby' Speed Graphic features separate control of tension and slit-width

GRAN VIEW

This is a surpassingly ugly but very strong and economically priced scale-focused rigid-bodied camera, with a unique design of back; not all models can accept all types of roll-film holder, though most can accept most cut-film holders and many Polaroid backs. Interchangeable 'nose cones', each with its own focusing helical, are provided for different focal lengths. Focusing can be checked with the built-in ground-glass back.

Other current rigid-bodied 4 x 5 cameras

These are made by Sinar, Cambo and others, and are designed mainly or exclusively for wide-angle lenses set in focusing mounts on cones of different sizes: the lens-plus-cone is changed as a unit. Some can accept extreme wide-angles, such as 47mm on 4 x 5in: a 47/5.6 Super Angulon XL will cover the format and is roughly equivalent to 14mm on 35mm. Others go out to 90mm (similar to 28mm on 35mm), and a few offer cones for 150mm and longer (150mm is similar to 45mm on 35mm). All current models are scale-focused: the longer the lens, the harder it is to focus accurately.

Graphic/Speed Graphic

The greatest handheld 4 x 5 of the past (though it was also made in 6 x 9cm (2 x 3in) guise) was arguably the famous Speed Graphic. It was so-called because of its focal-plane shutter, hence 'speed': plain Graphics had only the front (leaf) shutter in the lens. The usual objection to Graphics is that they have only very limited movements, but for handheld use this is a minor consideration: a little front rise is all that is normally used, and seldom that.

MPP

British-built MPP (Micro Precision Products) Micro-Technical cameras borrowed a great deal from both Linhof and Graflex. With a flourishing Users' Club, a surprising number of parts are available, and the truly determined can even file their own cams from blanks the club can supply: Roger cammed his 150/4.5 Apo Lanthar (a legendary lens) to his Mk. VII.

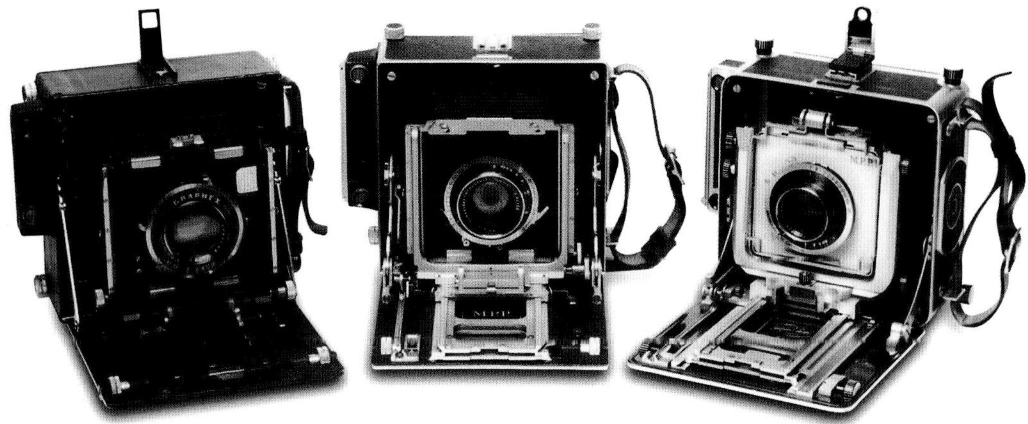

Very briefly, Mks. I to III had bodies that were entirely covered with leather and are the least desirable; Mks. IV and V were experimental and were not sold; Mks. VI and VII have a square-cornered die-cast body with the leather sunk in panels and bright alloy edges; and the Mk. VIII, the last, has wide-radius rounded corners in a fabricated body. The main differences between the VI and VII are the provision of an international back on the VII, along with a track lock and other minor changes. There is also the wood-bodied Micro-Press, with very limited movements, a shorter bellows, and non-rotating back.

MPP I, II and III bodies were covered in leather; the VI and VII had panels; and the VIII had large-radius corners

Other formats

Although there were some very lovely cameras made in quarter-plate format (3¼ x 4¼in, 83 x 108mm) – many of them scaled-down versions of 4 x 5in or 9 x 12cm – the film is virtually unobtainable today (and then only in black and white) so they are not worth considering unless you are very determined.

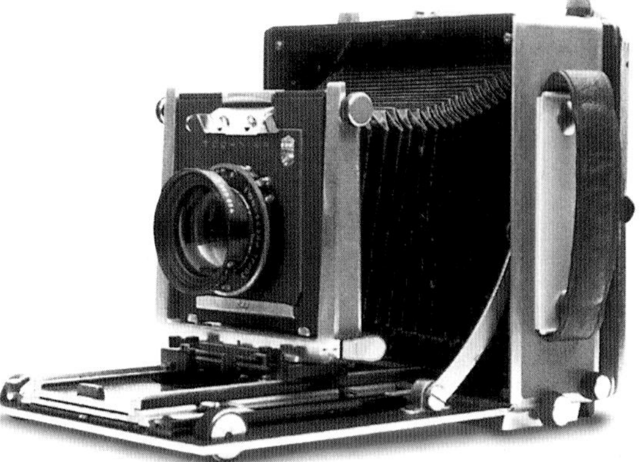

The 13 x 18cm (5 x 7in) version of the Linhof Technika V can be handheld by those determined enough

Going in the opposite direction, to 5 x 7in (13 x 18cm), Linhof Technikas (no RF) and Super Technikas (CRF) were made in this format for decades and are still reasonably often encountered today. Otherwise, there are just a few very old doppel-klapp cameras in this format or in half-plate (4¾ x 6½in, 121 x 165mm). All standardized holders for these three formats have the same external dimensions and can be used interchangeably in the same cameras.

There has to the best of our knowledge only ever been one 8 x 10in DV camera designed for handholding: the rigid-bodied Gran View, similar to the 4 x 5in described above. For ease of focusing it is normally used with wide-angle lenses, and there is a ground-glass option. It was still in production at the time of writing.

POLAROID CAMERAS

Polaroid cameras are something of an aside, but they warrant mention for two reasons. One is that peel-apart Polaroid prints have a charm all of their own, and the other is that P/N (Pos/Neg) film allows a big, beautiful, recoverable negative: 'recoverable' rather than 'instant' because it has to be soaked in sodium sulphite solution for a few minutes to remove the developing jelly, then washed and dried like any other negative.

The NPC 195 doppel-klapp Polaroid camera formed the basis for the 4 x 5in prototype

Although there have been several Polaroid cameras that allow manual control of exposure, the only two that are both commonly encountered and take modern film sizes are the NPC 195 (still in production) and the Polaroid 600, which ceased production just before the end of the twentieth century.

Both take standard quarter-plate pack films. The former is a doppel-klapp and indeed formed the basis of the NPC 4 x 5in doppel-klapp, while the latter is a big rigid-bodied camera. The base 600 has a fixed 127/4.5 lens, while the SE accepts interchangeable 75mm and 150mm lenses as well. The viewfinder for the 150mm is built in and the 75mm takes a separate finder.

The 600 is particularly interesting, because in addition to Polaroid there are two other film options. One is the NPC 4 x 5in back for 4 x 5in Polaroid as well as QuickLoad and ReadyLoad: you lose about 6mm (¼in) all around the edge of the image, but it's still a wonderfully big picture. The other is a roll-film adapter for 120. With either, you can still use the coupled rangefinder (the lens-to-film register is the same), but you can have fun with the viewfinder. With 4 x 5in you can guess pretty well, while with 6 x 9cm you will do well to use a separate add-on finder. A 127mm lens on 6 x 9cm is exactly equivalent to 54mm on 35mm; 75mm, to 32mm; and 150mm, to 64mm. We use a Tewe zoom finder, approximating 32mm with 35mm (the widest the Tewe goes) and with the 127mm adjusting the zoom to a pencilled-in mark that corresponds to 54mm. We don't own a 150mm.

Quite honestly, we don't use our LF or Polaroid RF/DV cameras very much, but they are tremendous fun and we strongly suspect that for the right photographer something from this range could be the basis for a unique personal style that could win competitions or earn money. But given what we do, which is mostly writing about different types and techniques of photography, we sometimes can't afford to explore a particular technique as much as we would like. This doesn't mean that you can't!

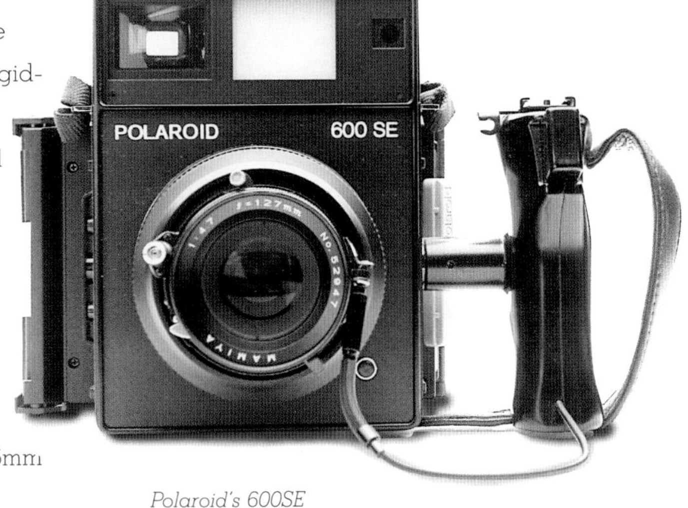

Polaroid's 600SE can be used (with adapters) with 4 x 5in Polaroid/Readyload/ Quickload and with roll film

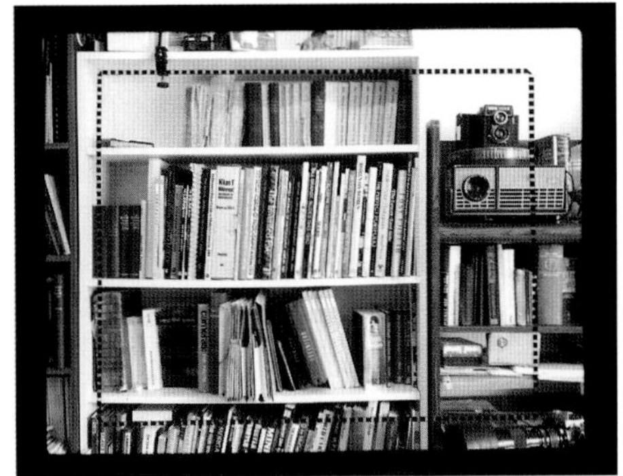

The area covered by the viewfinder in the 600SE is shown by the dotted line on this 4 x 5in Polaroid

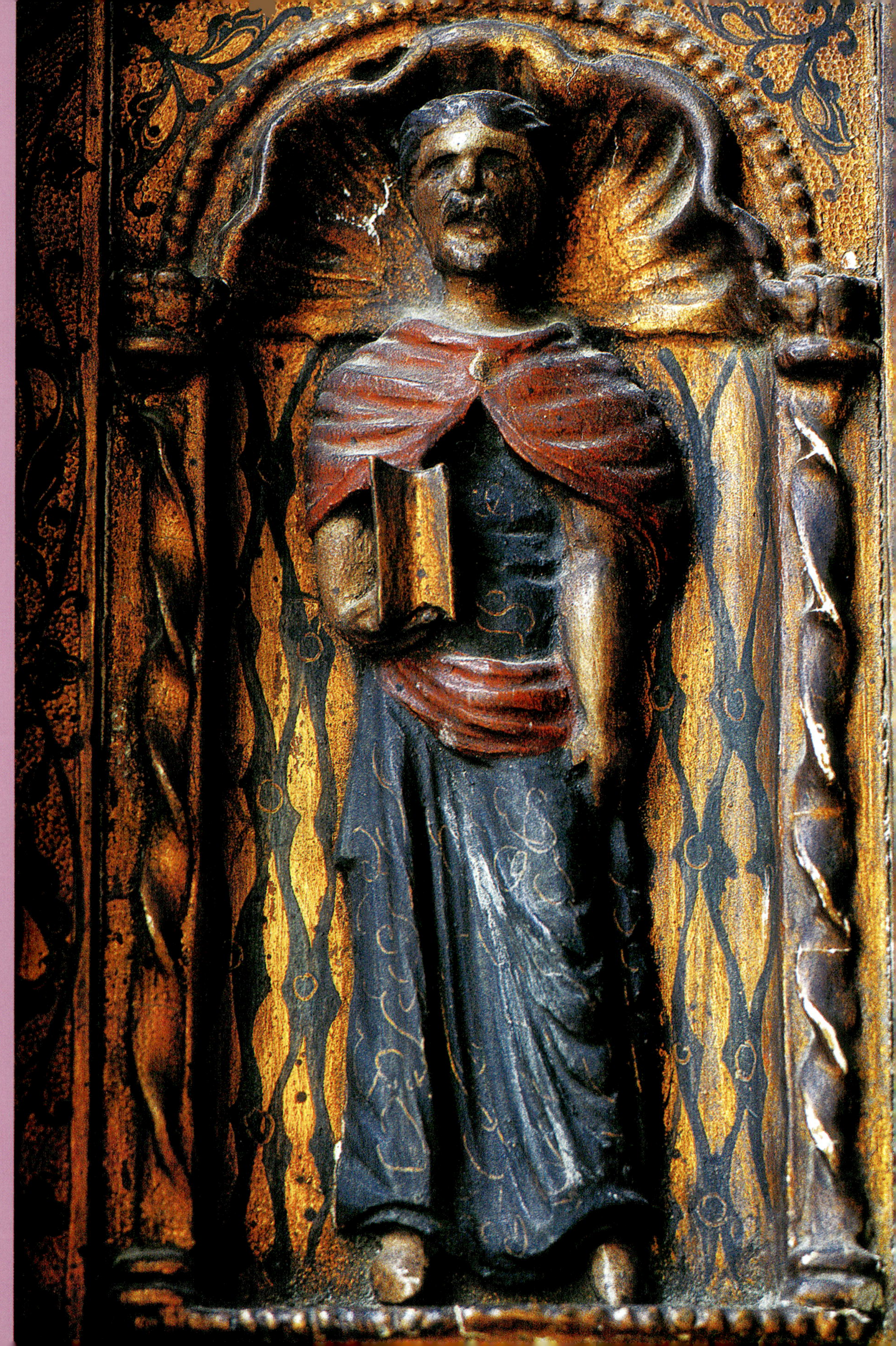

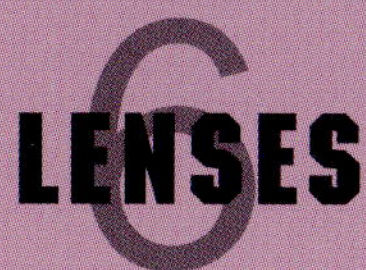

LENSES

SLR users and RF users tend to have different appreciations of which lenses are best, and how they are best employed. For fairly obvious reasons, RF cameras rarely have zooms, though there is one for the Contax G-series. There are also two 'multifocus' lenses: Leica's Tri-Elmar gives three focal lengths (35-50-90), and there is a Konica that gives 21 and 35. Quality is surprisingly good for these, but the lenses are rather slower than single focal lengths.

The emphasis, for the most part, is on sheer image quality (for which RF/DV lenses easily outstrip comparable reflex lenses), and on convenience and ease of handling – which includes compactness.

As already noted, lenses for RF/DV cameras can be smaller, lighter, faster, sharper, more contrasty and cheaper than lenses for reflexes. But the enormous choice available, right back to the late 1920s, means that there are some dogs. Also, even the finest lenses may have suffered wear and tear over the years (and indeed decades), quite apart from genuine progress in lens design.

Faced with such a choice, it is worth remembering that a lens that can't deliver the results you want will never be a bargain. We hope to make it clear which old lenses are likely to be usable and which aren't. With many collector lenses it is best to sell them for close to, or more than, the price of a newer lens as a replacement.

Centrepiece of Triptych, Romney Marsh

This is really just a technical shot, to show that you can frame precisely, close up, with a rangefinder. The trick is to use a 90mm lens – here, a 90/3.5 Apo Lanthar on a Bessa-R – which at the closest focusing distance of around 1m (3ft) gives an image about one-eighth life size. Kodak EBX

MONOCHROME AND COLOUR

Old lenses are often far more suitable for black and white than for colour. This has very little to do with colour correction, as even lenses from the 1930s were normally well corrected to bring both red and blue light to a common focus. Rather, it is a matter of contrast. Old lenses – especially old, fast lenses, and more especially still, old, fast, uncoated lenses – are 'flatter' and more prone to flare than newer ones. Of course, contrast is still further reduced if the lens is scratched or misty.

In colour, this not only means poor contrast, it also means a bluish tinge (out of doors) and a brownish tinge (under artificial light) as a result of unfocused light bouncing around inside the lens.

In black and white, the colour of the light doesn't matter, and you can increase contrast by increasing development slightly or printing on a harder grade of paper. You'll get a different look this way, but you may prefer it: many do.

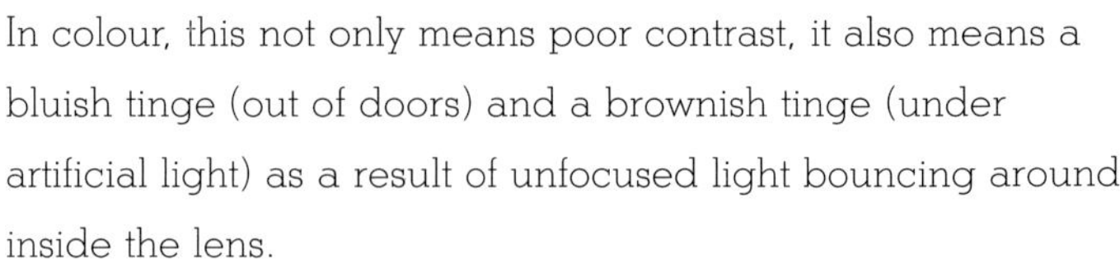

Although the 180/2.8 for Contaxes was initially released as a coupled lens, it was more use on a mirror box

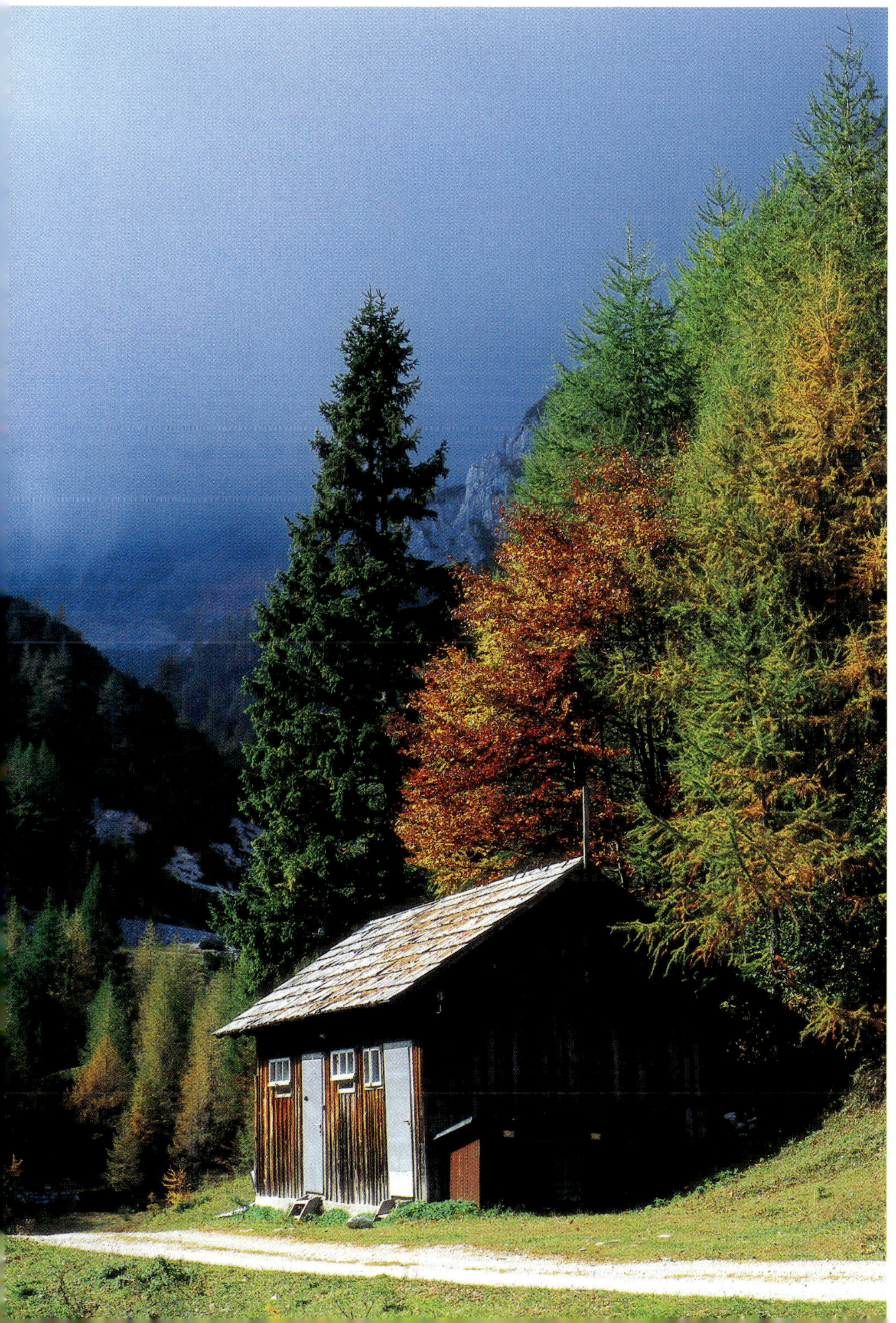

Hut and gathering cloud, Julian Alps, Slovenia

In about 2000 I started using a 50mm lens again, for the first time in maybe 20 or 25 years. I don't know why. We were loaned the 50/1.5 Nokton for a magazine test, and it was so useful that we cndcd up buying it. Bessa-R, Kodak EBX

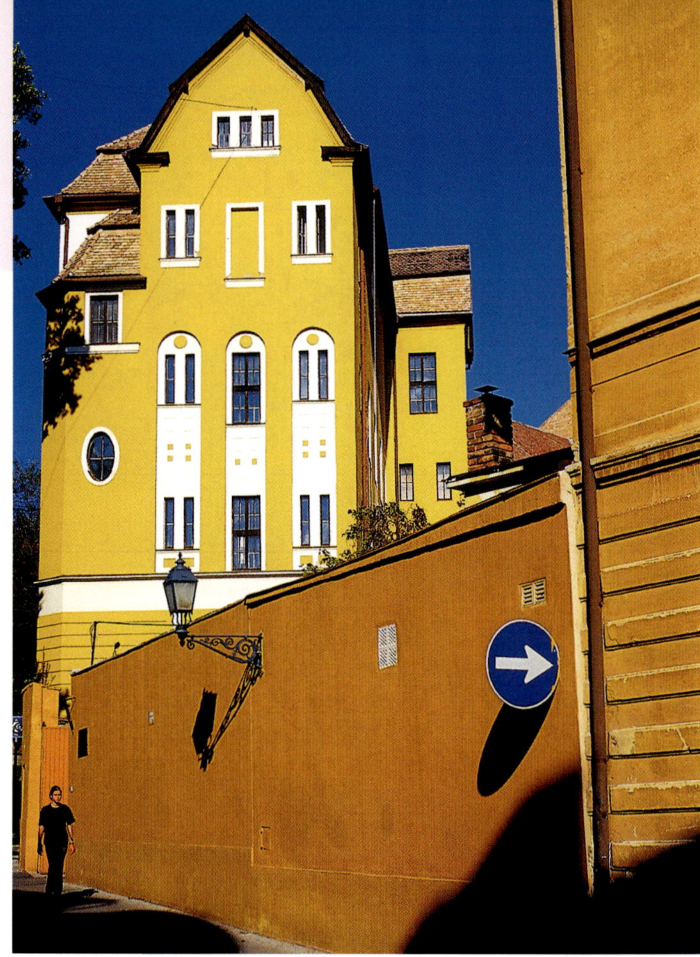

One-way street, Pecs, Hungary

Having too many lenses is a snare and a delusion. Even if I have a more extensive outfit with me, I'll often use just two focal lengths, normally 35mm (this was taken with the 35/1.7 Ultron) and 90mm. Bessa-R, Kodak EBX

WEAR AND TEAR

Scratches and chips in the lens often matter less than what are euphemistically called 'cleaning marks': a network of tiny scratches that reduce contrast dramatically. A scratch can be rendered more or less irrelevant if carefully filled in with matte black paint, but there is nothing you can do about 'cleaning marks' short of having the lens repolished. This is horribly expensive and is all too likely to take the finest edge off performance.

At least as destructive as 'cleaning marks' is the slight hazing seen in many old lenses, often the result of lubricants distilling onto the lens surfaces. Again, this is a terrible thief of contrast (and resolution). Fortunately, it is nothing like as expensive to have a lens cleaned as it is to have it repolished, and (for example) we have had Balham Optical Company clean both our 50/1.2 Canon (Leica screw) and our 35/2.8 PC-Nikkor (Nikon F, but with an adapter for Leica).

SPARS, COLLARS AND LOCKS

An unexpected feature of many lenses for RF/DV cameras is
that they are not focused with a collar, but with a short spar or
fingergrip. This takes some getting used to, but once you are
used to it, it is quicker than a collar and you can focus by
touch alone: a particular angle of the spar corresponds to a
particular focused distance. You can, therefore, focus the
camera without looking at it before you bring it to your eye, or
you can focus and shoot 'blind' without even using the viewfinder.

Some old lenses have infinity locks, which can be infuriating.
They can usually be disabled temporarily (by jamming a bit of
matchstick into the mechanism), semipermanently, or even
(with the aid of epoxy adhesives) permanently.

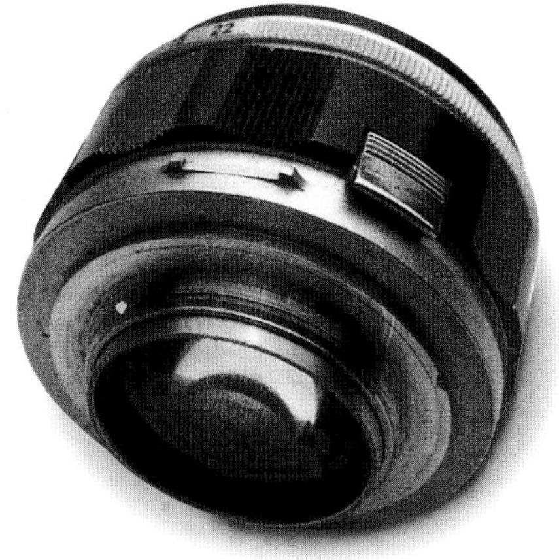

*Infinity locks are not confined to focusing spars:
this 50/1.2 Canon has one*

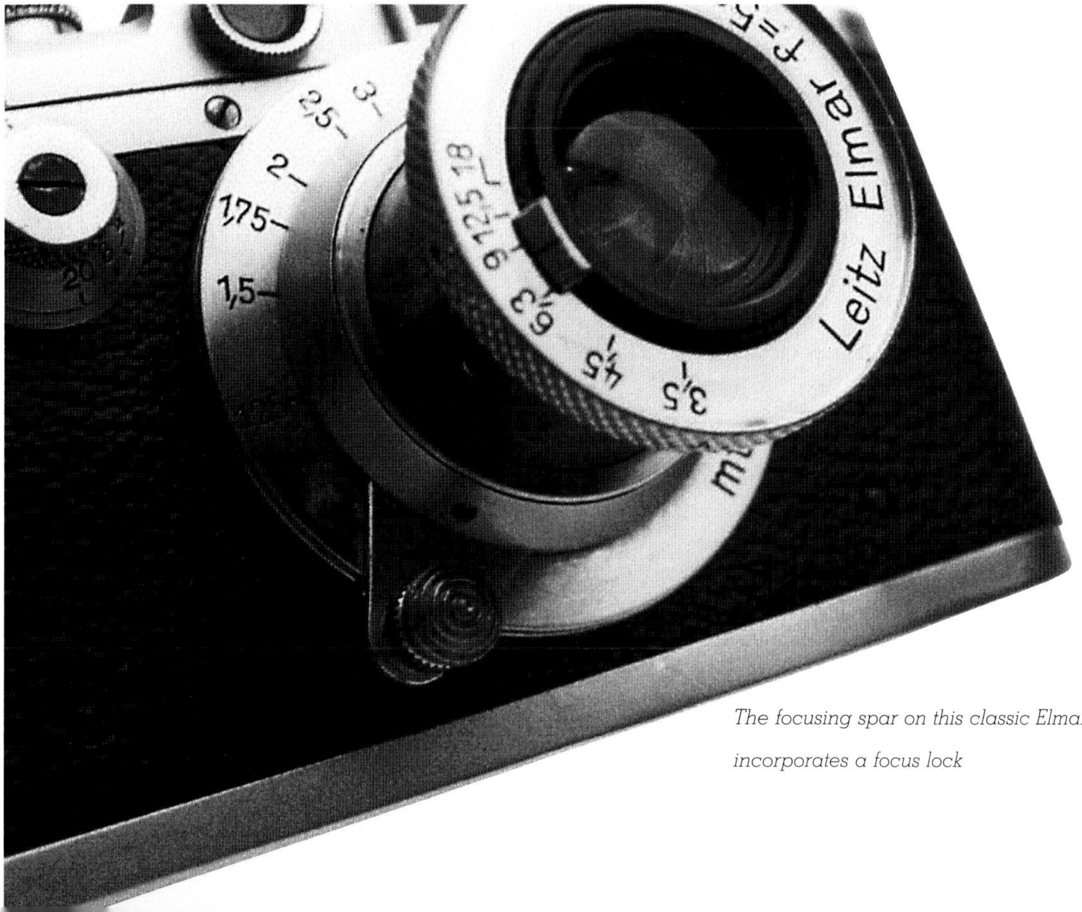

*The focusing spar on this classic Elmar
incorporates a focus lock*

Bride dressing

F *Modern reportage style wedding photography requires the photographer to be unobtrusive. Rangefinder cameras are ideal for this. Because I am an old and trusted friend of the bride and her mother, and because the camera is virtually silent, I could capture the intimacy of the occasion. The 50mm/1.5 gave me a useful increase in working distance to help put them at their ease. Voigtländer R, Ilford XP2 Super rated at ISO 400, MG Warmtone in selenium*

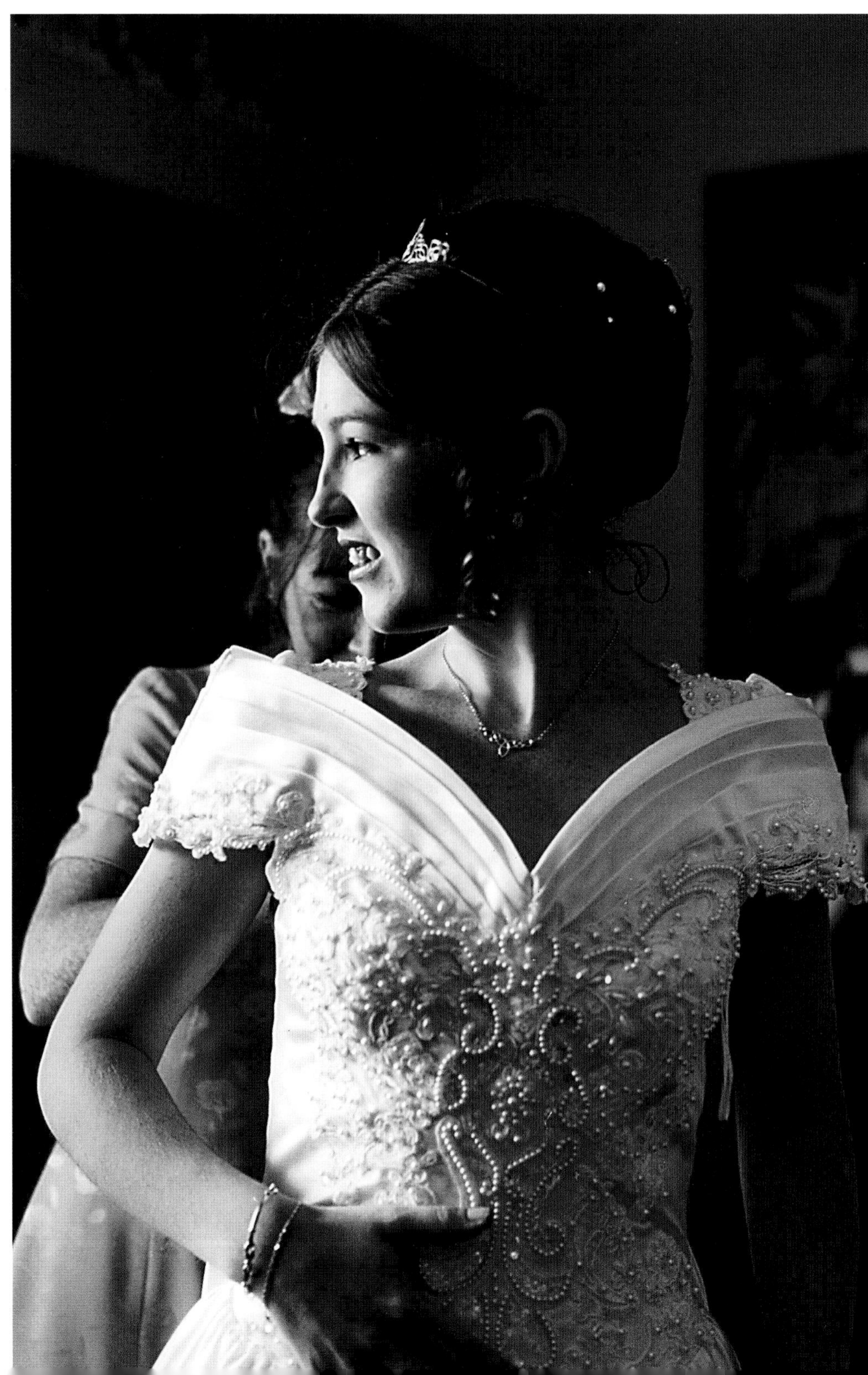

ADAPTING LENSES

Before the advent of Voigtländer's superb and economical lenses for Leica screw and (to a lesser extent) Contax cameras, it often made sense to adapt lenses from other systems – either because the lens you wanted wasn't available at any price (a 16/8 Zeiss Hologon for a Leica) or because you couldn't afford the new lens you really wanted. For example, our 21/4.5 Biogon is in Contax fit, but before it came into our possession it had been adapted for Leica. In the early 1990s this made an affordable and practical replacement for Roger's 21/2.8 Elmarit-M that was stolen in Moscow. But today, a new Voigtländer or Kobalux would almost certainly be a better buy.

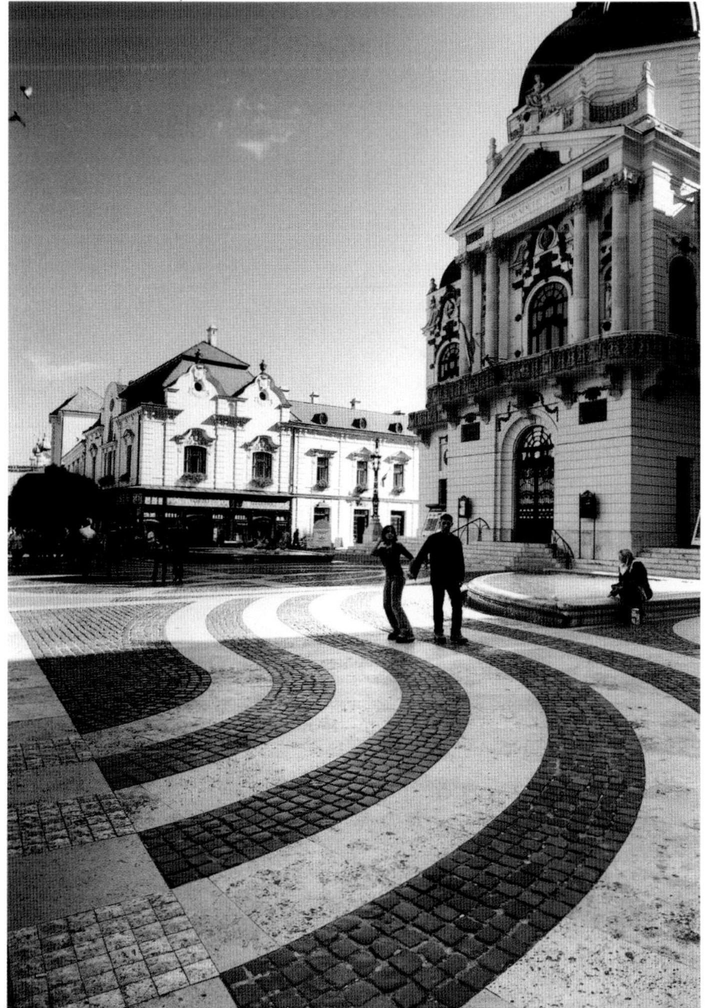

Young friends, Pecs

I was waiting for these two to move into the spot where I hoped they would go, but I was so amused by the girl's posing that I almost forgot to take the picture; a fraction of a second earlier, it would have been even better. Bessa-T, 28/1.9, XP2, MG Warmtone

We also had a Nikon-to-Leica screw adapter made by SRB of Luton, England. The primary purpose was to allow Frances to use her 35/2.8 shift lens (PC-Nikkor) on her Voigtländer. It is surprisingly easy to judge the viewfinder correction that is needed by reference to the scale on the lens. If you wind the lens up 6mm, for example, you know that you need to discount the bottom quarter of the viewfinder (6mm is one-quarter of the 24mm vertical dimension of the 24 x 36mm frame) and to add on a quarter mentally on the top. We also use it sometimes with our 15/2.8 Sigma fish-eye; an adapted 'Judas window' makes a tolerable finder.

As soon as you adapt a lens made for one system to another system, you are almost certain to lose the rangefinder coupling; with most lenses, of course, you don't have to worry about anything else, as this is the only communication between the lens and the body. With a Leica-screw-to-Leica-bayonet adapter, you not only retain rangefinder coupling, with the right ring you can also retain the automatic keying of the appropriate viewfinder frame.

Leica screw (39mm x 26tpi) to Leica 4-claw bayonet adapters are just 1mm (¹⁄₁₆in) thick

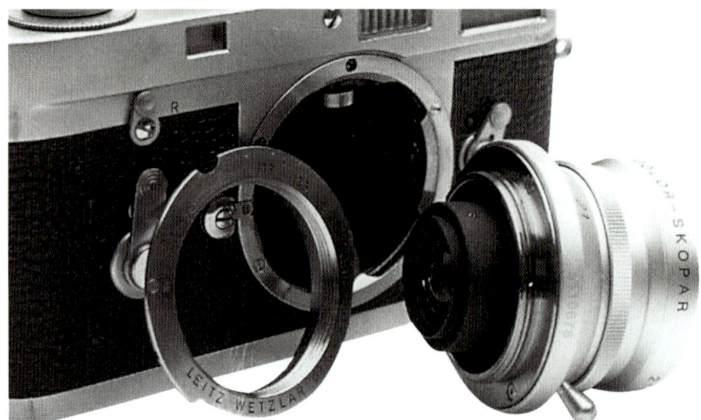

It now makes sense to look at the various focal lengths in turn, remarking on which lenses from the past deserve their legendary status, and which do not. It also makes sense to look at lenses for 35mm cameras first.

ULTRA-WIDES (21MM AND BELOW)

Modern 21mm lenses are mostly f/2.8: the Distagon for the G-series Contax, the bayonet-mount Elmarit-M for the Leica, the Leica screw Kobalux sold by Adorama. There is also a 21/4 Color-Skopar from Voigtländer in Leica screw mount: a stop slower, but much more compact. Remarkably, this was also issued in Nikon rangefinder mount.

All are astonishingly good and rangefinder-coupled. If you can afford an Elmarit-M, by all means get one, but we have both the Kobalux and the Color-Skopar, and the extra quality of the Leica lens cannot, in our eyes, justify what we would have to pay. But then, we're poor!

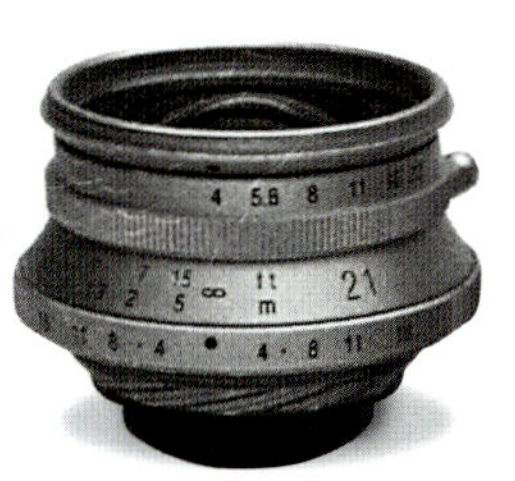
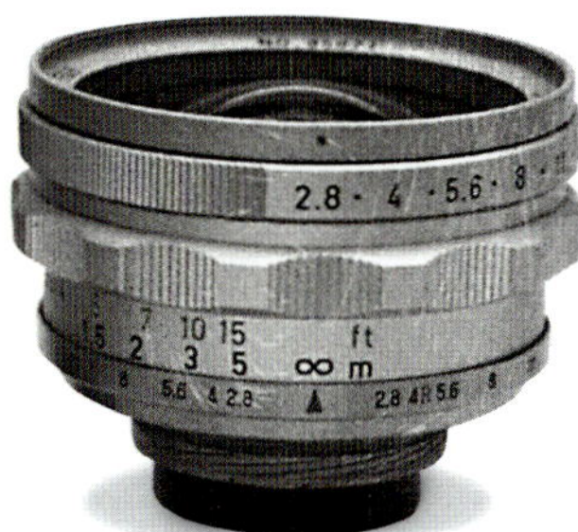

left, 21/4 Color-Skopar from Voigtländer; right, 21/2.8 Kobalux from Adorama

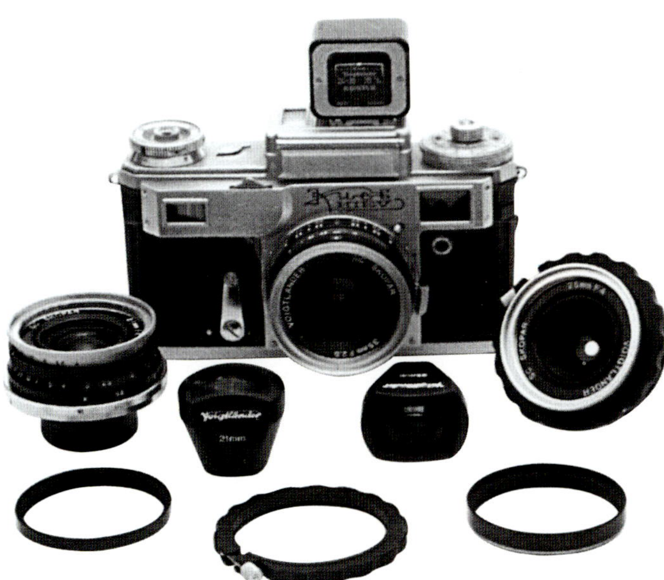

The Kiev can be transformed with the addition of one or more Voigtländer lenses

Among still wider lenses, the fixed-aperture Zeiss Hologons are fascinating. They first appeared in the fixed-lens Hologon camera (15/8), but later were made in Leica M-mount (15/8) and Contax G-mount (16/8); the latter was adapted unofficially (and uncoupled) for Leica M by Herwig Zorkendorfer.

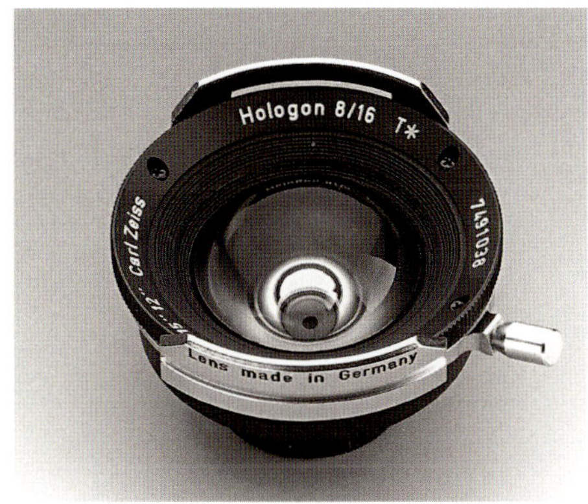

This is the Contax version of the Hologon; the earlier Leica version was 15mm, not 16mm

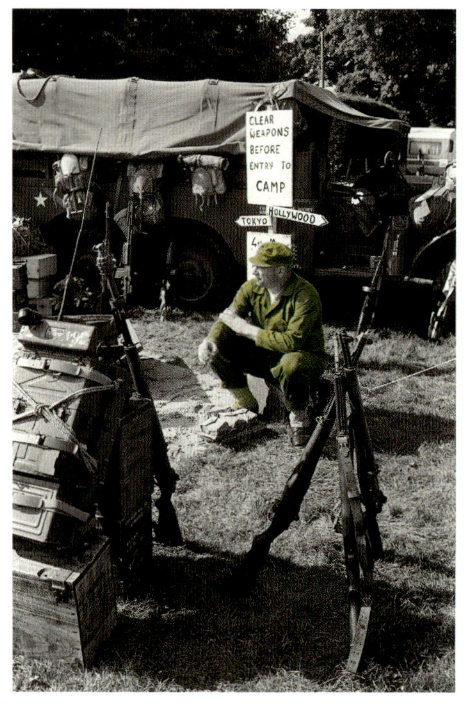

Clear Weapons

Most of our books tend to have a theme, depending on what we're shooting at the time, and there's a heavy re-enactors thread in this one

When I printed this picture of Roger's (I do all the conventional printing), I felt that the soldier cried out for hand-colouring; I used Zig-Pens. Bessa-R, 50/1.5 Nokton, yellow filter, HP5 in DD-X at 500, MG Warmtone

All who have compared Hologons directly with the 15/4.5 Super-Wide-Heliar from Voigtländer agree that the later, cheaper, faster lens is superior in sharpness and resolution, quite apart from having a variable aperture. The Heliar was introduced in Leica screw mount uncoupled, but has been adapted (uncoupled) for the Contax G, again by Herr Zork. A disadvantage of the Heliar is that it cannot accept filters of any kind.

The 12/5.6 Ultra-Wide-Heliar from Voigtländer in Leica screw mount is the widest production lens ever made for any 35mm camera, at any price. It delivers astonishingly good quality. There is some vignetting, it is true, but considerably less than you might expect, and it is possible (via an adapter) to use 82mm filters, including centre-grad filters to even out the vignetting.

Older ultra-wides

The very best of the old designs was the 21/4.5 Zeiss Biogon for the Contax, an excellent lens to this day. Another stunning lens was the 21/4 Nikkor, but collector demand has pushed the price of this through the roof. All are quite easy to adapt for Leicas, but it is unlikely to make economic sense.

In the more common Leica mount, the 'official' coupled Super Angulons (21/4, 1958, screw and bayonet, and 21/3.4, 1963, bayonet only) are very good, though arguably inferior to both the Biogon and the Nikkor. The 19/3.5 Canon (screw mount) has its devotees, but a modern 21mm is likely to out-perform it, and collector demand for the Canon means that it is likely to be a poor buy for the user. The 21/2.8 non-aspheric Elmarit-M for the Leica is excellent and more compact than the aspheric, but then it is a very recent lens.

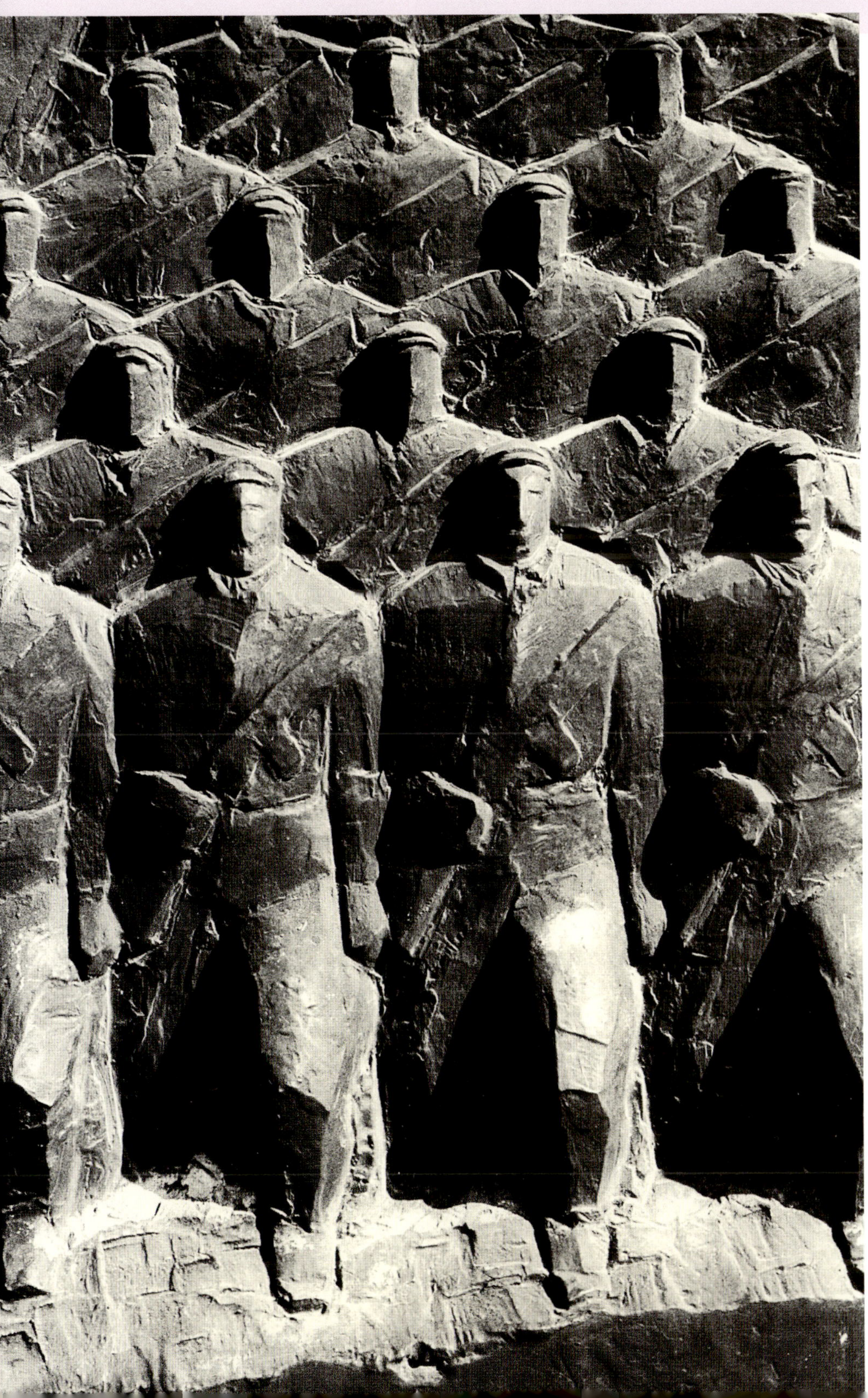

**Monument Park,
near Budapest**

This picture wouldn't work on an overcast day: the light and shade are an essential part of it. I could have taken this with just about any camera: there was no special merit in a rangefinder. But equally the rangefinder was at no disadvantage. Bessa-T, 50/1.5 Nokton, yellow filter, XP2, MG Warmtone

Otherwise, anything before about 1980 is likely to be an unwise choice. Only the very best are worth bothering with, and collectors will pay so much for these that it is far more cost-effective to buy a new or recent lens, which will normally deliver better results anyway. The 20/5.6 Russar (Leica screw) in particular is an appalling lens, reasonably sharp at the centre but hopeless at the edges.

WIDE-ANGLES (24–40MM)

Once again, the improvements over the years have been spectacular. The 'classical' focal lengths are 28mm and 35mm, though there have also been a few of 24mm, 25mm and 40mm.

Among modern 28mm lenses, there are offerings from Adorama (f/3.5, Leica screw), Konica (f/2.8, Leica bayonet), Leica (f/2, Leica bayonet) and Voigtländer (f/1.9 and f/3.5, Leica screw). All are excellent; the biggest question is how much speed you need. The earlier 28/2.8 Elmarit (Leica bayonet) from Leica was also a first-rate lens.

The same question – speed – is very much to the fore with 35mm lenses. The f/2.5 Color-Skopar from Voigtländer is slow but wonderfully compact and delivers superb quality. Curiously, it is made in both 'classic' and 'pancake' mounts: the former with a focusing spar; the latter rather bulkier with a conventional focusing collar.

At f/2 there are 35mm offerings from Konica (Leica bayonet), Leica (bayonet and screw) and Zeiss (Contax): all three are stunning and are among the finest lenses made today in any focal length for any camera. Then there is an f/1.7 from Voigtländer, a little lacking in contrast at full aperture but the equal of its slower brethren by f/2.8, while Leica's first 35/1.4 Summilux appeared in the 1950s: later models are better.

The fastest 35mm lens of all time is the 35/1.2 Voigtländer (2003), though it is rather bulky.

Voigtländer's 25/4 (Leica screw) is an astonishingly good and very affordable lens, if you don't mind scale-focusing: it isn't rangefinder-coupled. Of course, the enormous depth of field means that scale-focusing is entirely adequate. But it worries some people, which is presumably why the 21/4 (which had even less need of coupling) is coupled. The 25/4 is also available in Nikon rangefinder mount. Leica's 24/2.8 (bayonet only) is even better and faster and rangefinder-coupled; its only disadvantage is Leica pricing.

We were in two minds about whether to include 40mm in this category (wide-angle) or the next (standard), but opted for this category because 'standard' effectively means '50mm' in interchangeable-lens RF/DV 35mm cameras. There are three modern 40mm interchangeable lenses, all Leica fit: the 40/2 Summicron and the 40/2 Minolta for the Leica/Minolta CL and a 40/2.8 Zeiss from Rollei. They are of limited usefulness on other cameras as there are few 40mm finders – though you can 'fudge' 40mm with a zoom finder such as the Tewe.

Many users of 35mm RF cameras (quite probably the majority of them) regard a fast wide-angle as their standard lens. For years, Roger's choice has been the 35/1.4 Summilux, now supplanted to some extent by the 35/1.7 Ultron; Frances, who switched from 35mm reflexes to Voigtländer RF cameras only in 2000/2001, prefers the 28/1.9 Ultron. This is only a quarter of a stop slower than the 35/1.7, which would be the natural alternative, but it is a focal length with which she is more comfortable. Neither of us can really imagine working without a fast wide-angle.

Having said this, we also use the 35/2.5 Color-Skopar simply because it is so compact. If you don't need the speed of an f/2 or faster, why pay the extra money and carry the extra bulk? But if one of our 35mm lenses went, it would be the slowest. For the same reason, we've never really felt the need of a 28/3.5, though Adorama's is one of the sharpest, most contrasty lenses we have ever used.

Older wide-angles

The vast majority of older wide-angles are slow, or of indifferent quality, or both. Leica's 28/5.6 Summaron (1956, screw mount only) is one of the best, but even it has some curvilinear distortion; and many other old 28mm lenses are also lacking in contrast. The 28/6.3 Hektor (1935, redesigned 1952) is definitely best left to collectors, as are the 28/8 Tessar and post-war 25/4 Topogon for the Contax; 25mm Nikkors and Canons are good lenses but command very high collectors' premiums. The Russian 28/6 (Leica screw and Kiev/Contax bayonet) is hardly even worth collecting.

At 35mm, each succeeding generation has shown a clear improvement over its forebears; the faster the lens, the more true this is. The last generation of Leica's 35/1.4 non-aspherical Summilux (which we use) is often unfairly damned by those who have never used it, mostly for lack of contrast wide open, but the original 1959 35/1.4 that preceded it was detectably inferior. Leica's 35/2 Summicron (1958, screw and bayonet) seems always to have been one of the finest 35mm lenses ever made, but it was redesigned in 1969 for even better quality. Leica's 35/2.8 Summaron (1958, screw and bayonet) and 35/3.5 Summaron (1948, screw) remain both usable and, at least for the 35/3.5, affordable, but a 35/2.5 Color-Skopar is better, faster and usually cheaper, even new. In addition, with pre-1970 lenses you are running into an ever-increasing risk of haze and an expensive clean-up.

All those other than Leica are best left to collectors: even where the performance is tolerable, a new Voigtländer will deliver better performance, cheaper. Once again, the Russian or Ukrainian 35/2.8 in Leica screw or Kiev/Contax mount is scarcely even worth collecting.

STANDARD LENSES (50MM)

The 50mm 'standard' lens has almost completely disappeared from the 35mm SLR, replaced by the 'standard zoom'. Among rangefinder cameras, though, the 50mm is curiously persistent. Even those who have little or no time for this focal length on a reflex often find, if they can bring themselves to try it, that it can be uncommonly useful.

Part of the attraction, of course, is speed. The long-discontinued 50/0.95 Canon Dream is legendary (and wasn't very good), but you can still buy a new 50/1 Noctilux in Leica bayonet mount, and there are or have been several f/1.2 lenses and lots of f/1.4 or f/1.5.

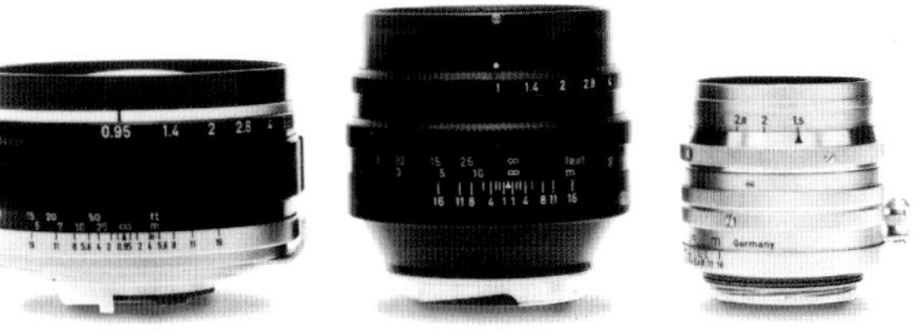

Left to right: 50/0.95 Canon, 50/1 Leica, 50/1.5 Leica

Inevitably, the very fastest lenses are less contrasty at full bore than slower lenses, but they are significantly more contrasty than those for reflexes, as well as smaller, lighter and cheaper.

How fast you go is very much a matter of personal choice. But from experience, we find that the problem with f/1.2 or faster is depth of field, or rather lack of it. That and the price: an f/1 or f/1.2 can cost twice as much as an f/1.4 of comparable quality. We therefore use an f/1.5 Nokton. But you may have other priorities: slower lenses are cheaper and more compact, and speed has no influence on ease of focusing.

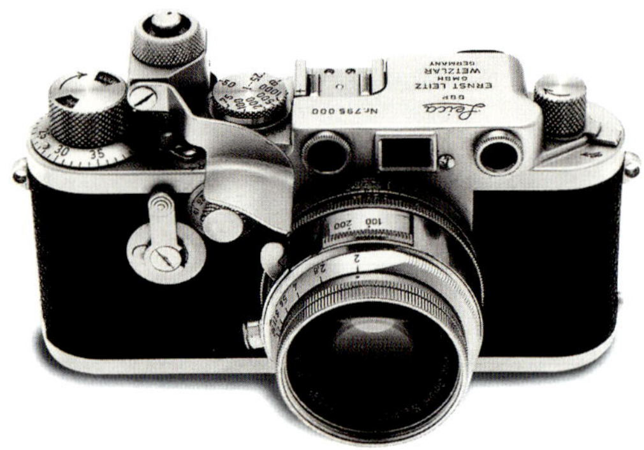

The very rare 'Blitz' Summicron incorporated a leaf shutter to allow flash synch at high speeds

Older 'standard' lenses

There are still plenty of uncoated, pre-war f/3.5 Leitz Elmars in use delivering excellent results, and many, many other 50mm lenses deliver results that range from acceptable to excellent, especially in black and white. Only the cheapest, nastiest lenses are likely to be unusable, or exotica such as the Russian 50/1.5 which is mercifully rarely encountered.

Even the Russian/Ukrainian 50/2 Jupiter (Leica screw), about the price of a roll of film on the used market, is capable of acceptable (if somewhat vintage-looking) results in monochrome, as well as a certain misty charm in colour.

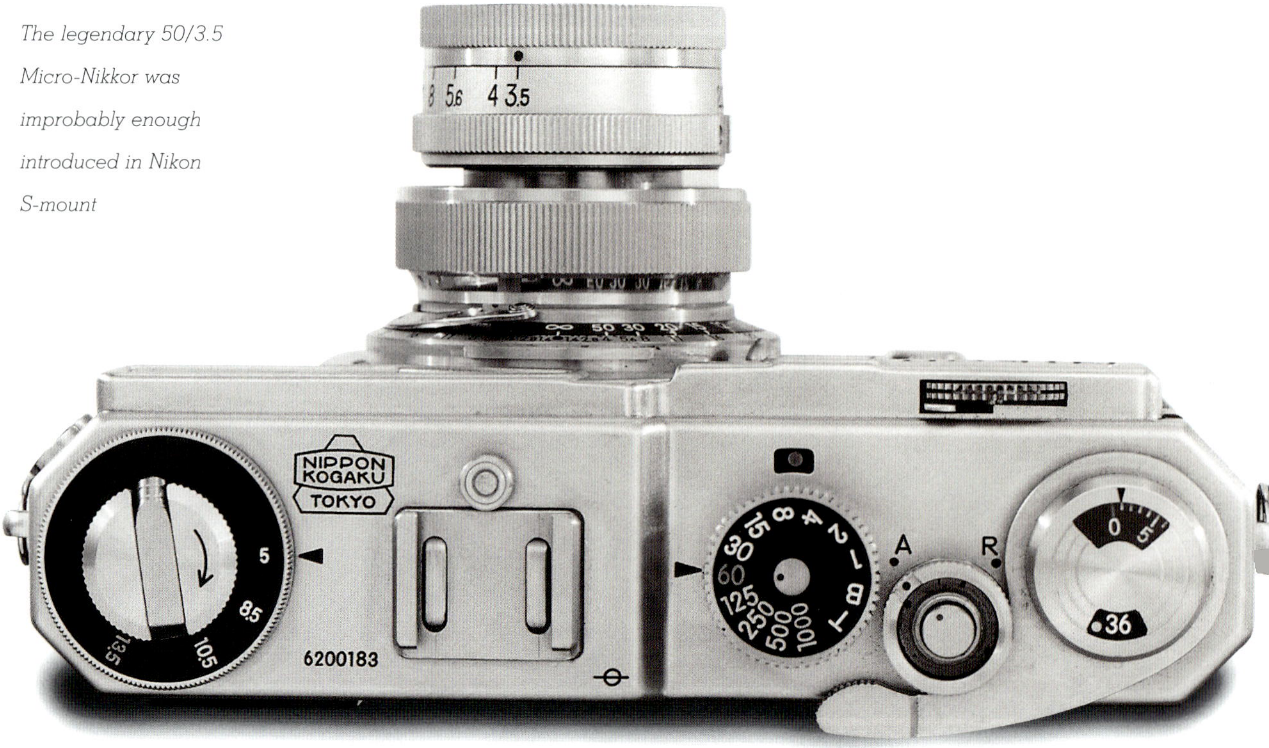

The legendary 50/3.5 Micro-Nikkor was improbably enough introduced in Nikon S-mount

'SHORT TELE' LENSES (73–108MM)

Most modern lenses in this group are either reasonably fast (90/2.8, 75/2.5) or very fast (90/2, 75/1.4), though the 90mm Voigtländer Apo-Lanthar is a mere f/3.5. To users of zooms, these focal lengths may seem modest, though the speeds of the faster ones will be eye-openers. It is, however, worth remembering that the area covered by a 75mm lens is about half that covered by a 50mm, or under a quarter of that covered by a 35mm lens, while a 90mm covers only 30 per cent of the area of a 50mm or 15 per cent of the area of a 35mm.

Anything much longer than 90mm tends to lose the advantages of the RF camera: immediacy, ease of focusing, and ease of use. 'Masking' finders, or small bright-lines in a large finder, make composition more difficult, though this can be overcome to a considerable extent by the use of dedicated single-focal-length finders (as with Voigtländer) or zoom finders (as with the Contax).

As with 50mm lenses, the big problem with increased speed is depth of field. This is exacerbated by the joint difficulties of focusing very fast longer-than-standard lenses and of holding them still for long exposures.

The difficulties of focusing are twofold. Accuracy is limited, partly by the ability of the human eye to see when the two images in the rangefinder are superimposed, and partly by the length of the rangefinder base and the mechanical construction of the rangefinder. A 75/1.4 taxes a Leica to the limit, and a 90/2 is not far behind; this is why Voigtländer, with their shorter rangefinder base, restricted themselves to 90/3.5 and 75/2.5, while Zeiss, with the electronic 'rangefinder' of the G-series, chose a 90/2.8. It is, however, surprising that Konica offered only a 90/2.8 when the Hexar-M was introduced.

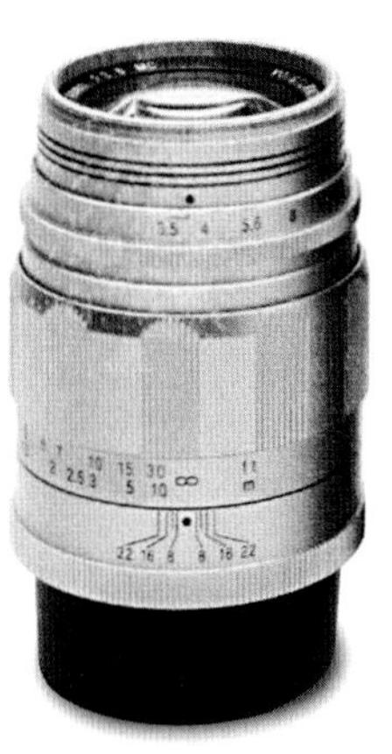
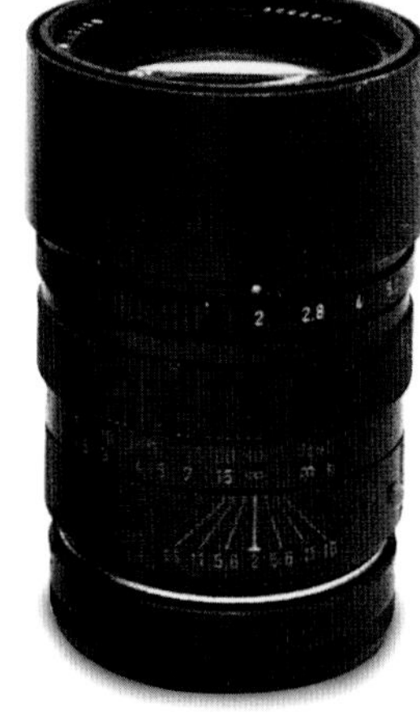

Left, 90/3.5 Apo Lanthar from Voigtländer; right, 90/2 Summicron from Leica

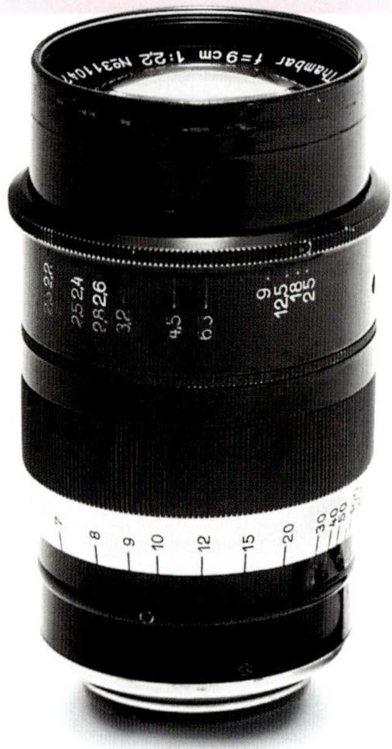

The 90/2.2 Thambar from Leitz is the only soft-focus lens we know of for 35mm RF cameras

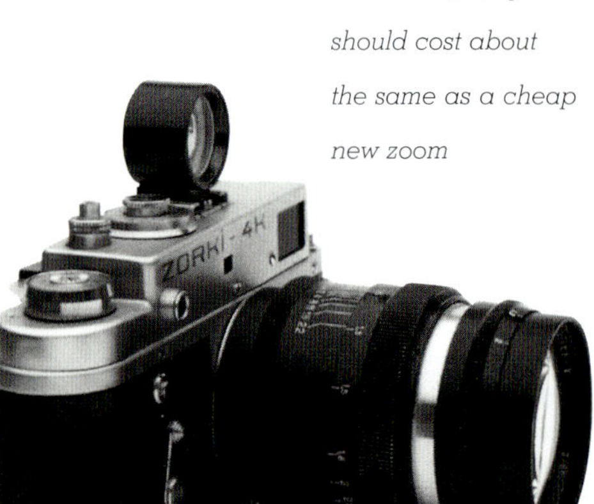

A used Zorkii 4K and an 85/2 Jupiter should cost about the same as a cheap new zoom

Incidentally, the reason that 'short tele' is in quotation marks is that many of these lenses are not telephotos at all, but simply long-focus lenses. This means that while they may be a little longer than lenses of tele construction, they can be sharper, cheaper and faster, and less bulky, too, if they are fast.

If you are into low-light reportage, a fast 90mm or 75mm lens is all but indispensable. For landscapes, a slower lens is more compact and less expensive. Either way, an unexpected advantage of the 90mm is for close-ups. A 90mm typically focuses to the same 1m (3ft) or so as a 50mm or 35mm lens, which allows a much tighter crop at the closest focusing distance.

A lot depends, too, on which other focal lengths you have. If you use 35mm as your 'standard' lens and omit the 50mm, then 75mm may be a more logical next step than 90mm.

Older 'short teles'

As with 'standard' lenses, the majority of old 'short teles' deliver results that range from acceptable to excellent. Very old fast lenses may be prone to flare, but perhaps because of this they can deliver wonderful results, especially in black and white, or even in colour, for tight portraits: lenses like Zeiss's 85/2 Sonnar (1932, Contax mount) or Leica's 85/1.5 Summarex (1941, Leica screw). Even the Russian 85/2 Jupiter, effectively a coated pre-war Sonnar that can often be picked up for a song, has its charms. Slower lenses, such as the immortal 90/4 Elmar for the Leica, can deliver excellent results, even in colour, and even from pre-war uncoated lenses, though a deep lens shade is advisable.

Although 85mm and 90mm were the 'canonical' lengths, introduced by Contax (1932) and Leica (1931) respectively,

other lenses in this group ranged from the 73/1.9 Hektor
(1931, but so sought-after that it is mainly a
lens for collectors) to 100mm and 105mm.
The former was popular with Canon, while
the latter was offered by Leica (f/6.3, 1933,
screw mount), Nikon (f/4, Nikon S-mount),
and Fed (f/6.3, Leica screw). There were
also 4in (101–102mm) lenses from Ross
(1931) and 4¼in (108mm) lenses from
Meyer (1934). Most are worth so much to
collectors that you might as well sell them
and buy something newer. Even so, most
remain very usable to this day.

LONG CRF LENSES (125MM AND BEYOND)

This is where RF/DV cameras run out of steam. They are let
down by focusing problems (see above) and by the
deficiencies of the viewfinders, which are seldom very precise.
The only lens remaining in this group today is the 135/3.4
Tele-Elmarit-M for the Leica (bayonet), half a stop slower than
the complicated 135/2.8 that incorporated a pair of
'spectacles' to magnify both the rangefinder image and the
image frame on M-series Leicas.

Older long CRF lenses

The lenses themselves are not difficult to make and almost all
deliver very good to excellent results; the difficulties are as
noted above. Some years ago we sold our 135/2.8 Elmarit-M,
and we now use reflexes if we want longer lenses than 90mm.
Although most long CRF lenses are 135mm, another popular
length after World War Two was 127mm (5in). Any f/4 or
slower lens (including the Russians) should be fine.

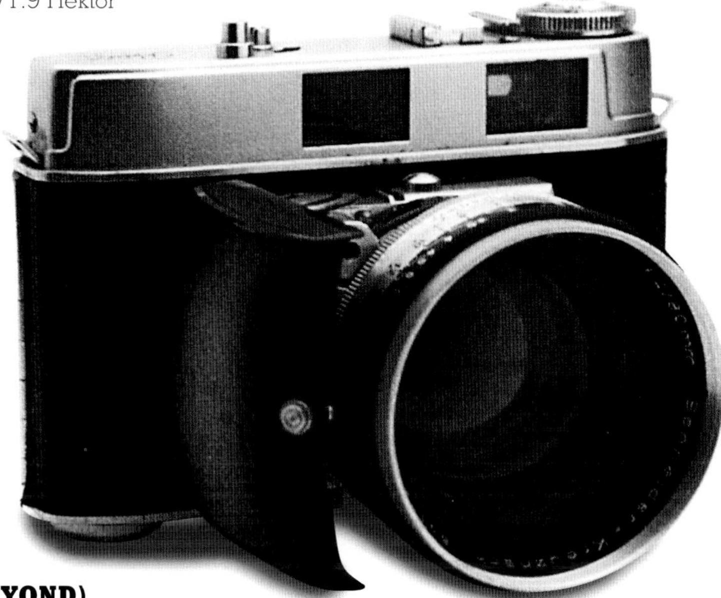

*The front group of the
50/2 on the Retina
IIC could be removed
and replaced to make
an 80/4*

For the 1936 Olympics, Zeiss offered a rangefinder-coupled 180/2.8 lens. This now commands a fortune from collectors, and some idea of its usefulness may be gauged from the fact that it was soon re-released for use with a reflex housing.

LENSES FOR REFLEX HOUSINGS

As noted elsewhere, most top-flight RF systems used to offer mirror boxes which transformed a CRF/DV camera into a reflex. There is more about the mirror boxes themselves on page 132.

The shortest production lens that focused to infinity with any mirror box was the 65/3.5 Elmar for a Visoflex-equipped Leica; the odd focal length was made necessary by the very long flange-to-film distance of the Viso/Leica sandwich. It's a good lens and we still use one for copying. Voigtländer allegedly made a 25mm prototype for the Prominent with a mirror box, but we have only ever heard about it: we have never seen it. It was of course of Retrofocus design.

Plenty of longer lenses have been offered. Leica, for example, made short-mount 'Viso' versions of rangefinder-coupled 85mm, 90mm and 135mm lenses (some had removable heads and could be used either coupled or on a Viso); the 125/2.5 Hektor (effectively an adapted projector lens); and a range of tele lenses including 180mm, 200mm, 280mm, 400mm, 560mm and 800mm. Other manufacturers offered a wide choice too, including 'independents' who didn't always make cameras: Astro of Berlin, and Kilfitt and Novoflex of Munich. Most were among the best of their day, and if they are clean, they remain usable – though like any long lenses, atmospheric haze can create the impression that they are less contrasty than they really are. Novoflex lenses are particularly contrasty, but sacrifice edge definition to central sharpness.

There are also special macro lenses, again for mirror box use, that do not focus to infinity; but these are the same as are used on reflexes. An alternative to such lenses is an enlarger lens on a bellows: generally, an 80mm will focus to infinity and will give excellent results in the close-up range. For still more magnification, switch first to a 50mm enlarger lens and then to a C-mount or D-mount cine lens of as little as 10mm.

Frankly, though, there is little reason not to use a reflex: an old Nikon F body is comparable in price with a Visoflex (easily the most common reflex housing) and there is a better choice of cheaper lenses for the Nikon than there is for the Viso.

LENSES FOR MEDIUM-FORMAT CAMERAS

The vast majority of MF cameras accept only those supplied by the camera manufacturer: the main exceptions are 'baby' technical or press cameras. The other (and notable) exception is Alpa, which, because it is a direct-vision camera, can be fitted with just about any lens in a focusing mount. As well as scale-focusing, of course, ground-glass backs are available for the Alpa, but they are not especially convenient. With all other currently available RF/DV MF cameras, the choice tends to be pretty small.

With older cameras, there is sometimes a choice of lenses available in the same focal length and even speed. For example, the Graflex XL offered a bewildering choice of lenses in the 80mm to 100mm range, from humble f/3.5 Tessars to mighty f/2.8 Planars. To a very large extent you get what you pay for, but there is such a jump in quality simply from going up in format from 35mm to 120 that even a modest lens – we have an 80/2.8 Rodenstock on our XL – can deliver quite stunning quality, particularly in black and white.

In general, old wide-angles for MF cameras are significantly superior to old wide-angles for 35mm, but this is principally because the images are rarely enlarged very much: even the old 65mm on the Envoy Wide 6 x 9cm is tolerable at a 5x enlargement, which is 28 x 42cm or about 11 x 16in. The only lenses we would caution you against are the first series for the Mamiya Press, which were very unimpressive indeed, though this was as true of the standard and long lenses as of the wide-angles. Later Mamiya lenses were superb, as were the lenses for the Koni-Omega.

Which focal length you choose will depend, inevitably, on what sort of photography you do. Because we use our MF cameras mainly for reportage, travel, and architecture, we tend to prefer wide or very wide lenses; if we were more into portraiture, we might be more inclined to use longer lenses.

LENSES FOR LARGE-FORMAT CAMERAS

Move up to large format, 4 x 5in and above, and you can fit pretty much any lens that will go into a lens panel, whether it is brand new and state-of-the-art or 100 or more years old: all you have to worry about is making up a focusing scale, and you can do that with adequate accuracy by reference to the ground glass.

Resolution and sharpness cease to be major concerns, unless you are making truly monstrous enlargements, above 16 x 20in (40 x 50cm). You rarely use movements when you are handholding the camera, so coverage is far less important than it is when the camera is on a tripod. In colour, there is the perennial question of contrast – we avoid all Wray lenses, even coated ones – but in black and white you can use just about anything (except possibly Wray).

Having said all this, if you do want to use colour, newer means better (unless some elderly lens gives an effect you particularly like), and more modern lenses are often a lot better at wider apertures than their forebears: a Schneider Super Angulon can be used wide open at f/8 or f/5.6, but the f/6.8 of a plain Angulon was intended for focusing on the ground glass only, with f/16 or f/22 as a working aperture.

Most 'technical' cameras have (and need) a drop baseboard for use with wide-angle lenses

For handheld use, which is really what we are talking about here, wide-angle lenses will give you a much better chance of scale-focusing with adequate accuracy. On 4 x 5in (9 x 12cm), where the 'standard' lens is 150mm (6in), the press photographers of yore commonly used 135mm or 127mm (5in) lenses: 90mm (equivalent to about 28mm on 35mm) is not too wide. For 5 x 7in or half-plate or 13 x 18cm, if you are brave enough to handhold such a monster, a 'standard' 210mm or 8in is about as long as you might reasonably dare to go, and something like a 121mm Super Angulon (roughly 25mm on 35mm) is a good idea. At 8 x 10in (18 x 24cm), a 210mm lens (30mm equivalent on 35mm) is as long as most people would essay, and the same 121mm Super Angulon (now equating to 17mm on 35mm) would be an interesting option.

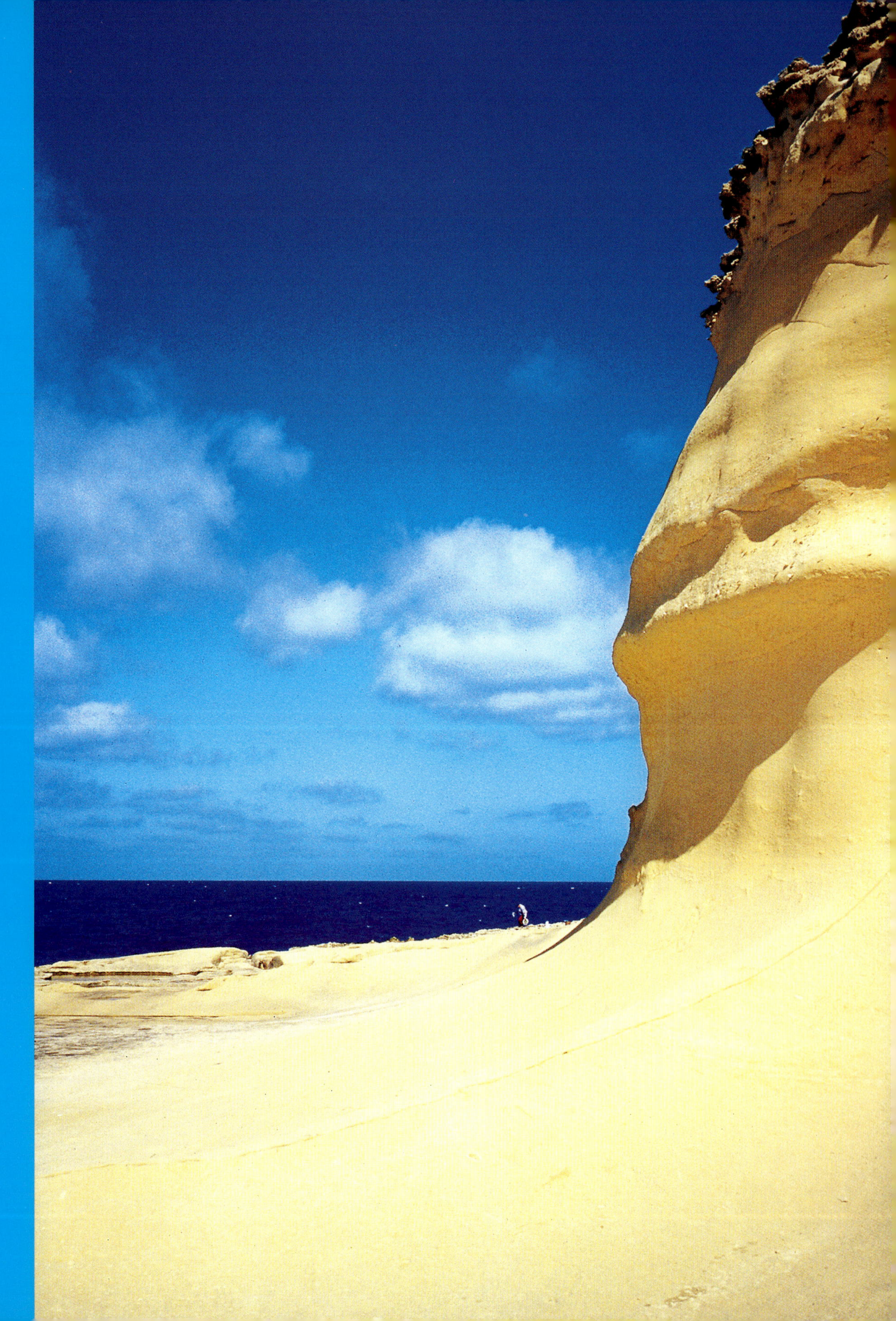

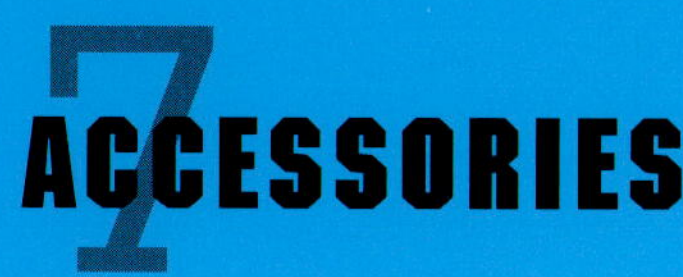

ACCESSORIES

On the one hand, an RF/DV camera is (or can be) a paragon of stripped-down simplicity. On the other, it can turn into a veritable Christmas-tree of accessories, which broadly fall into two groups.

The first group is designed to remedy the undisputed shortcomings of an RF/DV camera compared with a reflex: finders for different focal lengths, close-up devices, and reflex housings. These can all be lumped together under the heading of 'viewfinders'.

The second group is more disparate and can be loosely grouped together under the heading of 'customizing'. These are the things that reflect the personal preferences of the user or (sometimes, it seems) the inventive exuberance of a single individual. How else, for example, could you explain not one, but two separate varieties of baseplate adapter that allow you to hang an extra lens or lenses on the bottom of the camera?

Sandstone, sea and sky

Although RF cameras are more generally associated with reportage and the 'decisive moment', their sharp, contrasty lenses make them ideal for landscapes as well. This is in Gozo: the contrast of the colours, and the scale of the fisherman against the landscape, intrigued me. Bessa-R, 35/1.7 Ultron, Kodak EBX

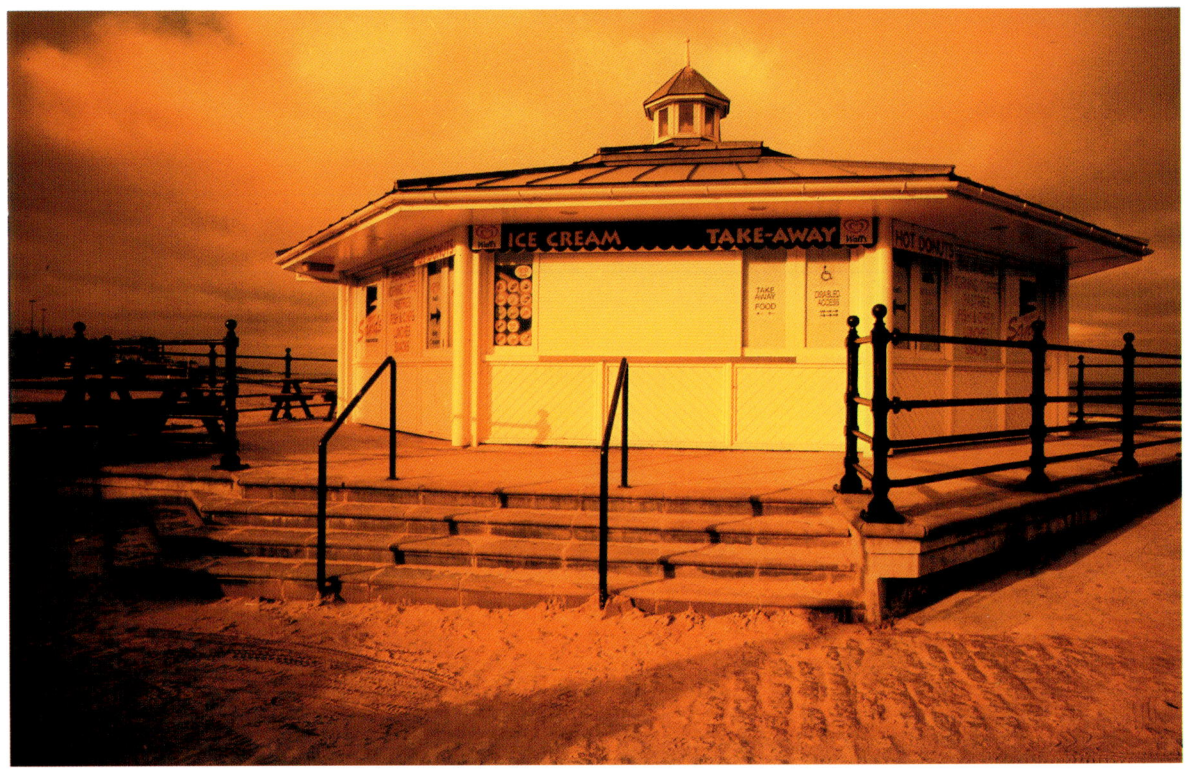

Cafe, Margate

To be honest, I didn't check the lens before I used it: Roger had been shooting black and white and hadn't removed the orange filter from the 35/2.5 Color Skopar. This is a danger with RF cameras. When I saw the transparencies, though, I liked what I saw – it's a sort of sepia colour shot. Bessa-T, Kodak EBX

VIEWFINDERS

Very few 'system' RF/DV cameras have built-in viewfinders for all the lenses that they can accept: many have only the 50mm finder built in, while a few have no built-in finders at all and rely exclusively on accessory finders.

The variety of finders is extraordinary. As well as finders for single focal lengths, there are finders with multiple frames; reversing finders; 'masking' finders; multiple turret finders; and zoom finders. Each of these has been made in several ways, including the wondrous Kontur finder that you can't actually see through.

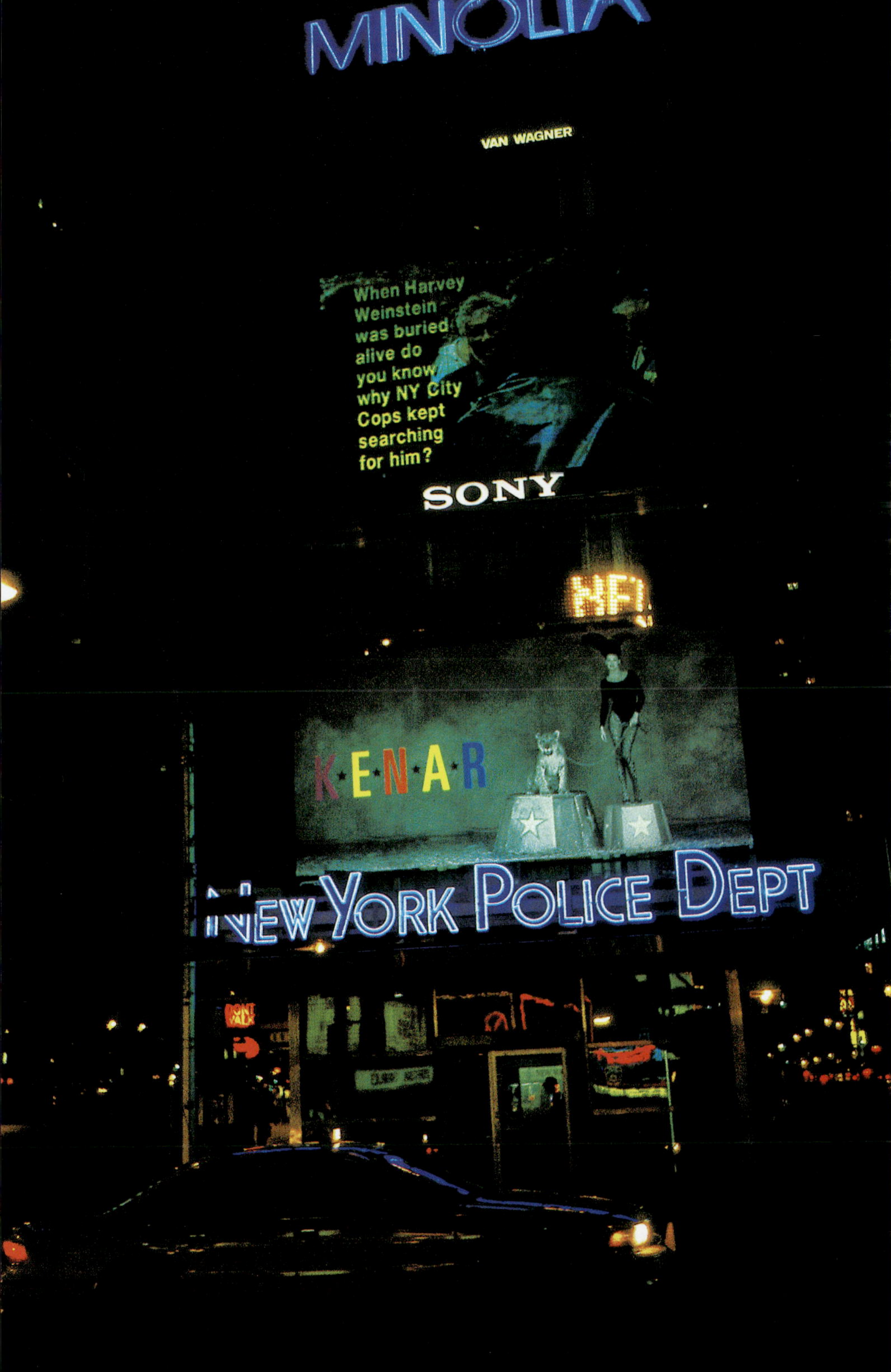

NYPD

I was intrigued by the idea that we 'consume' police services in the same way as electronics and cameras. Flash would have flared back appallingly, and not been powerful enough anyway. A 35/1.4 Summilux on my M4-P allowed a (barely) adequate exposure on ISO 100 Fujichrome

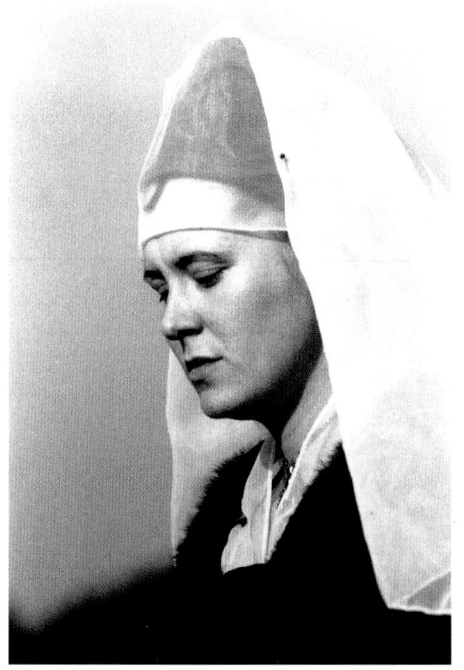

Lady

Most photographers associate RF cameras principally with 'people' photography – and they do make it a lot easier. I've taken more successful, close-up pictures of people since I've started using RF cameras seriously. Bessa-T, 90/3.5 Apo-Lanthar, HP5 in DDX at 500, MG Warmtone in selenium

For still further variety, there are several ways of compensating for parallax. In a few old cameras, the accessory shoe was actually tipped mechanically as the lens was focused closer. More often, there is a little lever on the foot of the finder that you can move for yourself, again tipping the finder forwards. Then there are the ones where you move the rear sight or rear window up and down. There are others that rely only on a second fixed line in the finder – the main frame is for 2m (6ft) and above, the secondary frame for 1–2m (3–6ft) – and plenty that make no parallax compensation at all. SLR users may find all of this alarmingly casual, but the thing is, it works.

Because accessory viewfinders have been made since the 1920s, there are countless examples available on the used market, and some offer advantages that are absent from modern finders. Most start at 35mm, because anything wider than that used to be regarded as an ultra-wide (even 28mm), so if you use wider modern lenses, you will probably have to stick with new finders or pay a fortune for old wide-angle finders.

Frame finders are no more than frames with a fore sight in the format desired and a rear peep sight: you can make one yourself from a wire coat hanger. Some have multiple flip-up frames at the front; some mark the front frame or frames on a sheet of Perspex or something similar; a few allow the front frame to be brought nearer to the rear sight or further away, to accommodate still more focal lengths. Frame finders are unparalleled for speed and are very easy to use with both eyes open, but they are not the most precise in the world and they are bulky. Few remain in production.

Reverse-Galilean finders are the simplest optical type, with
a negative front glass and a positive rear glass: the whole
frame indicates the image area. They reduce the size of the
image somewhat but are compact, bright and reasonably
accurate. Few if any are made today, but they are common on
the used market.

Engraved optical finders are similar to reverse-Galilean
(though optically more complex) but have fixed, engraved
frames: several offer multiple frames for different focal lengths.
Because the frame lines are thin, they are less distracting than
multiple bright-lines, but they are still harder to use than
single-frame finders. A very few engraved optical finders use
interchangeable front masks or cells: the Alpa, in particular,
offers a choice of focal lengths (35-38-47-58 as standard)
and a choice of formats (66 x 44mm, 6 x 7cm, 6 x 8cm,
6 x 9cm), and optional enhancements such as cross sights
(which make it much easier to level the camera) and shift
indicators (for the 12 S/WA only).

Bright-line finders are like engraved
finders, but with bright-lines, and are
generally reckoned to be best.
Multiple bright-lines can,
however, be very distracting:
there can sometimes seem to
be more bright-line than finder.
The vast majority of modern
finders are bright-lines for single
focal lengths.

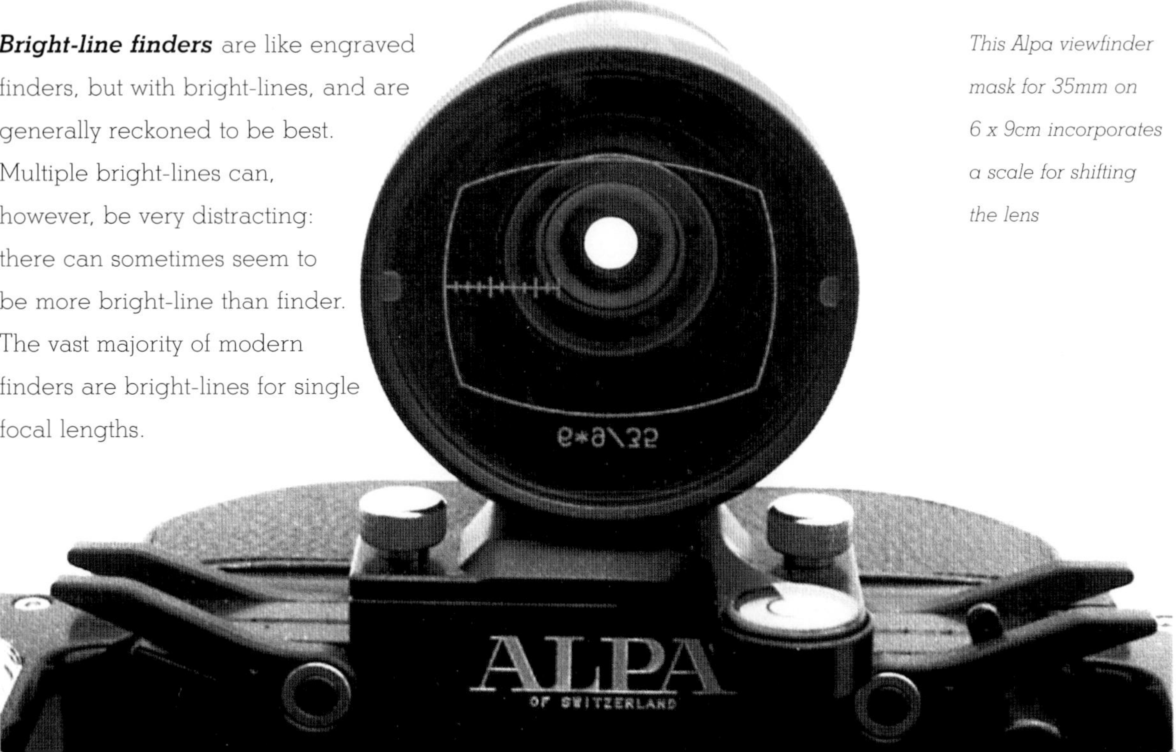

*This Alpa viewfinder
mask for 35mm on
6 x 9cm incorporates
a scale for shifting
the lens*

Kontur finders from Voigtländer (the old company, not the new one) are the finders you can't see through. They consist of a strong magnifying glass and an opaque front mask with a clear frame engraved upon it. To use one, keep both eyes open: one eye sees the frame, the other sees the scene, and the brain superimposes one on the other. They are superb for use in poor light, but some people never get the hang of them. Kirn of Dunoon, Scotland, made something similar.

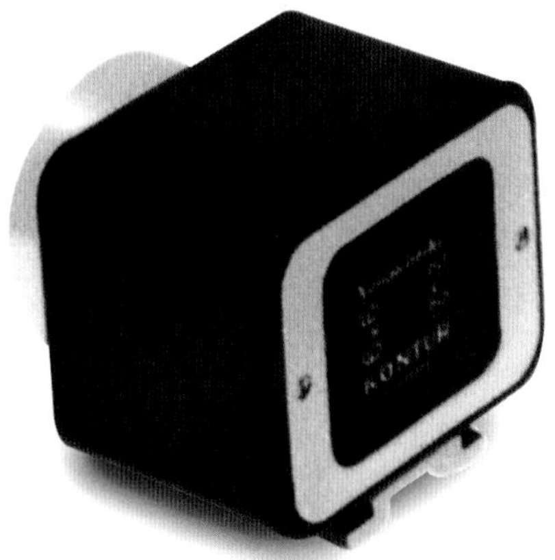

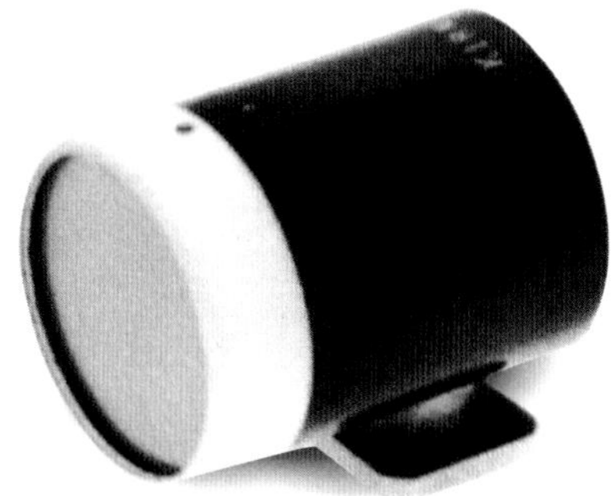

Kontur and Kirn viewfinders are impossible to see through, as described in the text

Reversing finders are used one way round for one focal length, and the other way round for another. Voigtländer's long-discontinued 35/100 Turnit is an example.

Masking finders are of two kinds. The simple kind pops an opaque mask over the front of the finder to suit the format or focal length in use – Linhof's Universal finder is an example – while the more complex kind uses a pair of sliding L-shaped masks for an infinitely variable image area. The drawback, of course, is that if you start out with (say) a 35mm field of view, and by the time you have masked it down to 135mm, the image area is pretty small. Leica's old VIDOM (laterally reversed) and VIOOH (right-way-round) finders are of this type; a Wray knock-off added the refinement of transparent yellow masks so you could see what was going on outside the actual field of view. All are long-discontinued.

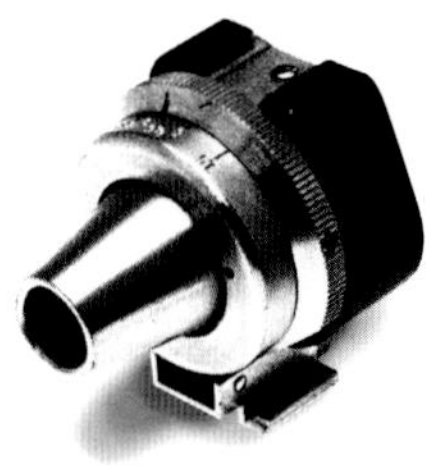

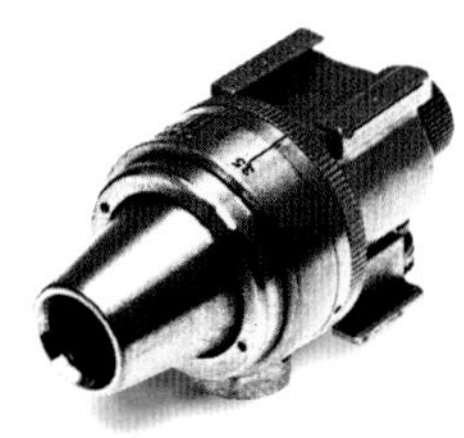

The earlier Leitz VIDOM gives a wrong-way-round image; the later VIOOH is the right way round

Turret finders are optical systems – effectively telescopes –
with a common rear end and multiple front ends mounted on
a turret, rather like a multiple-objective microscope. The most
desirable (and also the rarest and most expensive) is an old
Zeiss finder that starts at 21mm; the most common is a
Ukrainian finder for 28mm, 35mm, 85mm and 135mm.
Parallax compensation is by setting the turret to a subsidiary
index so that it is slightly offset.

Zoom finders are exactly what their name suggests. One of
the most common is the Tewe, which zooms from 35mm to
200mm. The great advantage of these is that you can set any
focal length: the Tewe (which was discontinued in the 1960s)
has the additional refinement of two index lines – one long,
one short – to compensate for the change in the field of view
as you focus closer. Linhof (for LF cameras) goes one further
and zooms for the same purpose as you adjust the parallax-
compensation knob.

Right-angle finders allow you to look along the long axis of
the camera and shoot sideways, allegedly unobtrusively,
though this is hard to believe. You can form your own opinion.
Leica made them in the 1930s; Voigtländer in the 1990s.

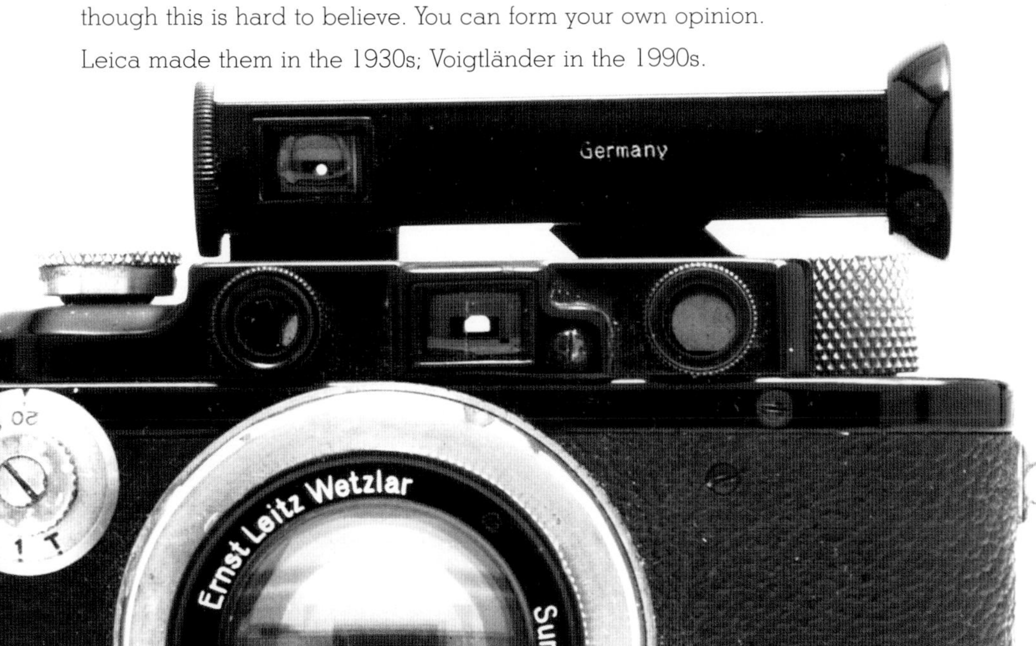

*Right-angle finders –
this one is from Leica
– never seem to us to
be particularly
unobtrusive*

Waist-level finders were popular in the 1930s and survived into the 1950s. Presumably they appealed to those who were used to the horrible old waist-level finders that were so common on roll-film cameras. They were normally used at chest level, rather than waist level, as the image was too miserably small to see otherwise, and the Zeiss 'lighthouse' finder, with its very tall eyepiece, was more like a right-angle finder for use from above, rather than a waist-level finder.

Focuspot viewfinder projectors were an altogether wonderful invention, normally found only on Graphics and Speed Graphics, though they were available on a few other cameras. They allowed the rangefinder to be used backwards in poor light: instead of looking through the finder and fusing two images, the photographer used the Focuspot to project two spots of light onto the subject. When the two spots fused, the subject was in focus.

Megoflex finders from Hugo Meyer converted the Leica I into a sort of twin-lens reflex, and are mentioned here only for completeness. They are very rare and are of much more interest to collectors than users.

Close-up devices

These are also generally of more interest to collectors than to users: today it is quicker, easier and cheaper to buy an old reflex and use that for close-ups than it is to use a complex and not very satisfactory adapter with an RF/DV camera.

The classic close-up adapter is probably the Leica NOOKY (honestly!), which incorporates prisms, masks and a built-in variable extension tube to allow the rangefinder and viewfinder to be used with an Elmar 50/3.5 at distances down to about 0.5m (1½ft). A later Leica stab at the same problem

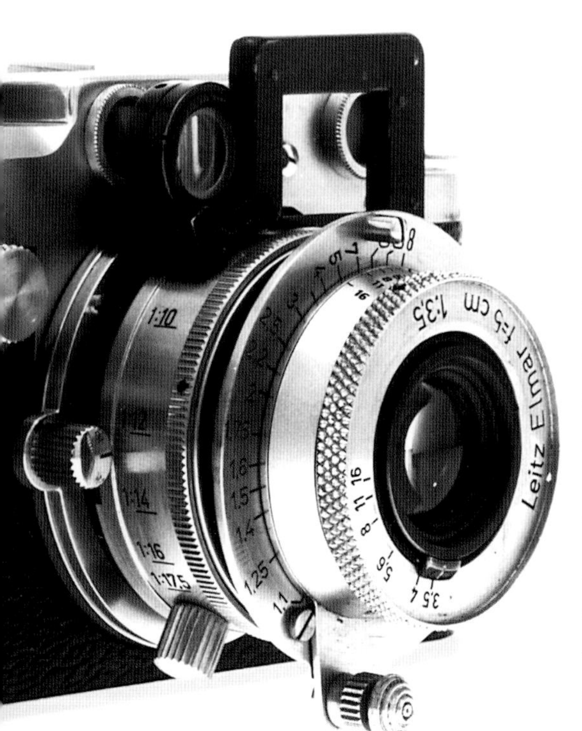

The Leica NOOKY accepted a collapsed Elmar and allowed focusing down to about 50cm (19in)

was the 'Spectacles' 50/2 Summicron, which had a pair of prisms-cum-lenses which could be slipped on and off a specially adapted lens with an extended focusing mount.

Kodak and Zeiss used a much simpler approach, with a combination range/viewfinder in the accessory shoe and a (two-glass achromatic) close-up lens on the taking lens. Others offered variations on these themes, including Voigtländer (see page 154) and Canon.

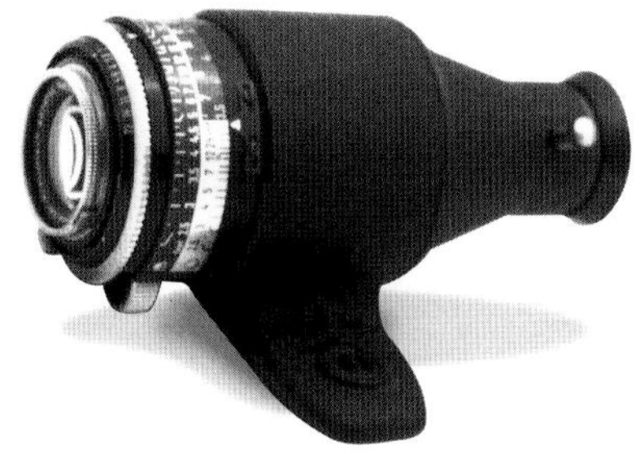

This Retina close-up accessory replaces the camera and half the lens with a focusing unit

Both Zeiss (left) and Kodak (right) offered close-up range/viewfinders to use in conjunction with close-up lenses

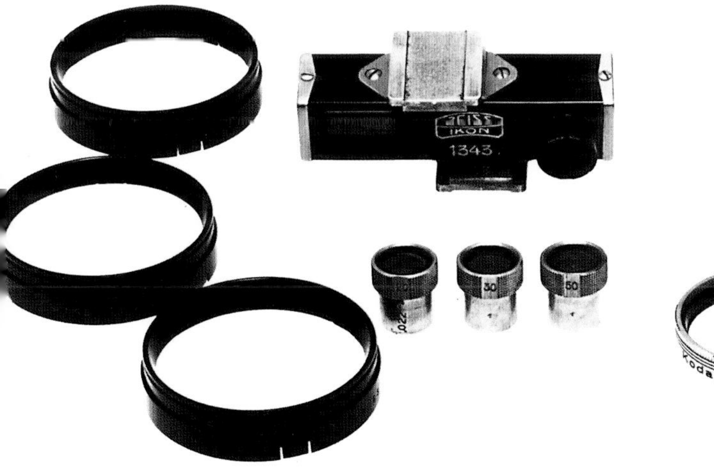

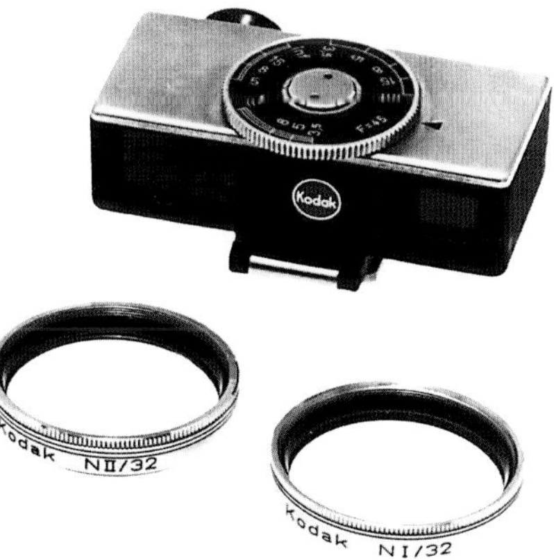

There is, however, one type of close-up adapter that is surprisingly convenient: the 'spider'-type copy stand. This consists of a collar that attaches either to the camera (where it functions as a short extension tube) or to the lens (which must also be equipped with a close-up lens) and has four legs. The ends of these legs correspond to the corners of the field of view. Usually, the length of the legs is adjustable to correspond with different strengths of close-up lens or thicknesses of extension tube.

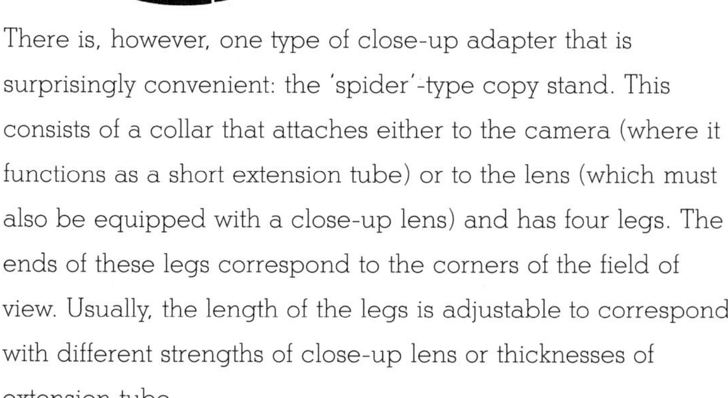

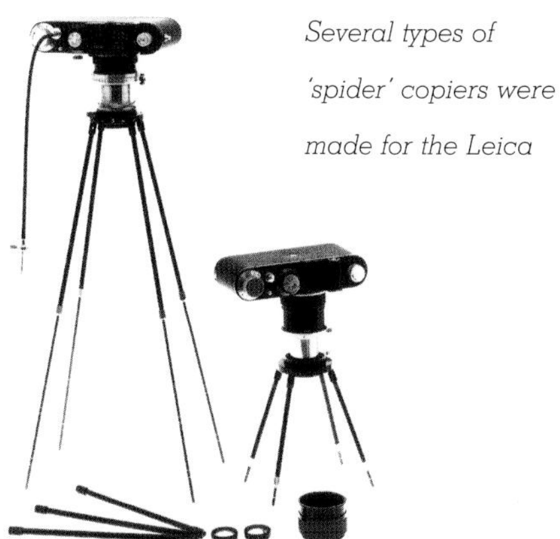

Several types of 'spider' copiers were made for the Leica

The applications for 'quick-and-dirty' flat copying are obvious, though shadows from the legs can be a problem. A less obvious, but arguably even more useful, application is for photographing three-dimensional subjects such as flowers, or even insects: once the subject is in the plane defined by the tips of the legs, it is in frame and in focus. As ever, Leica's various models (for both screw and bayonet) are the most often encountered.

Reflex housings

The easiest way to make a CRF/DV camera behave like a reflex is to turn it into a reflex by sticking a mirror box on the front. This allows parallax-free close focusing and the use of long lenses, but the problem is that the camera/mirror-box sandwich is necessarily rather thick, so short focal lengths cannot be used without radical Retrofocus designs, which seem never to have made it into production.

The definitive mirror box is the Visoflex III for the Leica, which also, intriguingly, fits straight onto the Voigtländer Bessa-T. It was discontinued a long time ago, probably in the 1980s, and despite bearing the magic name of Leica, it is not terribly expensive. The III (1963) has an auto-return mirror, which the similar II (1958) lacks. The I (1952) and its similar predecessor PLOOT (1933) are much bulkier and less convenient, and at 62.5mm thick are over 50 per cent thicker than the II/III.

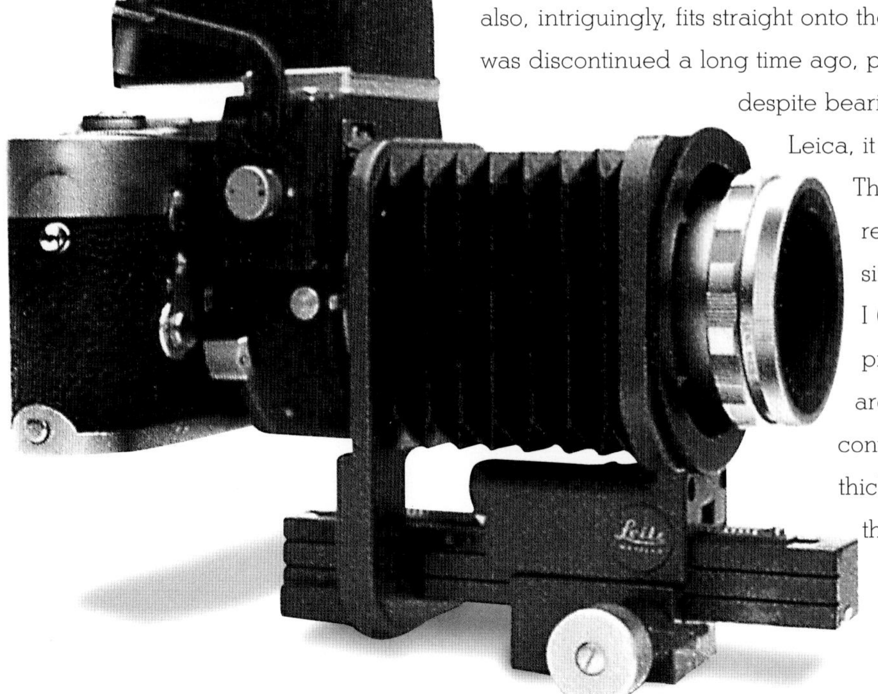

Left to right: Leica M2, Visoflex III with prism, bellows unit, 65/3.5 Elmar

Other mirror boxes were made both by camera manufacturers
(Canon, Nikon, Voigtländer and Zeiss) and by independent
manufacturers, especially Astro, Kilfitt and Novoflex. The
Canon, incidentally, fits on an external bayonet on late Canon
cameras: it is not Leica screw-fit. The f/0.95 Canon 'Dream'
lens shared the same mount and cannot be used on other
Leica screw-fit cameras.

Although mirror boxes are at first sight a clumsy and
inconvenient way of doing things, they do have a certain
charm, and the Visoflex has the advantage of showing the full
24 x 36mm image area (minus, for some reason, rounded
corners) unlike many reflexes that crop a bit off the edge.
With a 'stovepipe' (vertical) finder, they make excellent copy
set-ups; with the right-angle prism finder, you can even
handhold the whole set-up. The Viso II and III have an
actuating arm that fires the camera, thereby removing the
need, usual among others, for a dual cable release, one for
the mirror box and one for the camera.

*The telegraphic order
code for this
magnificent Leica
mirror-box outfit was
RIFLE*

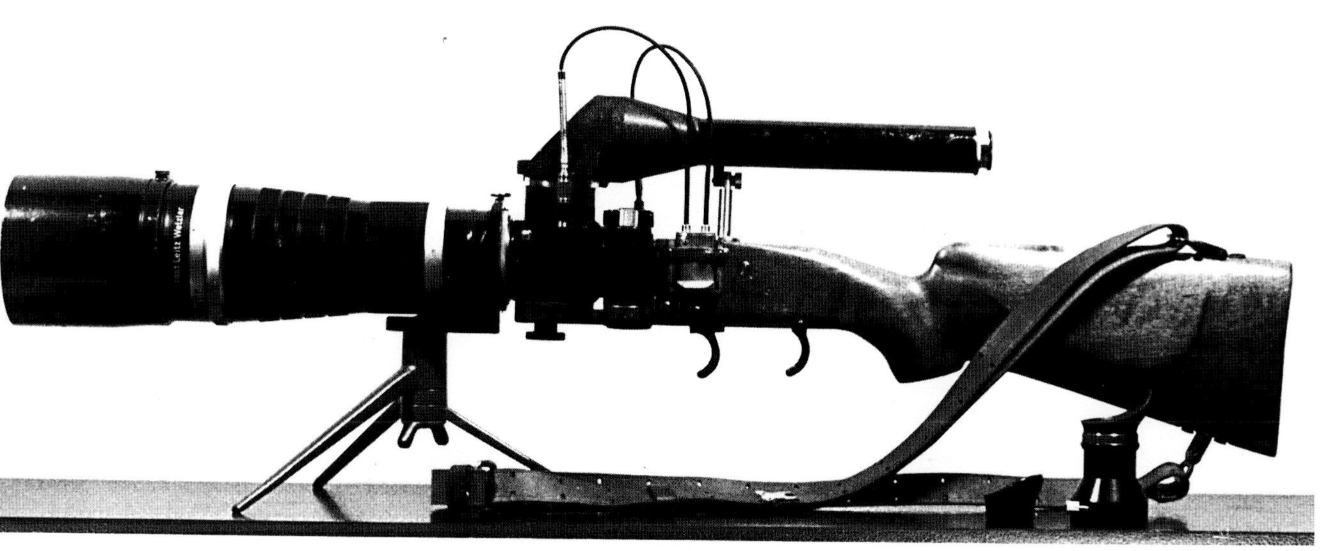

Notre Dame de Paris

Very heavy red filtration, such as I used here with HP5, can make it unnecessarily hard to focus an SLR. With a rangefinder, of course, there is no problem, even with visually opaque IR filters. Bessa-R, 35/2.5 Color-Skopar, MG Warmtone with local bleaching

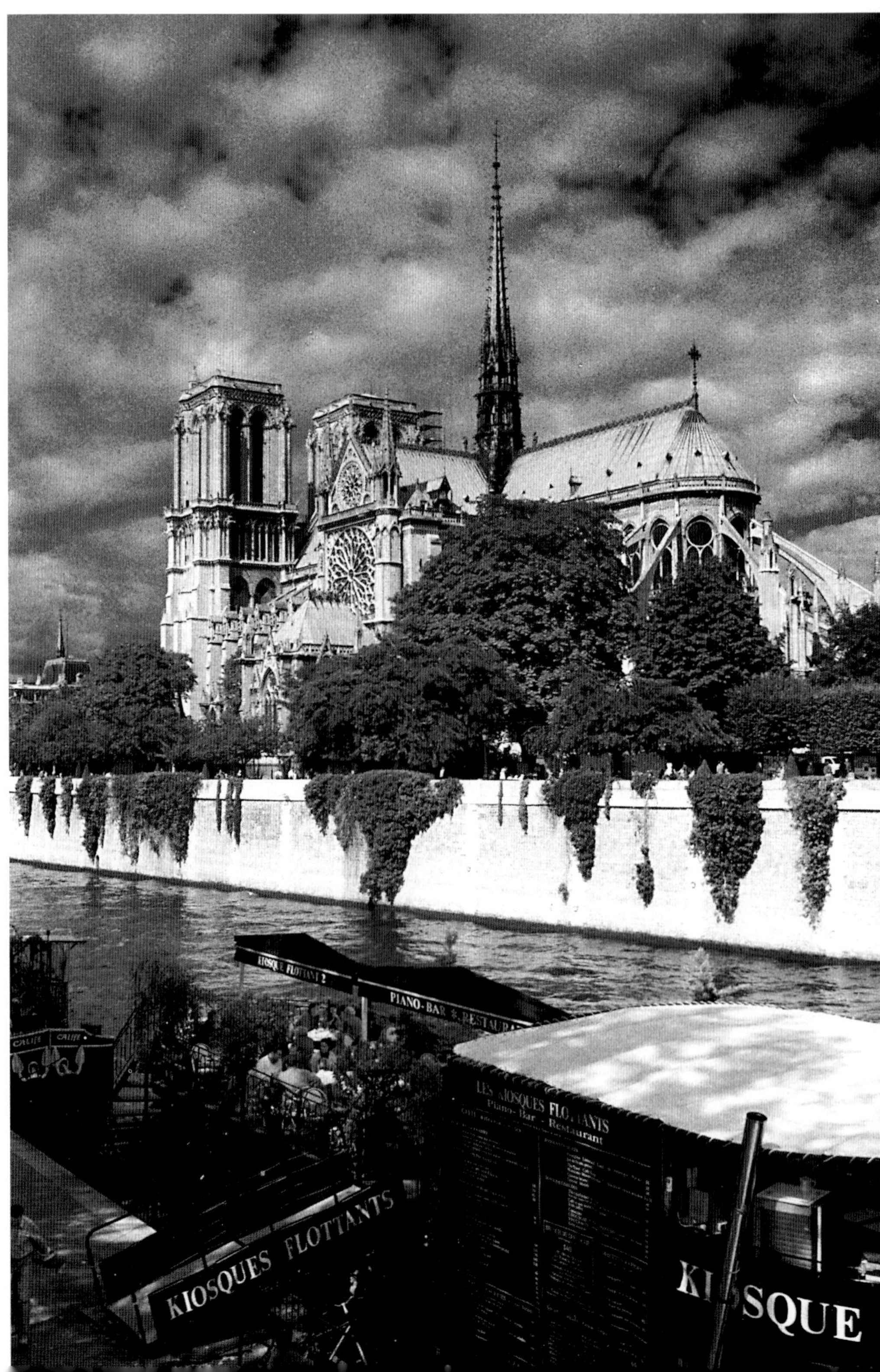

Combine a Viso II, or better still III, with a 65/3.5 Elmar (the shortest lens that will focus to infinity) and a bellows or focusing ring, and you have a top-quality macro outfit that will go from infinity to about 1.5x life size at surprisingly modest cost.

Ground-glass backs

Several medium-format cameras offer these as an option (Alpa, Graflex, Linhof Technika, Mamiya Press), and of course they are found on almost all large-format cameras as standard. They rather negate the advantages of the RF/DV camera, but they are ideal for maximum precision in focusing, close-ups and where lens rise is employed. Close focusing with a bellows cameras such as a 'baby' Linhof is obviously not difficult, but a few manufacturers of rigid-bodied cameras (most notably Graflex) offered extension backs, which move the film plane further and further from the lens, in the same way as a conventional extension tube but at the other end.

CUSTOMIZING

Leica used to offer a left-handed shutter release, allegedly for those who had lost their right arms during the Great War; it fitted in the accessory shoe. There was also a mouth release, squeezed between the lips, though this was only a modified conventional release. Even so, it gives some idea of the degree of specialization that accessories for RF/DV cameras have reached on occasion.

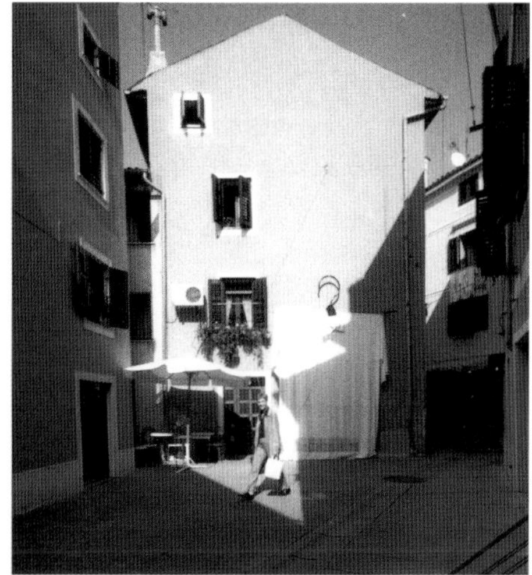

Big T

The giant T-shirt caught my eye, but doesn't read well in the final picture. Continuous viewing and the rapid response of my Bessa-T allowed me to shoot just as someone walked into the light. The foreground is slightly cropped: I often do this with non-shift wide-angles. Today I'd probably use my 35/2.8 PC-Nikkor on an adapter. 28/1.9 Ultron, XP2, MG Warmtone

Leica's left-hand release was allegedly intended for handicapped veterans of the Great War

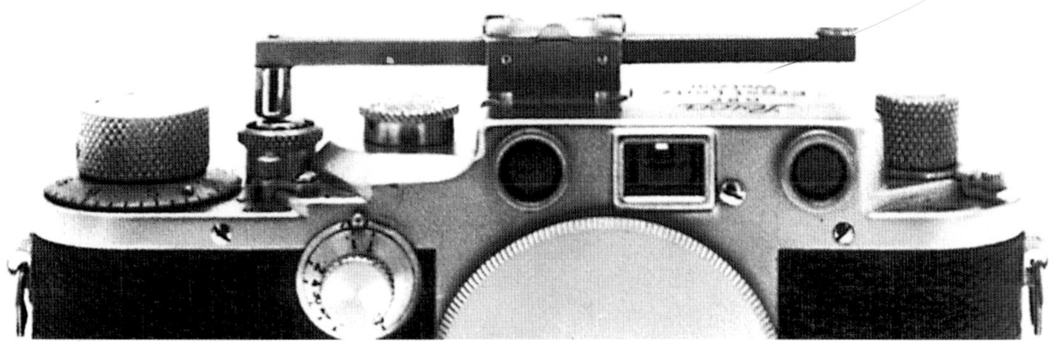

The accessory shoe, of course, was originally intended for an accessory, an uncoupled rangefinder; few people realize that the original Leica rangefinder, FOFER, was actually launched in 1924, before the camera.

Next came viewfinders, and then over the years, a variety of other things: the left-handed release, exposure meters, flash synchronizers (in the days when this was not necessarily built in), bubble levels, and more. Now, of course, the accessory shoe is so closely identified with flash that it is often known as a hot shoe; the term 'cold shoe' is an altogether ridiculous back formation.

An idea that has periodically been revived is accessory-shoe multipliers: you stick a two-shoe adapter into the one shoe on the camera. A rather better idea, and one that Voigtländer would do well to revive at least on the L and T, is twin shoes on the camera itself. Twin-shoe adapters are useful when you want to fit both a bubble level and a viewfinder on the same camera, or a meter and a finder. Voigtländer makes a particularly fine bubble level that can be used at eye level. Another way to avoid using up the accessory shoe is a flash bracket secured to the camera by the tripod screw, with an accessory shoe on the bracket.

Voigtländer supplied a shoe doubler to allow the use of finders and other accessories simultaneously

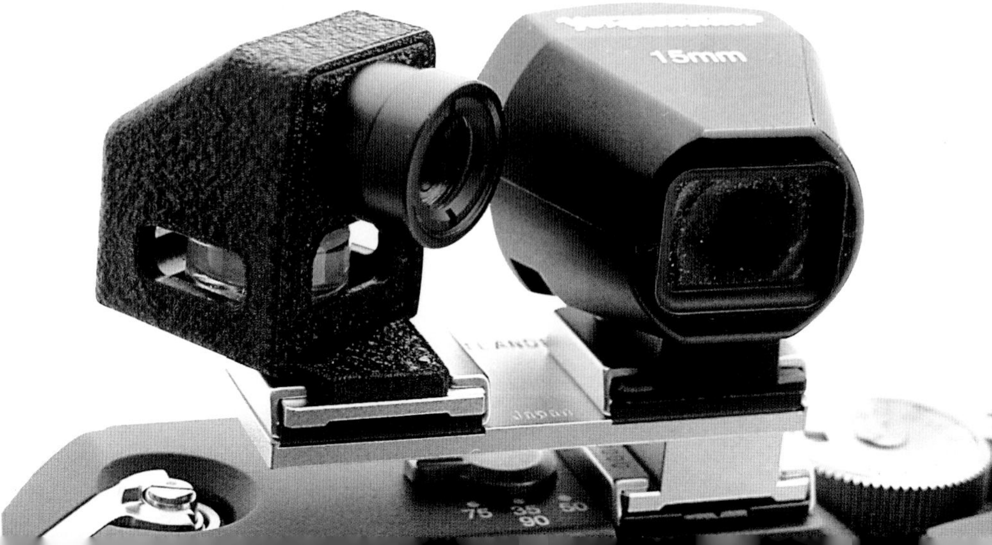

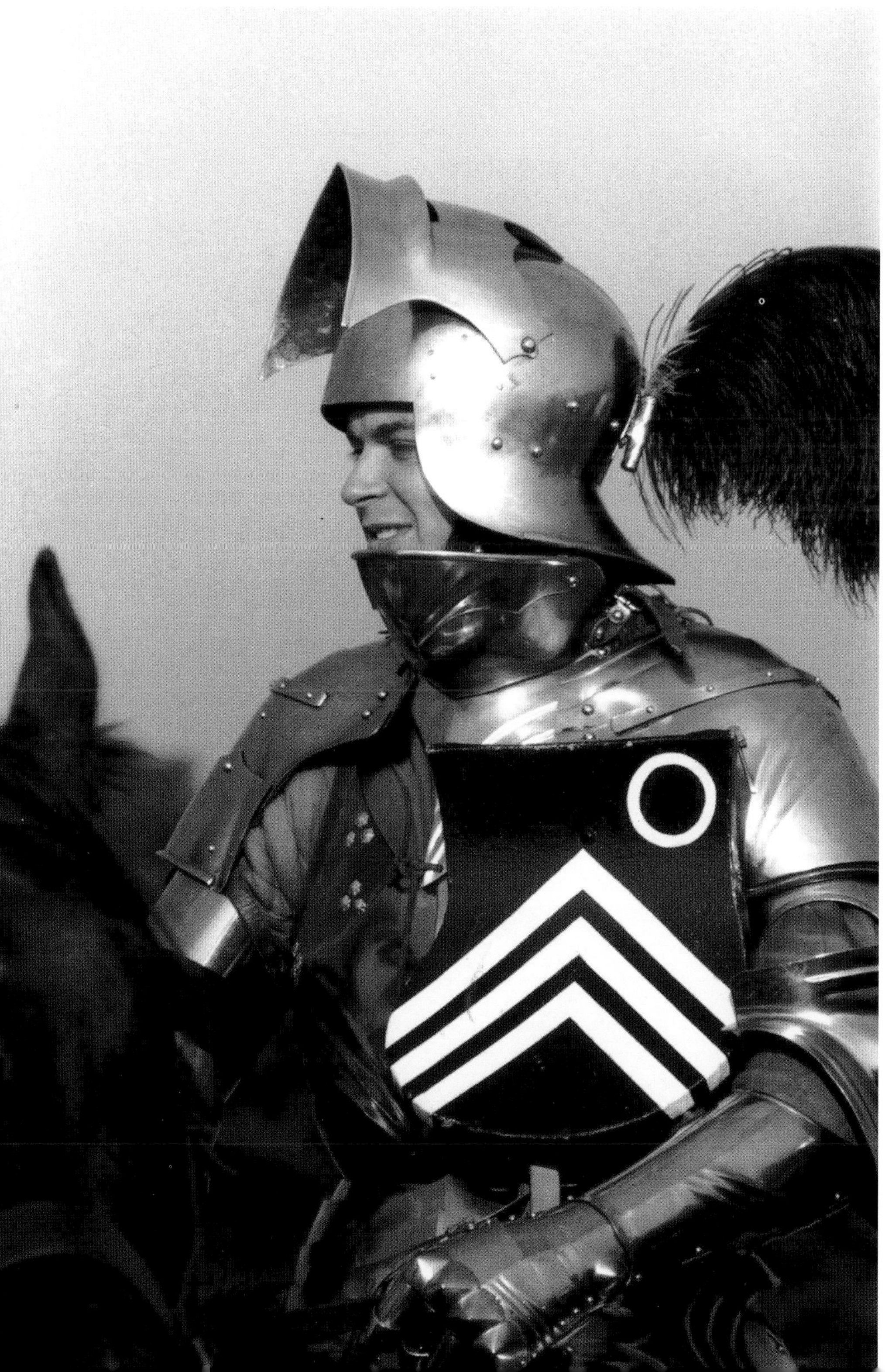

Knight

This wasn't an important shot: it didn't matter whether I got it or not. But what I learned about exposure and printing long brightness ranges came in very handy for the wedding shots elsewhere in this book. I always prefer to practise on non-urgent subjects before I shoot something unrepeatable. Bessa-T, 90/3.5 Apo-Lanthar, XP2, MG Warmtone in selenium

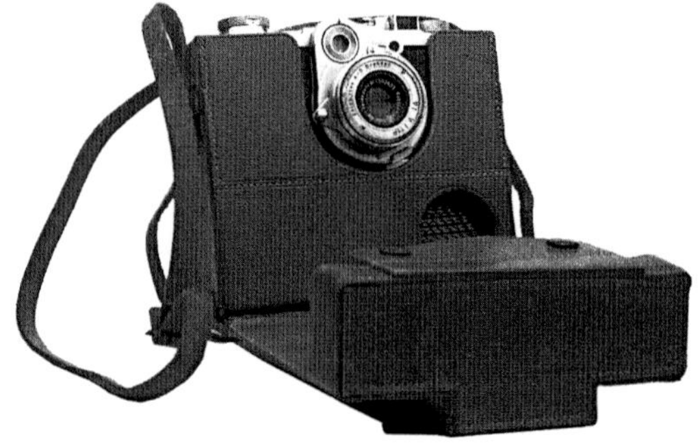

An enormous compartment under this Nettax incorporates an original Weston exposure meter, with the cell at the front

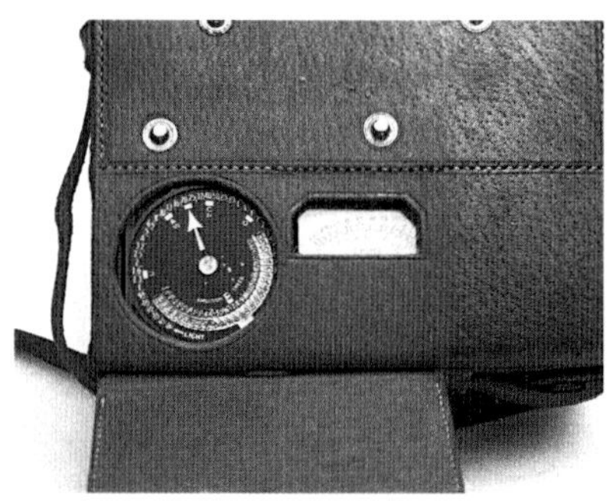

From the back, you can set the film speed and read the dials

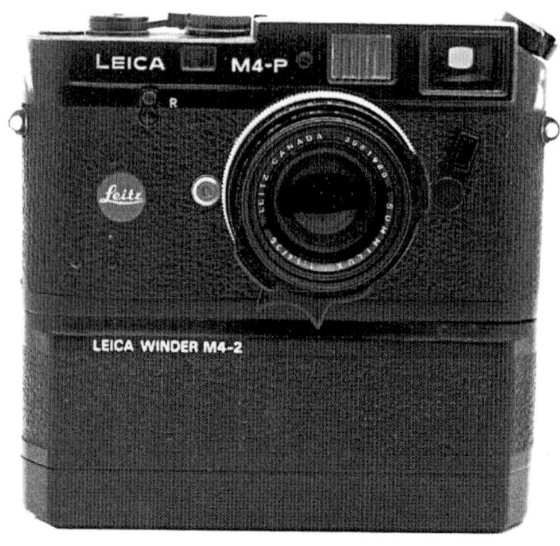

*Purists understandably
feel that the motor wrecks
a Leica M-series*

There is not much that is worth saying about flash – one of the great attractions of an RF/DV camera with fast lenses and fast film is that you don't need flash, after all – and the main thing that is worth saying about exposure meters is that while there were plenty of shoe-mount meters in the old days, most have now died of old age, and the cells are rarely replaceable. But the Voigtländer meter is more reliable and more accurate than any of them, so it reintroduces this option. The Leicameter MC (selenium cell) and MR (CdS) couple with the shutter-speed dial of M-series Leicas and give a direct read-out in stops, but are not as reliable as they should be.

Grips

We have to confess that these rather puzzle us – we prefer unadorned cameras – but they come in two flavours. The Leica-fit variety provides a finger ridge for the right hand, down the side of the camera, while Voigtländer offers both this kind and ones that screw into the tripod socket and provide little handles to hang on to.

Motors and winders

Add-on motors are surprisingly rare accessories for RF/DV cameras, though Leica offered them as early as the 1930s, originally in spring-driven guise and then later with electric power. The only other noted accessory motordrive was for late Nikon rangefinder cameras,which were electric from the start. The Nikon F drive was derived from it and wasn't very good, as it tended to fire a complete roll when you least expected it.

An unexpected alternative is the baseplate trigger: the fingers of the left hand drag the trigger along parallel with the baseplate, thereby winding on the film and cocking the shutter. Leica introduced these in the 1930s, too, but the real surprise was when Voigtländer introduced a similar device with the Bessa-T in 2001 (it also fits the Bessa-R2 series).

Compared with the knob wind of an old Leica, a baseplate trigger offers a very significant increase in rate of fire – at least twice, and possibly three times or more – but compared with the lever wind of the Bessas, the advantage is more modest: maybe 50 per cent faster, or twice as fast at most, but it's a great gadget, and it's not battery dependent.

Then again, experienced users of screw Leicas wind on by dragging the side of their right index finger smartly backwards along the outer side of the knob from knuckle to fingertip. With a little practice, it's a good deal faster than the regular knob wind, though not as fast as a trigger.

Before they devised the trigger base, Leica made a marvellous string-pull device that fitted around the wind-on knob and resembled the self-starter for a lawnmower or outboard motor – the latter accounting for its nickname.

There have been several rewind adapters for earlier M-series Leicas, transforming the knob into a crank. None has ever been official, and they have generally been made in small batches by enthusiasts. One of Roger's M2 cameras is fitted with one.

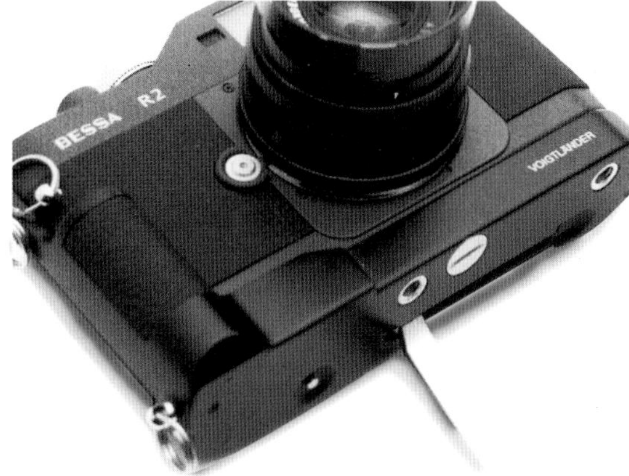

The Bessa-T and Bessa-R2 series all accept a rapid-wind trigger

This improbable rapid-wind device for the Leica is often known as the 'outboard motor'

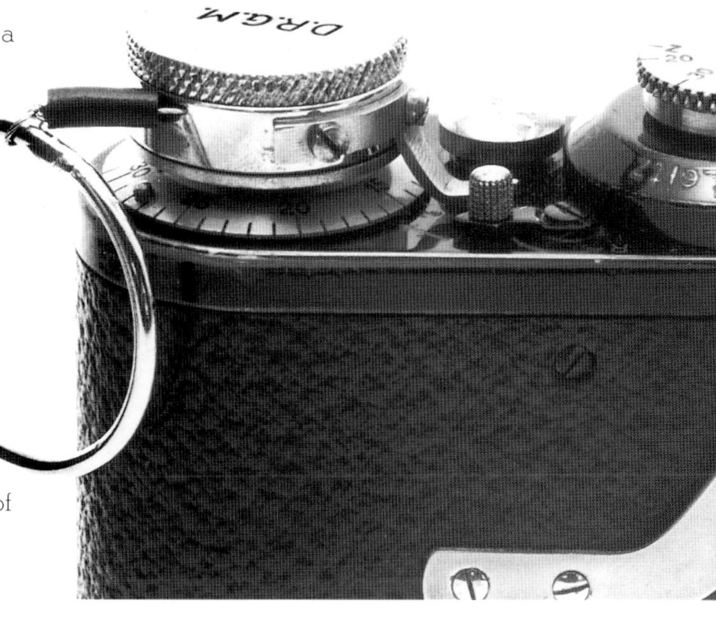

Lens holders

Walter Benser was a Leica aficionado who bubbled over with ideas. One was a baseplate that fitted over the existing M-series baseplate and had two lens-mount sockets: the lenses hung down from the baseplate, readily to hand and easily changed. Although it was an excellent idea in theory, even the lightest lenses can start to strain the neck when you are carrying three of them, plus a camera body, all on one strap. Roger had one but got rid of it because of this.

A decade or three later, Leica started selling their own version with just one lens socket; this was still available at the time of writing. A lot depends on how long you carry your Leica around your neck!

Lens turrets

This was a seriously weird Leica accessory (left). Looking like a giant cloverleaf on a stick, it took an M-series Leica on the back and three screw-mount lenses on the front. Turning the knob rotated all three of the screw-to-bayonet adapters that were built into the turret, releasing whichever one was locked on the camera. Turning it further moved the three lenses forward clear of the camera, and turning it some more rotated the whole turret, bringing another lens into place. Twisting the knob the other way reattached whichever lens was now in front of the camera. It weighed a ton, it was an invitation to camera shake, it cost a fortune to make and it was a hopeless idea; in short, it had 'Collector's Item' written all over it. Roger swapped his for a new 90/2 Summicron.

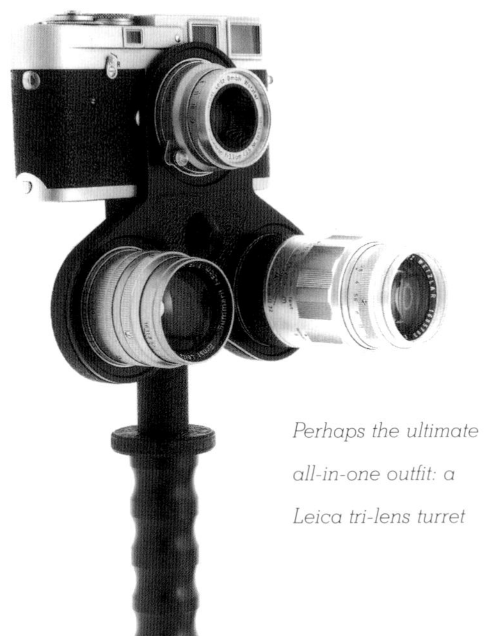

Perhaps the ultimate all-in-one outfit: a Leica tri-lens turret

A clamp-on focusing collar makes Voigtländer's Nikon-fit lenses easier to use, but less elegant

Stereo

Hard though it may be to believe today, stereo adapters were once offered for a surprising number of cameras. Most used twin prisms to create a single image through the standard lens – Leica and Retina stereo sets are the most commonly encountered, along with (unexpectedly) those for Pentax SLRs – but Leica's Stemar actually had two lenses side by side, plus a prism stereo assembly for normal shooting distances where greater interocular distance was needed. A simpler solution was the stereo slide set at 90 degrees to the subject-camera axis: two pictures were taken in quick succession, one at one end of the slide, one at the other.

Inverter bar

This only just qualifies as a camera accessory – you could equally well classify it as a tripod accessory – but as they were made by at least two camera manufacturers, Alpa and Linhof, they deserve mention here. An inverter consists of a stout bar, one end of which attaches to the camera, the other to the tripod. The camera can now be hung upside down. The reason why you might want to do this is that if your camera has a rising front and you are shooting (for example) down a flight of stairs where you want a falling front, the inverter bar ensures the necessary role reversal. Needless to say, both manufacturers' examples are beautifully made, with Alpa having the slight edge, and both are very, very expensive.

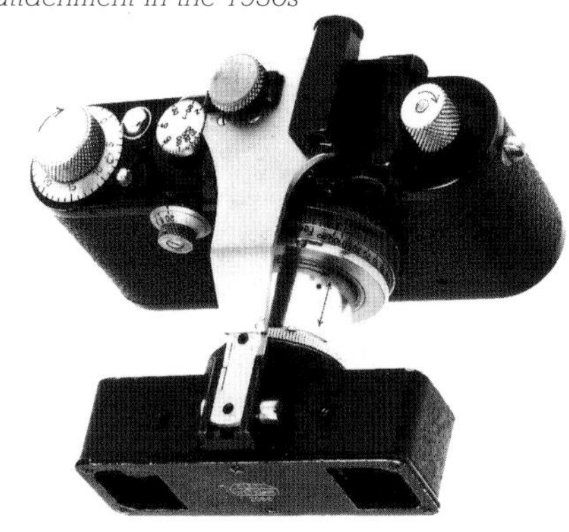

The Stereoly was the first Leica stereo attachment in the 1930s

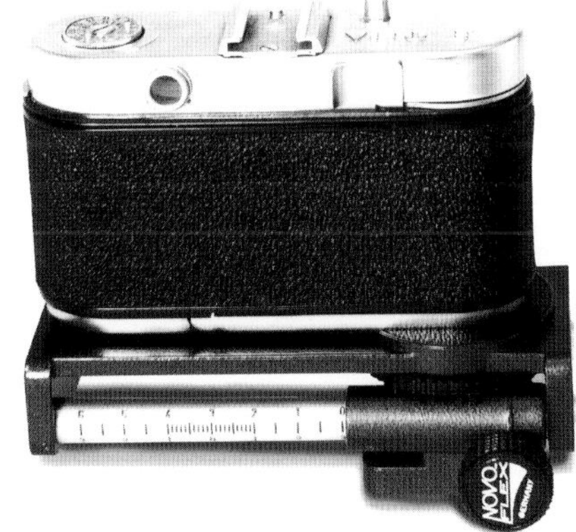

A cheap and easy way to get stereo is by taking two pictures in quick succession at either end of the slide

Voigtländer's clip-in meter is beautifully designed and quite at home on a Leica

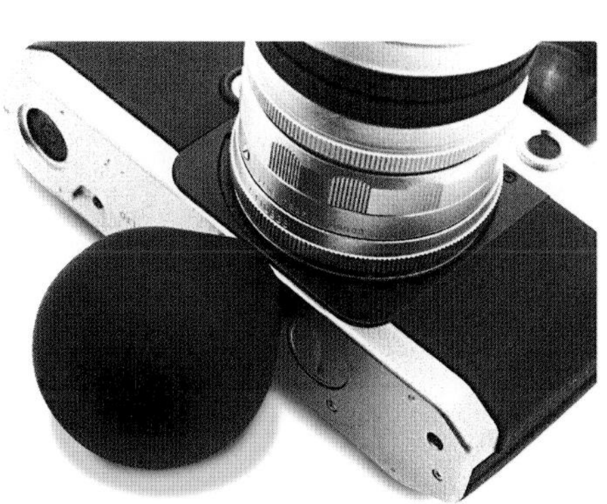

Frances likes this improbable Voigtländer grip; Roger can't see the point

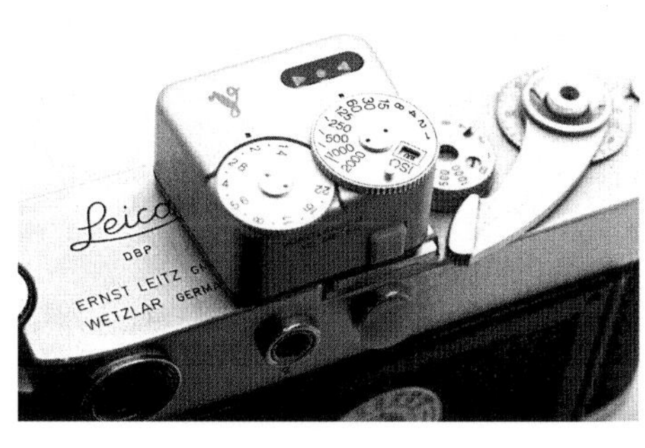

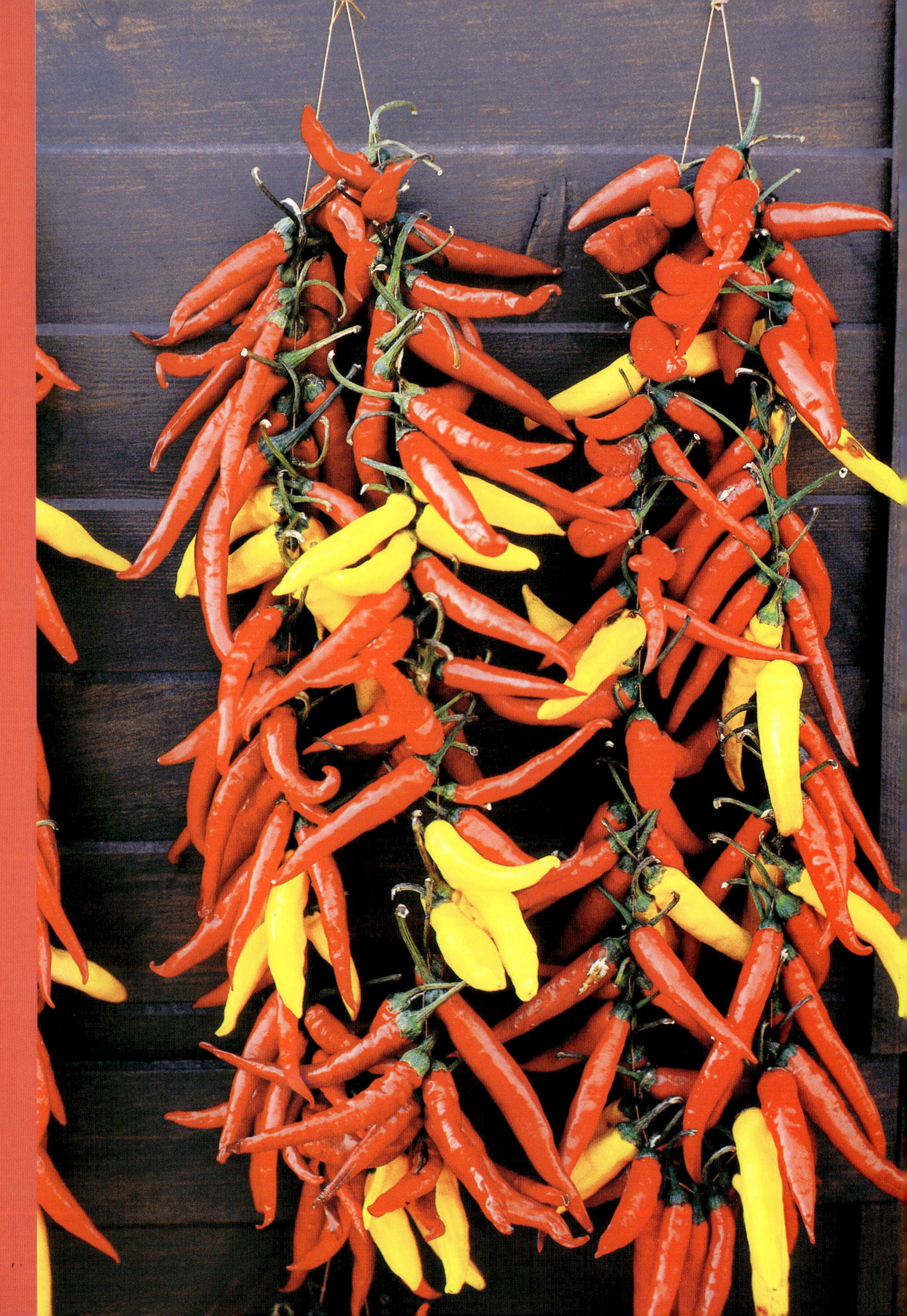

TECHNIQUES AND OUTFITS

By now, we hope, you will be champing at the bit: if you have not already bought an RF/DV camera or outfit, you will be on the point of buying one; if you already own one, you will be ready to rush out and take pictures. This chapter deals with techniques, hints and tips for using RF/DV cameras and with assembling an outfit.

It may seem odd to refer to 'rangefinder technique' as if there are significant differences between using rangefinder cameras and reflexes. In one sense, there aren't: much of what is in this chapter is as applicable to SLRs as to RF/DV cameras. Even so, there are some techniques that bring particular benefits, and there are points of difference between SLR and RF/DV where the voice of experience can provide reassurance or save time.

For example, a lot of people get bent out of shape by the base-loading of a Leica. There is absolutely no reason for this. Sure, it's unfamiliar. But it isn't difficult, so don't let anyone tell you it is. With minimal practice, you can learn to do it (as generations of Leica users have) even at a dead run, or by touch alone in the dark. With older M-series Leicas, tucking the film end under the tab on the take-up spool is a bit time-consuming. But, if you are lucky, you should be able to find a rapid-loading spool that makes early M-series cameras as quick to load as later ones. Do remember, though, that screw Leicas require a long film leader, as shown on page 20.

Changing lenses on screw cameras can be a hassle too, until you learn a simple trick: set the lens to its nearest focusing distance before you try to put it on the camera. If a lens is reluctant to seat properly, it's usually because the rangefinder coupling cam on the lens is hanging up on the cam follower in the camera, tipping the mating surfaces slightly out of

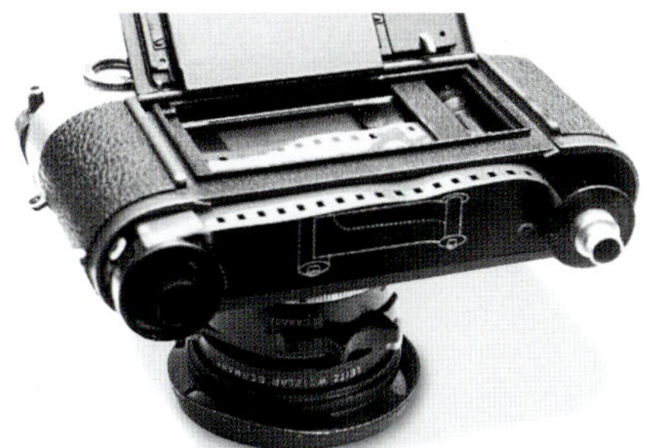

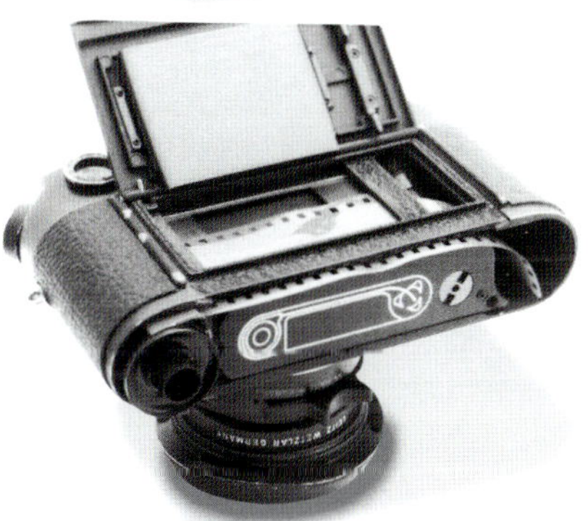

Loading a Leica through the base really isn't difficult

Peppers, Hungary

I want a camera I can use quickly and easily, without really having to think. The 90/3.5 Apo Lanthar on my Bessa-R allowed me to shoot this close-up of peppers near Lake Balaton without hassle. EBX

parallel. At the closest focusing distance, the cam is fully retracted, so this isn't a problem.

Another point that exercises some people about RF/DV cameras with fabric focal-plane shutters is the danger of the sun burning a hole in the blind: unlike a reflex, of course, there is no mirror in the way. This is a minor risk – we have never had it happen – and the usual recommendations are that the lens should be set at its nearest focusing distance or at its minimum aperture, or both, to remove it entirely. Repeated experiment with a piece of black fabric (we didn't actually risk a shutter) indicated that at f/1.4 with the lens at infinity and pointed straight at the sun, the fabric began to smoulder in 30 seconds to one minute. At f/8 or less there was no risk at all: the 'hot spot' moves faster than the fabric heats up to danger point.

METERING

Something that makes many newcomers to RF/DV cameras nervous is metering. Some cameras (such as older Leicas) have no meters at all, and those that do may seem to be rather primitive and casual to photographers brought up on multisector, multimode, multi-everything systems. Well, there are three approaches.

First, you can use the built-in meter. You are likely to find it astonishingly accurate for colour slides, though, as with reflexes, you will often get better results with negatives by setting a film speed that is slower than the ISO speed: the higher the subject contrast, the bigger the compensation factor should be. We generally reckon on 1/3 of a stop overall, so an ISO 400 film is rated at EI 320, but on an overcast day you can use the full ISO speed or even 1/3 of a stop more, while on a bright, sunny day with deep shadows, you are

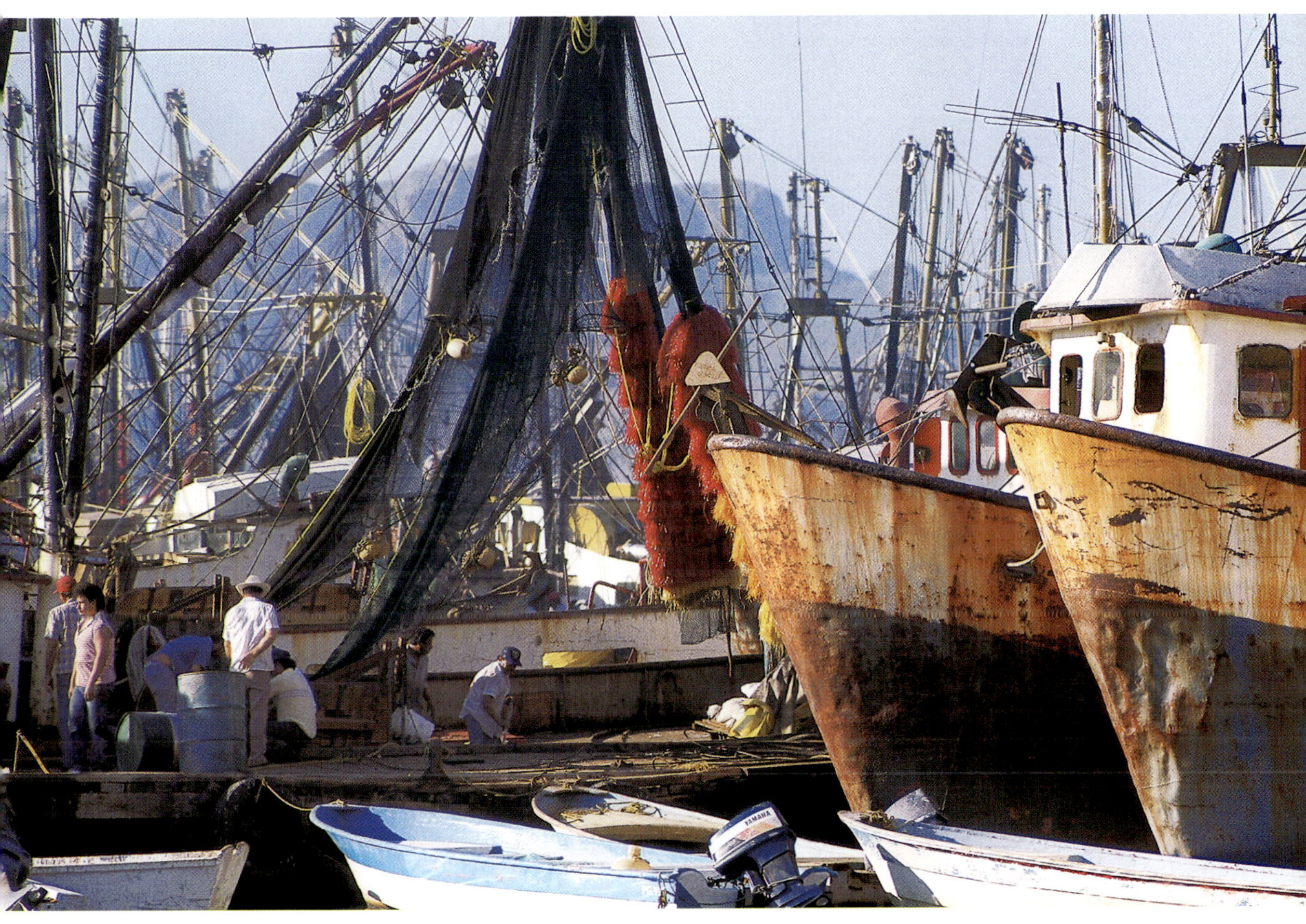

Fishing boats, Guaymas, Mexico

Early in the morning, I don't feel like carrying heavy kit around unfamiliar areas. An RF camera and a couple of lenses is light and unobtrusive – and 90mm (this was my 90/2 Summicron on an M4-P) is normally plenty long enough. Kodachrome 64

likely to do better with 2/3 of a stop or even a full stop less. This reflects the simple truth that exposure determination for slides is governed by the highlights, while exposure determination for negatives is governed by shadow detail. Amazingly many people do not understand this.

Second, you can use a separate handheld meter. The very best results with slides are obtained with an incident light meter, while the very best results with negatives are obtained with a spot meter. Something like a Gossen Starlite allows both types of reading with more accuracy and predictability than you will ever get with any in-camera meter, multisector or multi-anything else.

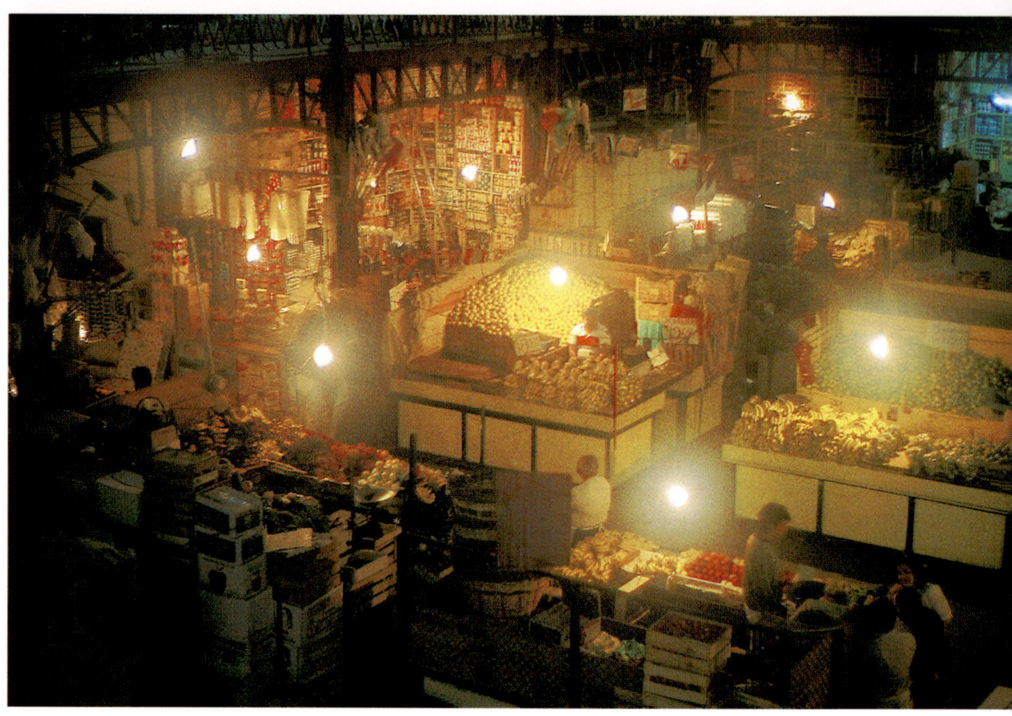

Market, Guanajuato

It's a pity they discontinued Scotch 640T and 1000D. They may have had grain like popcorn and poor colour saturation, but no one could deny that they had character. I shot this with my 21/2.8 Elmarit-M on an M4-P

Third, you can just guess. If you are shooting negative film and err on the side of overexposure, you may be amazed at the quality you get – just don't underexpose – and with a little practice, you can even learn to shoot slides at the right exposure nine times out of ten. Of course, the more you shoot, the better you will get.

This is one of the things that tends to unite RF/DV users: they know what they can get away with. They laugh at people who bracket negative films, colour or mono, half a stop either way. If they bracket negatives at all, it will be one frame at their best guess and another at one stop or (more likely) two stops over. The penalties for overexposure are a slight loss of sharpness and (with conventional mono films) an increase in grain; with chromogenic mono films such as Ilford XP2 Super, or colour negative films, grain actually becomes finer with overexposure, though sharpness still suffers.

Knowing what you can get away with is wonderfully liberating: you can worry about the pictures, not the technique. And let's be honest: it's all too easy to get obsessive about equipment and technique.

FOCUS

If in doubt, focus on the main point of interest in a picture: the eyes in a portrait, for example. But depth-of-field (d-o-f) scales make zone focusing very easy if you want to work quickly. The trouble is, if you are used to autofocus and zooms, where you often don't get d-o-f scales, they may look a bit complicated. They aren't.

Let's say you're shooting out of doors, at f/8. Set the infinity mark on the lens against one of the f/8 d-o-f markings and the other will indicate the closest distance at which things will still be in acceptable focus: with a 35mm lens, typically around 2.5m (8ft). You can now use the camera without bothering to focus at all, provided the subject is more than eight feet away. This is a lot quicker than any autofocus can ever be!

In the light of experience, especially if you habitually make big enlargements, you may decide to use the next scale down from the actual aperture you are using: f/5.6 for f/8, for example. In this case, just set infinity at the f/5.6 mark; the other f/5.6 mark will tell you that everything from just over 3m (10ft, maybe 11 feet) is in acceptable focus. Different manufacturers have different ideas of what constitutes 'acceptable' focus, which is why you may need to do this.

You don't always have to focus to infinity, of course: depending on what you are shooting, you might set the focus to 3m (10ft), so that with an aperture of f/5.6 everything from about 2–6m (7–20ft) will be acceptable. You can also pre-focus on a spot where you plan to take a picture: for example, where a runner will pass. The quick response time of an RF/DV camera cuts the need for anticipation to a minimum, by contrast with (say) a digital camera where the runner may well have breasted the tape before the camera condescends to take a picture.

***Door, latch and
handle, rural France***

*Maintaining
optimum aperture
can be a problem in
bright sun, especially
with fast film (this is
Ilford XP2 Super, ISO
400). Even so, there
are ways around it. If
I had not been using
an orange filter on
my 90/3.5 Apo
Lanthar (mounted on
a Bessa-R) I should
have shot at 1/1000
or even 1/2000. As it
was, the filter let me
shoot at 1/250 at f/8-
and-a-half (f/9.5)*

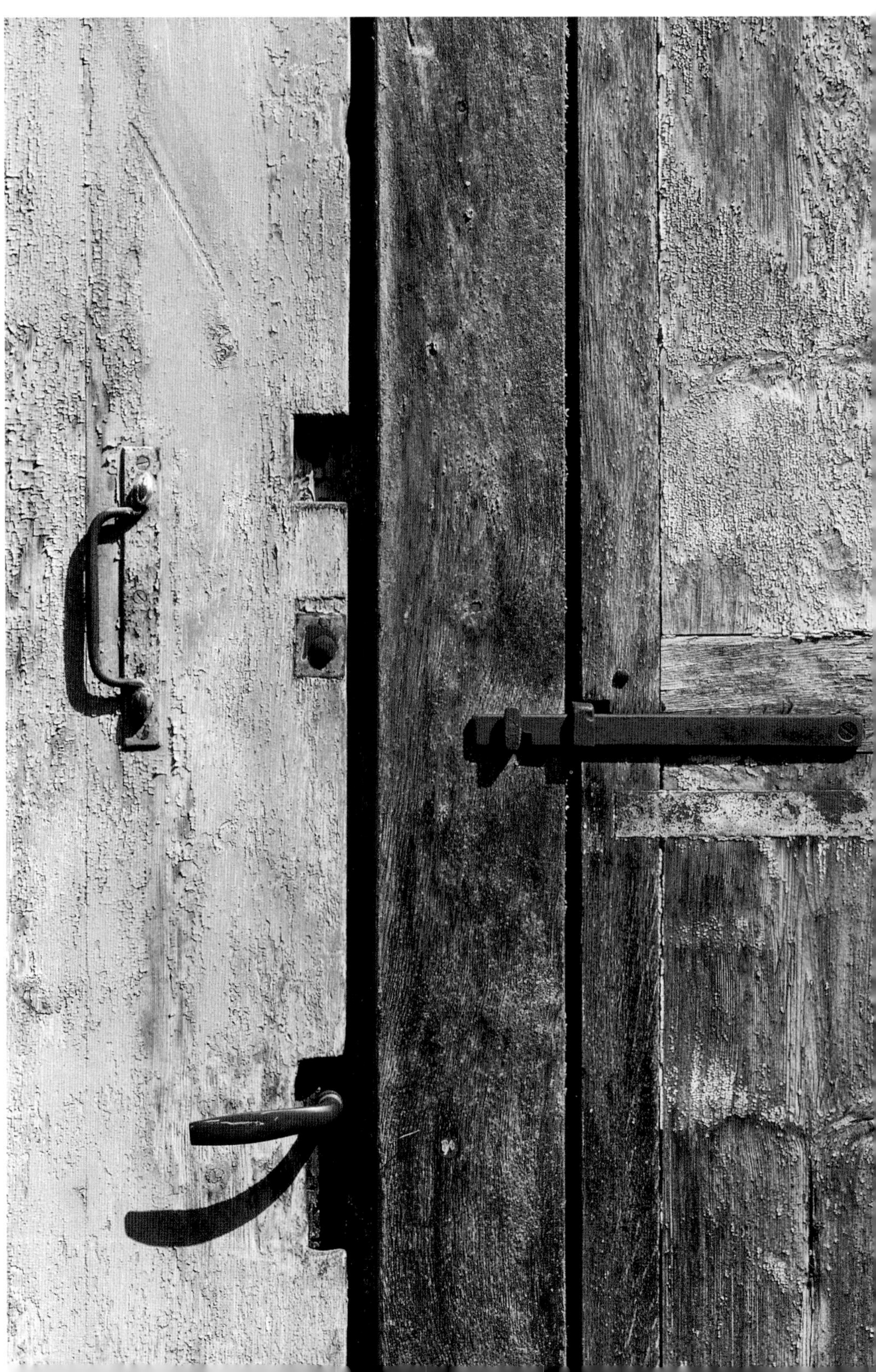

An intriguing feature of older M-series Leicas is two little cut-outs above and below the RF patch. These correspond to the depth of field of a 50mm lens at f/16 (top) and f/5.6 (bottom); as long as the split images are no further apart than this, d-o-f will be acceptable. But they are fiddly to use; apply only to the 50mm lens; and are ignored by (or unknown to) the vast majority of users, so they were dropped years ago.

OPTIMUM APERTURES

Many RF users tend to be more aware of the optimum aperture of their lenses – the one that gives the very best sharpness and resolution – and to use them at those apertures, adjusting the shutter speed to give the best exposure. With almost all lenses for 35mm cameras, f/5.6 and f/8 give the very best results, though a few are at the same standard by f/4, and deterioration at f/11 is only slight. Go to full bore, or stop down to f/16 or (worse still) f/22, only when there is no convenient alternative.

SHAKE-FREE RELEASES

We have already mentioned that most people find it easier to handhold RF/DV cameras for longer than reflexes, and that we are not quite sure why this is. What we are sure of, however, is a range of techniques for ensuring the steadiest possible hand when firing the camera. Here are our favourites:

Exhale – Many people hold their breath when they are trying to hold a camera steady for a long exposure, but a much more successful technique is to take a deep breath and then exhale slowly, releasing the shutter during the exhalation. Your whole body is more relaxed and there are far fewer muscle tremors than with any other technique.

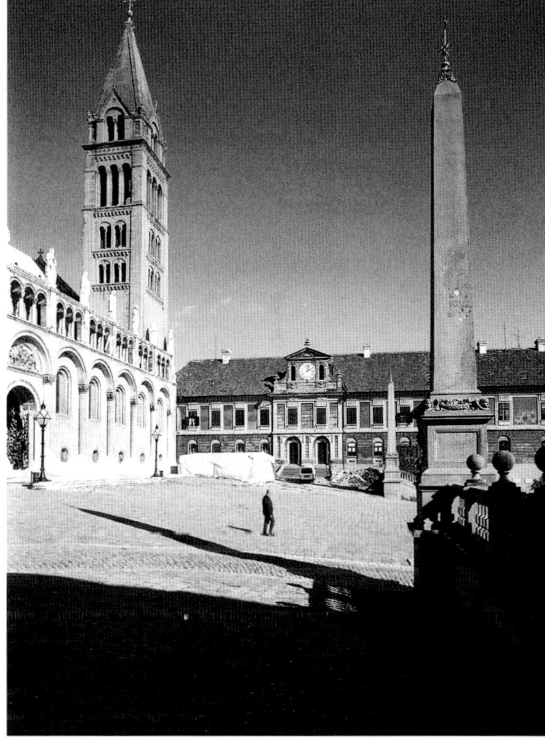

Cathedral square, Pecs, Hungary

This square really appealed to me, even with the building materials in the far corner, but the cobbles were bleak with no one on them, so I waited for someone to come along – without keeping my Bessa-T to my eye for too long and making my 'benign essential tremor' worse. 28/1.9 Ultron with yellow filter, XP2, MG Warmtone

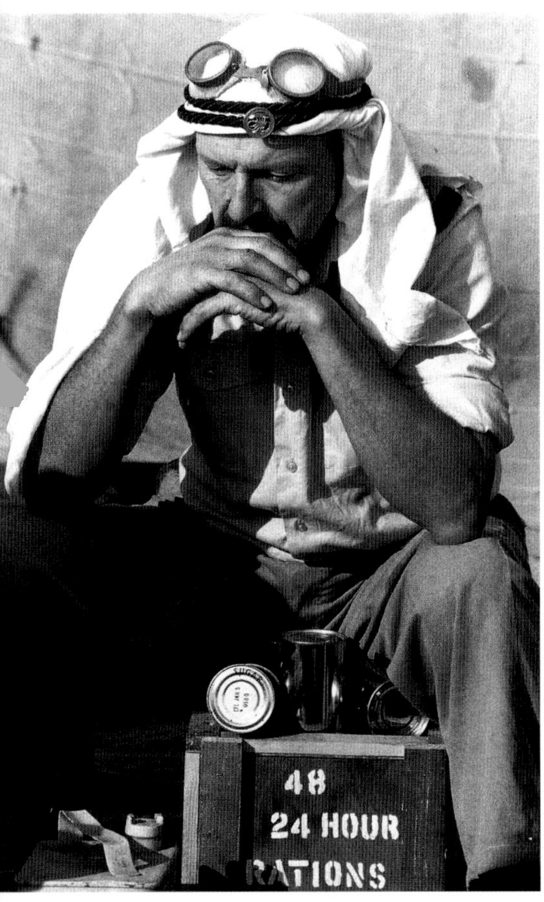

Long Range Desert Group

Someday, we hope to do a book about re-enactors. The opportunities for candid portraits are wonderful, and there's a lot of fascinating history behind many of the re-enactors' choices. When we do, we'll be using our Voigtländers and Leicas. M2, 90/2 Summicron, HP5 in DDX at 500, MG Warmtone

Slouch – Ideally, lean against a wall and relax. Slouching in a doorway is even better: the whole idea is that you exert as little effort as possible in standing still. If you can, brace one hand against the door frame. Or sit at a table and rest your elbows on the table.

Don't keep the camera at your eye too long – Sooner or later, your arms get tired and start to shake. Practice lifting the camera to your eye, shooting, and putting it down again. Not only does this give you sharper pictures, it's also less obtrusive.

Keep both eyes open – This tends to freak SLR users and it takes some getting used to with most RF/DV cameras, but after a while you can learn to take in the whole scene with one eye, while looking through the camera with the other. This is easiest with a finder such as the (original) Voigtländer Kontur, and next easiest with frame finders or any other kind of finder where the viewfinder magnification is 1:1 or close to it. But after a while you can learn to do it even with a 21mm or wider viewfinder, switching your attention from one eye to the other. We're not sure how this helps steadiness, but it seems to, perhaps because it relieves tension about what is going on outside the frame and when you are going to take the picture.

Balance the camera on your shoulder – This is a rare old trick from the days of 4 x 5in press cameras, preferably with wide-angle lenses (typically 5in/127mm or 135mm) and fairly loose composition, seeing that the camera is aimed without the viewfinder. Again, it relies on leaning against a wall or door frame. Focus, then rest the camera on your shoulder like a pirate's parrot. You should be able to get away with 1/10 or 1/5 of a second fairly easily, and 1/2 second or even a full second if you are lucky.

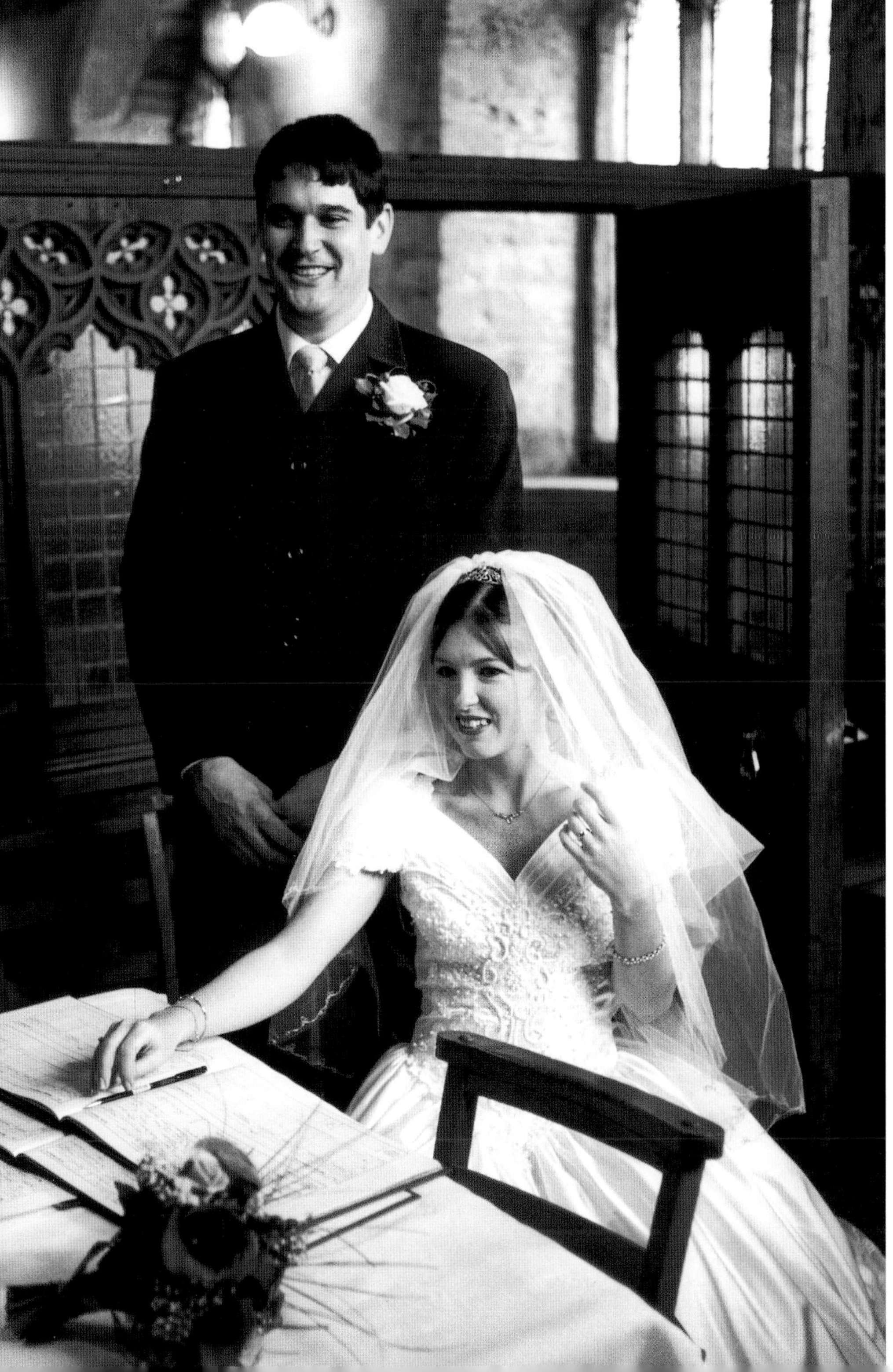

Signing the register

The first pictures I took of Louise on her wedding day, at the beautician's before she started to put on her wedding dress, set the theme of casual intimacy that characterized the rest of the set – a theme you can see even in this formal 'set piece'. Contrasty lighting plus (of course) a light dress and a dark suit meant that I needed grade 0 paper to make this print – but I still find the effect more natural than using flash. MG Warmtone in selenium

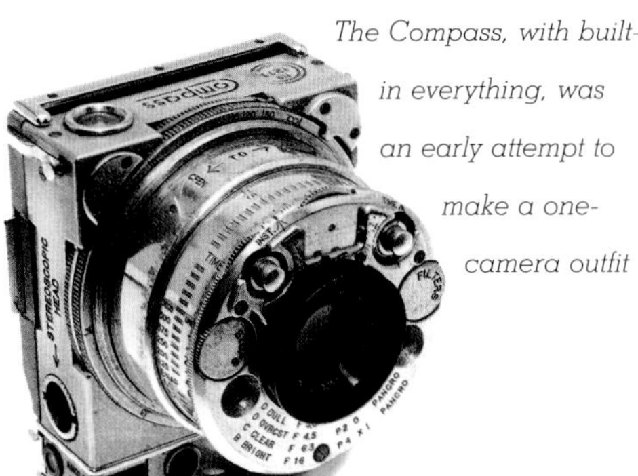

The Compass, with built-in everything, was an early attempt to make a one-camera outfit

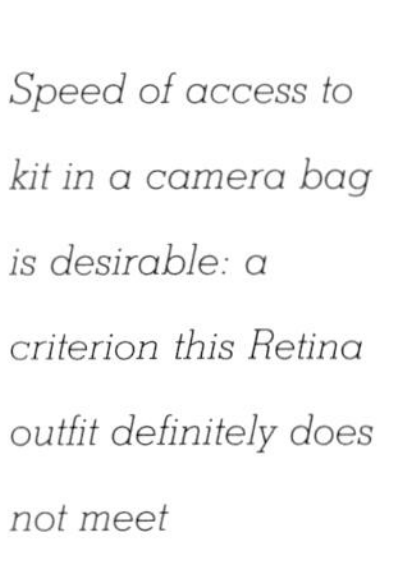

Speed of access to kit in a camera bag is desirable: a criterion this Retina outfit definitely does not meet

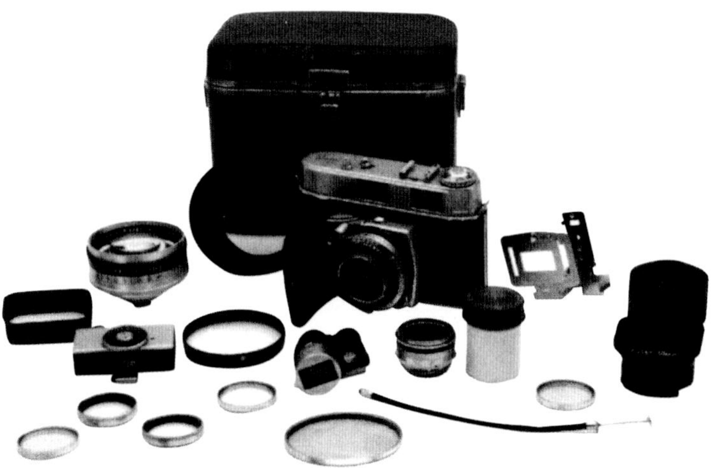

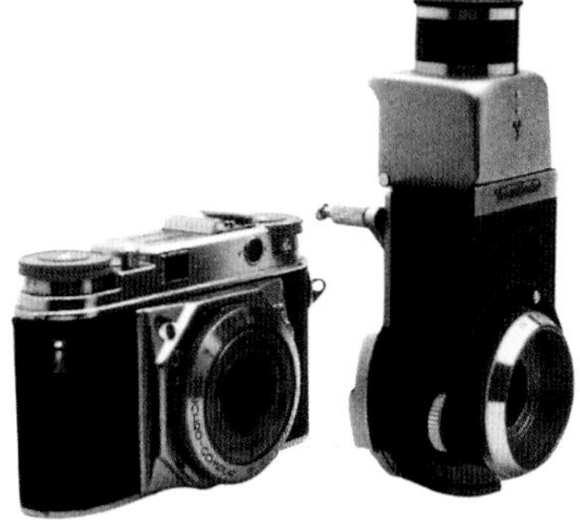

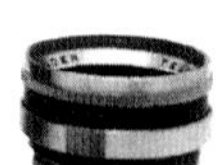

This Prominent reflex housing must have involved more unpacking, setting-up and re-packing than actual shooting

Do not neglect camera supports – Despite all the above, do not disdain camera supports when they are feasible, especially with 35mm. A bean bag, or even a rolled-up scarf or pair of gloves, can help promote the kind of relaxation we refer to above, as well as protecting your camera from being scratched when you rest it on a wall.

Very light monopods can be worth an extra step on the shutter speed dial, or even two, so that you can shoot at 1/15 of a second or even 1/8 where you would normally use 1/30. But if you are waiting for the decisive moment and you don't expect to have the time to raise the camera to your eye when it happens, an ultra-light monopod will allow you to keep the camera at eye level without too much discomfort and shake. We use Camcanes, now out of production; they weigh 350g (12oz) each.

And, of course, tripods will always give you the ultimate sharpness of which your camera and lens are capable. With small, light RF/DV cameras, you really can get away with small, light tripods – provided you go for the very finest quality. We use two: the Slik Snapman and the Hakuba Maxi 343e, which weigh about a kilo (just over 2lb) each. They cost around twice as much as some superficially similar tripods, but this still isn't a fortune, and they are much more rigid and more durable. Keep centre column extensions to a minimum for maximum stability.

For minimum weight and bulk, we use the ball-and-socket heads that come with the Slik and the Hakuba, though we do add a few more ounces with a Q-top quick release. These are the soundest and most reliable small-size QR system on the market; the plates can live on the cameras full time, ready to be clicked onto the tripod at a moment's notice.

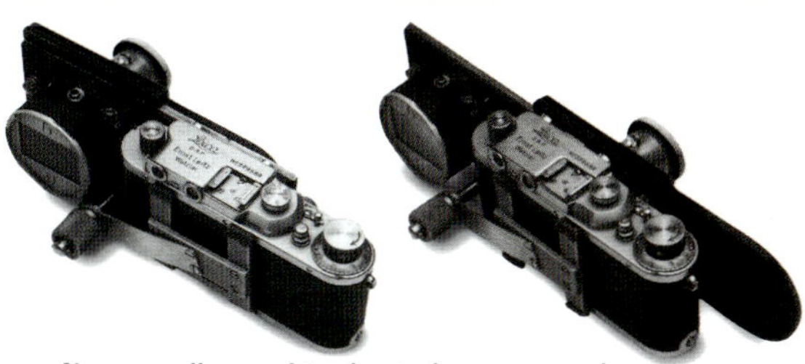

If you really need to shoot close-ups, a cheap used reflex beats the Focoslide hollow

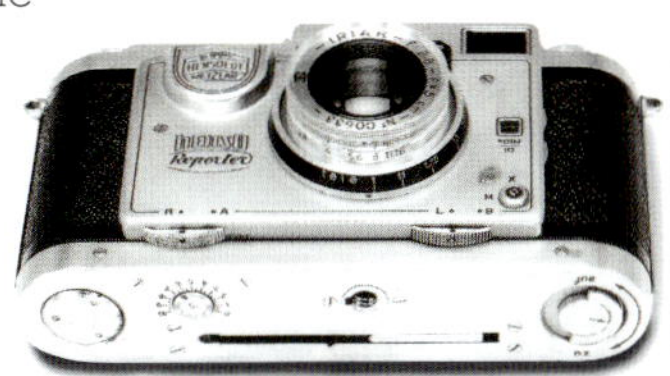

This Hensoldt has a built-in trigger base: another attempt at the 'integral outfit'

YOUR LEGS ARE YOUR BEST ZOOM

The non-availability of interchangeable zoom lenses (except on the Contax and some 645 cameras) may be distracting at first to people who learned their photography either with a zoom compact or an SLR and a 'standard zoom'. There is, however, a very strong argument that by forcing you to move closer or further away in the search for the best composition, prime lenses on RF/DV cameras also encourage you to put rather more effort into looking for the best possible viewpoint, be it high or low, left or right, as well as closer or further away.

USE AVAILABLE LIGHT

The unobtrusiveness of RF/DV cameras is completely nullified by flash, and besides, you don't need it anything like as much as you do with an SLR. Lenses are faster and sharper, especially compared with zooms. And, as already noted, most people can hold an RF/DV camera still for a full shutter-speed step longer than an SLR. This may be quite unlike your habitual way of working with an SLR, but once you have got used to even moderately fast film in an RF/DV camera – Ilford HP5 Plus at ISO 650, for example – you may be amazed: first, at how little you need flash, and second, at how much more atmosphere your pictures have.

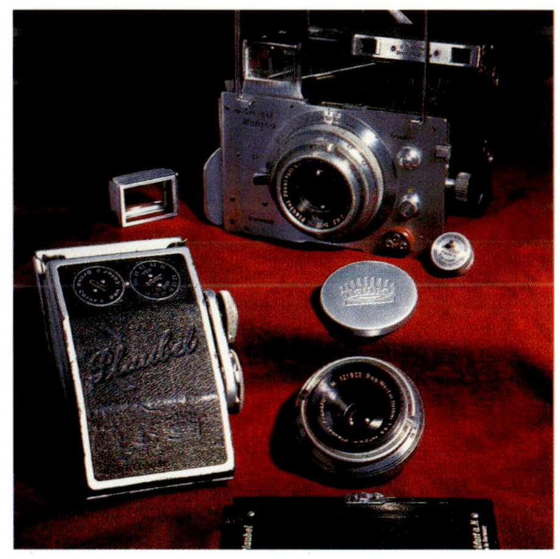

This handsome post-war Plaubel outfit is wonderfully compact, but results are, alas, mediocre

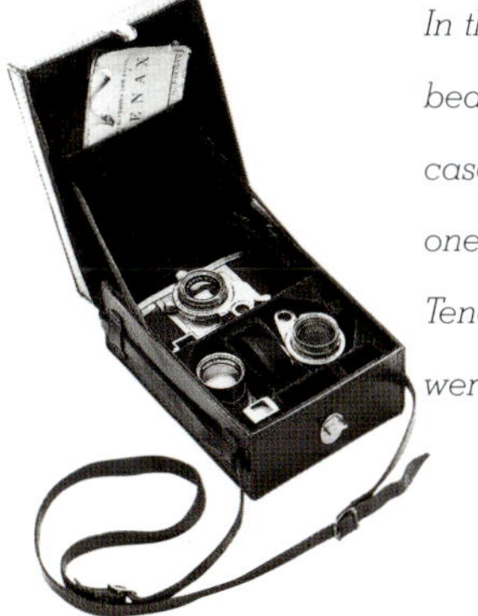

In the 1930s, beautifully fitted cases, like this one for a Zeiss Tenax outfit, were popular

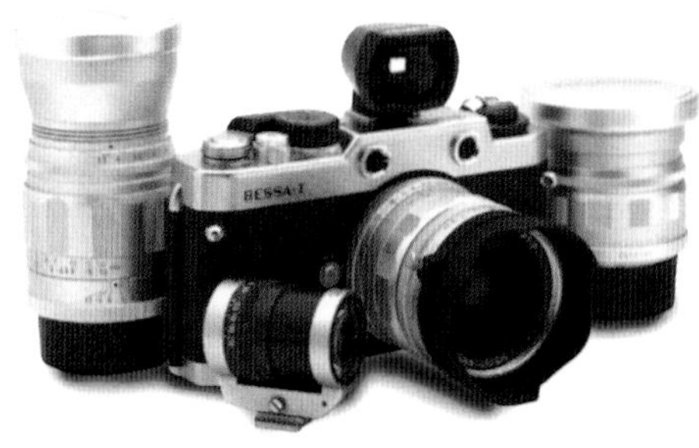

Frances's outfit:
Bessa-T, 28/1.9,
50/1.5, 90/3.5 and
two finders

If you want to use
classic cameras,
finding accessories
like this Prominent
close-up device can
be difficult

TAKE CARE WITH FILTERS

With an SLR you can see in the viewfinder whether you have a filter in place. With an RF/DV camera you can't. This is especially true if you use Voigtländer lenses, many of which have an internal female thread for the filter and an outer male thread for the hood (shade): you can't even see the filter sandwiched between the lens and the shade. This has led to some interesting (mostly yellow-tinted) colour slides – some of which, to our surprise, have been remarkably successful.

DON'T CARRY TOO MUCH KIT

One of the great attractions of an RF/DV camera, next to an SLR, is that it is so much smaller and lighter. Add in a few interchangeable lenses, where the difference in size and weight is even more marked, especially with 35mm, and you can save a great deal of back strain. You can also carry your kit onto an aeroplane a great deal more easily: an important point in these days of ever-increasing security checks.

The trouble is, you can be tempted to add another lens (or two, or three) and soon, the savings in weight and bulk are nothing like as impressive as you had hoped. If you can, restrain yourself to a maximum of three lenses, or four if you absolutely must. Yes, it would be nice to have the full set of lenses for a Voigtländer (12-15-21-25-28-35-50-75-90) plus a 135mm Elmarit-M, but that's ten lenses, and some of them are a bit close together. We actually have 15-21-28-35-50-90, though both the 12 and the 75 tempt us from time to time, and we have mentioned elsewhere the old Nikon F with a 200mm lens.

But even though we have such a large range of lenses, we try
to keep to three lenses, or even two, each. This is because we
don't want to spend all our time changing lenses – which we
regard, not unreasonably, as the mark of the rank amateur
who is obsessed with equipment rather than with taking
pictures. Watch a good photographer, and he or she spends
very little time changing lenses and fiddling with equipment.
Partly this is down to practice, but an important component is
that a good photographer plans to carry and use the right
equipment, rather than trying everything they possess.

Admittedly, we cheat. If we are fully laden, Roger carries
21-35-50-90 and Frances carries 15-28-35-90, which is
six focal lengths (and eight lenses, with the 35mm and 90mm
duplicated). We quite often share the 15, the 21 and the 50,
but Roger very rarely uses the 28, and our 35s are quite
different: Roger's is either his 35/1.4 Summilux or his 35/1.7
Voigtländer, while Frances's is her 35/2.8 PC-Nikkor
for tripod use.

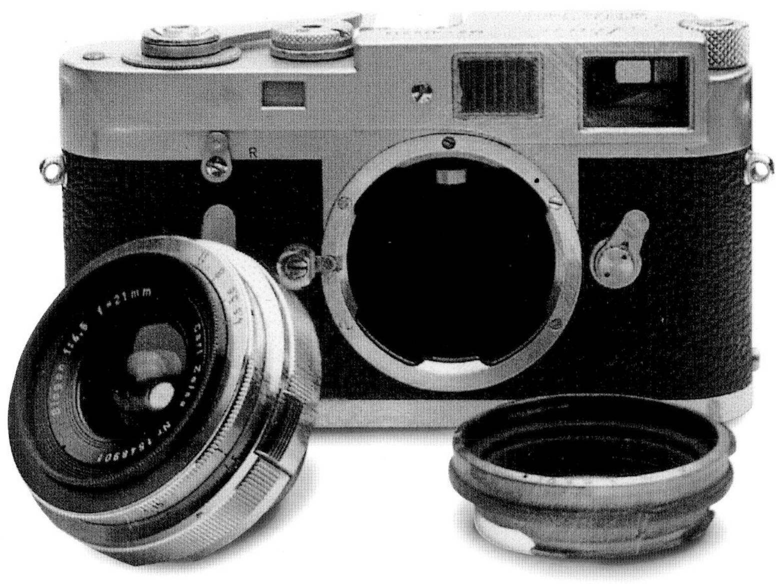

*Until we got the 21/4
Color-Skopar and
21/2.8 Kobalux, this
adapted 21/4.5
Biogon was our
standard 21mm lens*

A good deal depends, too, on what we are shooting. Habitually, for travel photography, we carry three bodies. These may be allocated as one each, and a spare, or Roger may carry two (one colour, one mono) while Frances carries one (she normally shoots only mono).

If we know we are going to have to switch lenses a lot, we carry two bodies each. Just before we delivered this book, for example, we photographed a friend's wedding. Roger used 35/1.4 and 90/2, while Frances used 28/1.9 and 50/1.5. Changing lenses between bodies is quick and easy, if you have to do it, and if you adopt the right mind-set, you just don't need more than two lenses – at least, not very often.

Having said this, a typical day's travel shooting in Malta might involve 15mm for interior shots, 21mm and 28mm for wide-angle landscapes or archaeological sites, 28mm, 35mm and 50mm for people shots, and 90mm for landscapes or picking details out of crowds. Plus maybe a 200 on the Nikon for really long shots.

But then we go out with our Alpas, where we so often use just one lens each, and we really don't miss the other focal lengths. It doesn't seem to do our picture-taking any harm. If anything, the opposite.

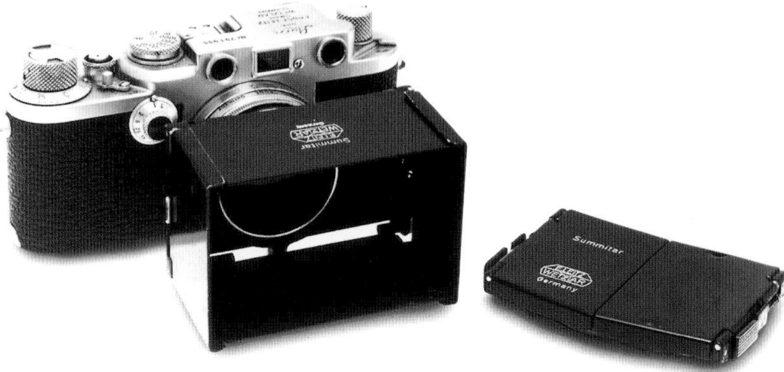

Lens shades are an invaluable accessory in any outfit: this 'rat-trap' Summitar hood is effective but slow

This is the most important point of all: cameras are for taking pictures. RF/DV cameras can be wonderful things to collect, and we'd be the last to deny that there are some absolutely fascinating old accessories which, although they are almost completely useless, we simply like to own. But at the end of it all, if we could have just one general-purpose camera each, to shoot pictures for fun, an SLR wouldn't get a look-in. Roger's leading contenders would be either a Leica or a Voigtländer in 35mm; or an Alpa in 120; or a Linhof 5 x 7in in large format. Frances's would be a Bessa-T in 35mm or an Alpa in 120.

Fortunately, we don't have to choose. Nor do most of our readers. Don't chop in your Nikon or Canon or whatever: try a rangefinder camera alongside it instead. We believe you'll be hooked. Whether that's good or bad is a question of perspective. But we can pretty much guarantee this: it will be fun.

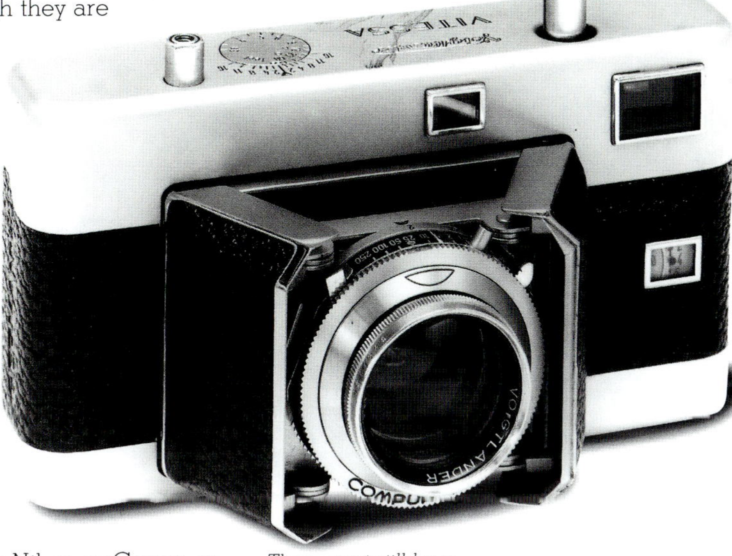

There must still be a market for a high quality folding pocketable camera like this 'bomb doors' Vitessa

More or less whatever outfit Roger is carrying, or wherever he goes, his Pen W is his ultimate back-up camera

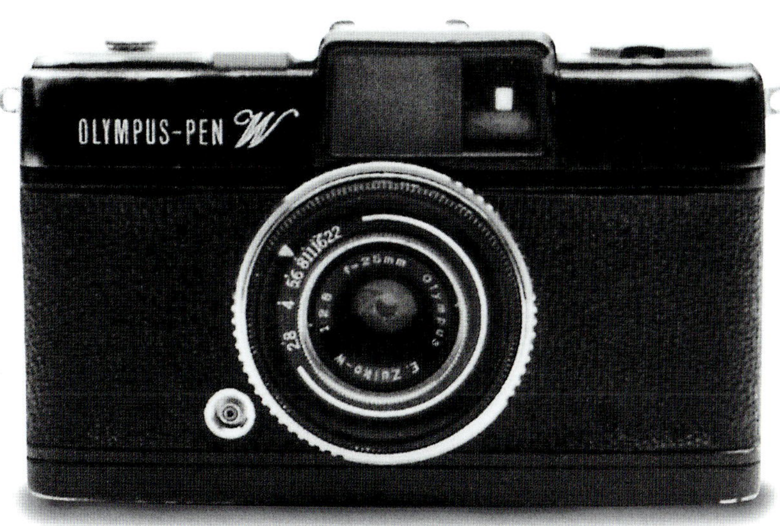

Alpa started making cameras in the 1940s, as described in the text. As befits a Swiss product, they were always extremely expensive, and later reflex models had other eccentric features apart from the combination rangefinder/reflex focusing on the earliest **Alpa Reflex** cameras. For example, the eyepiece for prism finders on 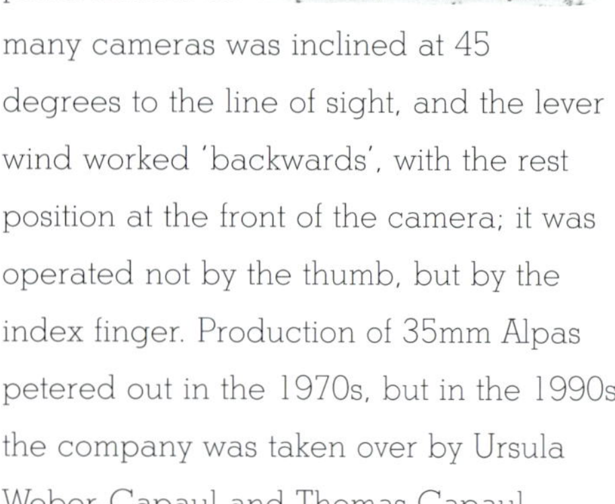 many cameras was inclined at 45 degrees to the line of sight, and the lever wind worked 'backwards', with the rest position at the front of the camera; it was operated not by the thumb, but by the index finger. Production of 35mm Alpas petered out in the 1970s, but in the 1990s the company was taken over by Ursula Weber-Capaul and Thomas Capaul-Weber. The **Alpa 12** 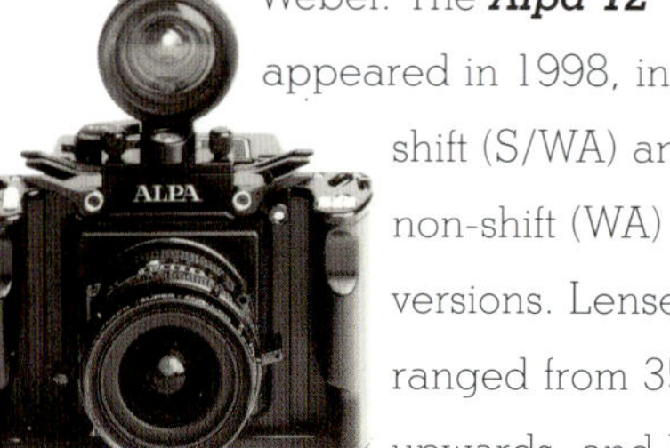 appeared in 1998, in both shift (S/WA) and non-shift (WA) versions. Lenses ranged from 35mm upwards, and backs from 6 x 9cm downwards. It is probably the best-made medium-format DV camera of all time, and one of the most basic.

Kodak's Autographic films incorporated a sort of carbon-paper backing. After opening a trap-door in the back of the camera, it was possible to make notes on one end of the negative using a stylus supplied with the camera: where the carbon was removed by the pressure of the stylus, light coming through the trap-door printed the note on the film. Kodak paid a fortune for the patents in the early twentieth century, but hardly anyone ever used the feature and it was soon dropped. The **Autographic IIIa** was the first ever camera with a coupled **rangefinder**, but it was hopelessly inconvenient: the rangefinder, at the base of the front standard, was not only separated from the viewfinder but was also at right-angles to the line of sight.

Kodak Bantam was a roll-film size based on imperforate 35mm film; it gave 28 x 40mm exposures, and was also known as B.S.0, 88, 828 and 888. It would be forgotten today if it were not for the beautiful **Bantam Special**.

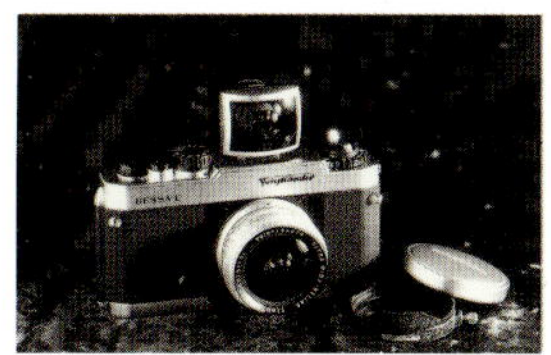

Bessa cameras from Voigtländer/Cosina are fully covered in the text: here are the **Bessa L** (no rangefinder or viewfinder), the **Bessa R** (coupled range/viewfinder), the **Bessa T** (coupled rangefinder, no viewfinder) and the **Bessa R2** (Leica M-bayonet compatible).

In the 1950s and 1960s, leaf-shutter cameras such as the Voigtländer Prominent and Kodak Retina were widely used professionally because they allowed 'synchro-sun' flash at all speeds. This **'Blitz' (flash) Summicron** was a less than fully successful attempt to extend the same convenience to Leicas.

Bronica introduced their Bronica 645 rangefinder camera at photokina 2000, with a standard 65/4 lens and optional 45/4 (separate finder) and 135/4.5 (selectable frame). The rangefinder and film advance are fully mechanical, but the shutter is electronic, allowing both aperture priority and programmed auto-exposure as well as manual metering – all through-lens, of course. The camera accepts both 120 and 220; the only disappointment is perhaps that the lenses are a little slow for reportage, though the camera would be ideal for weddings.

The **Cam-Watch** was a short-lived German sub-miniature from around 1990. It took Minox film, and was reputedly the smallest and lightest sub-miniature ever made. It is also very, very basic: a frame finder with only a front frame, a fixed-focus lens and only two shutter speeds.

Both the **Canon 7** (selenium meter) and Canon 7S (CdS meter) offered multiple, manually-selected bright-line finders, plus an enlarged rangefinder-only option for maximum focusing precision. The legendary f/0.95 'Dream' lens fits on an external 3-tab bayonet that surrounds the Leica screw-compatible main throat.

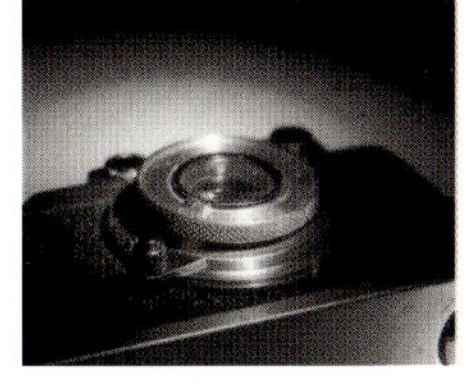

Collapsible lenses normally work with a simple non-locking bayonet inside the main mount: pull out and twist to shoot, twist and push back in to carry the camera. The only reflex ever to have them was the Alpa – and of course the mirror had to be locked up.

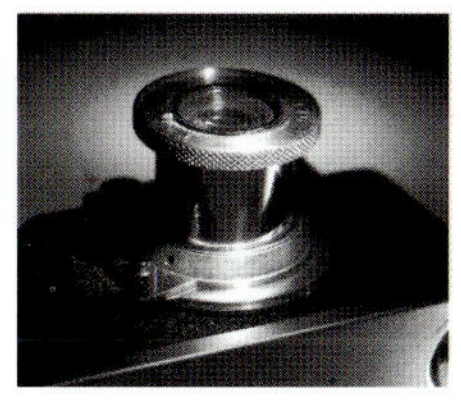

The 70mm **Combat Graphic** was

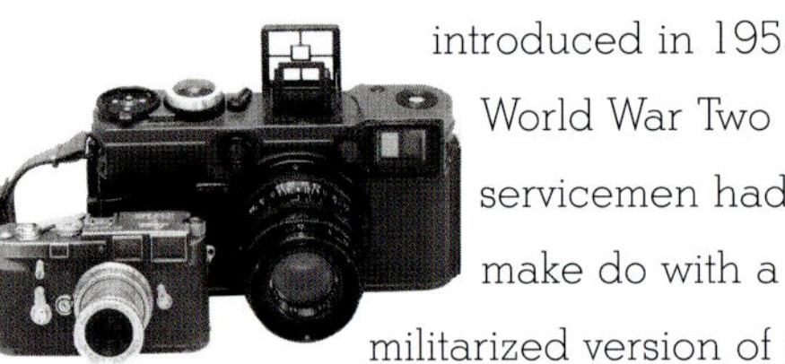

introduced in 1953 – World War Two servicemen had to make do with a militarized version of the 4 x 5in press camera, also known as the Combat Graphic – but had gone out of use by the time of the Vietnam conflict. The standard lens was a 120/2.6, and there were also wide-angle and tele lenses. Military versions were in olive drab, civilian in black. It was apparently rather heavy to carry on parachute drops.

Noel Pemberton-Billing designed the **Compass**, and Jaeger-le-Coultre made it in 1937.

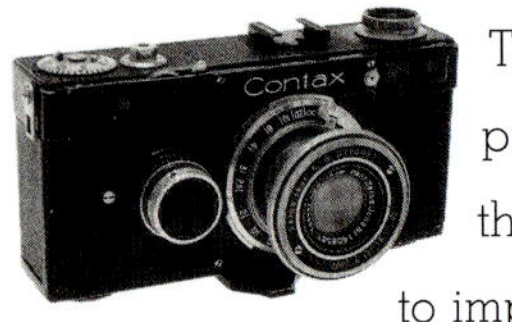

It had a rangefinder, an (extinction) exposure meter, built-in filters, direct and right-angle finders, provisions for stereo and panoramic photography, a 22-speed shutter and a ground-glass back. It took special 24 x 36mm glass plates and a 6-exposure roll film, both specially made by Ilford; a 35mm back was available from a third party, T.A. Cubitt.

The Contax is quite properly a legend, but if they break, they are next to impossible to repair – and the original **Contax I** was not too reliable

to begin with. The pre-war II and post-war IIa were unmetered; the III and IIIa were the metered versions. Contaxes are covered reasonably comprehensively in the text. See also Zeiss.

The **Corfield WA67** (c. 1990), also known as the Architect, had a fixed 47mm Super Angulon with a rising front and tilting viewfinder: it took 6 x 7cm Mamiya backs and was designed for very quick architectural photography ('From the middle of the road', in Sir Kenneth Corfield's own words).

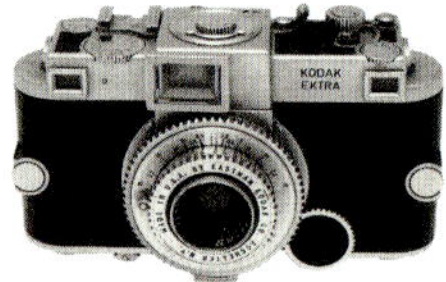

Kodak's **Ektra** looked magnificent and was very well specified (even with interchangeable backs), but it was over-complicated, unreliable and overpriced. And the fact that it was launched in 1941 meant that it was never developed fully. The few that survive do so in the hands of collectors.

Early Fed cameras were cheap Leica knock-offs, but even the **Fed 2** shows how they began

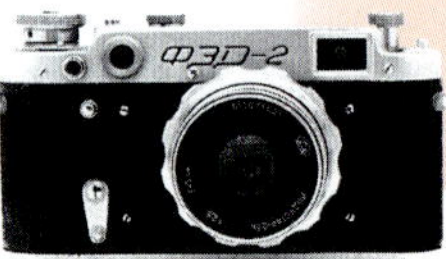

to evolve in their own way. They were named after Felix Edmundovich Dzerzinsky, the notorious secret policeman, and some of the earliest pre-war models are engraved with 'NKVD'. By the time of the Fed 5, the only real link with the Leica ancestry was the 39mm x 26tpi mount. They were always rather roughly finished, but remained intermittently available new even in the early twenty-first century,

Film cassettes play a more important role

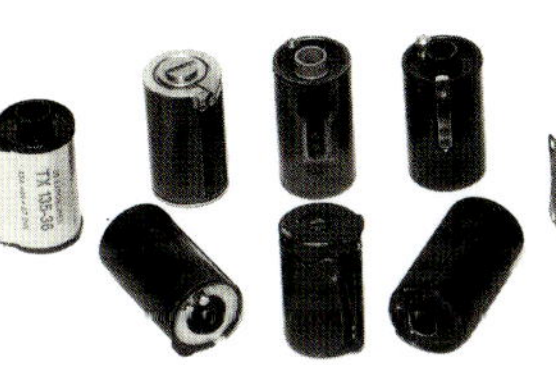

than one might expect: cameras that do not accept the standardized cassettes introduced by Kodak in about 1933 have seldom enjoyed the wide acceptance of those that have. Several manufacturers have, however, offered self-opening reloadable cassettes that could be used interchangeably with standardized disposable cassettes. Most have been for a single camera, though Shirley Wellards can be used in almost any camera with a pull-up rewind knob.

For close-ups and copying, there have been a number of accessories like the *Focoslide* for the Leica. The two pictures on page 153 make it clear how it worked. In one position, there is a ground glass behind the lens, which can be used with close-up lenses or extension tubes; in the other, the camera body slides into place for shooting.

Bell & Howell's *Foton* boasted a built-in film advance that could hit six frames per second – quite arguably the fastest

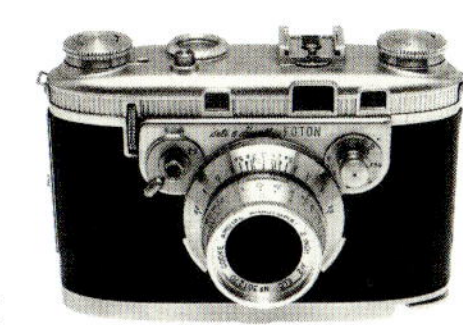

mechanical advance of all time, never mind 1948 when it was introduced – and was beautifully finished, though some of the control layout was eccentric. It had excellent lenses too, calibrated (unexpectedly) in T-stops, which measure the actual transmission of the lens rather than its mechanical aperture: common enough in the movies, but unique in still cameras. But at $700 (about £450) it cost more than a Leica, and it lacked the cachet.

When it comes to RF/DV, Fuji is best known for its roll-film rangefinder cameras, from 645 models through 6 x 7cm to 6 x 9cm. The earliest 645s were manual, including the GS 645 folder with 70mm lens, and the rigid-bodied GS645S (60mm) and GS645W (45mm). Later autofocus rigid-bodied cameras, with a very high degree of automation, included the GA645i (60mm lens), GA 645Wi ('Wide' – 45mm lens) and GA 645Zi ('Zoom' – 55–90mm lens). Early 6 x 9cm G690 and GS690 models featured interchangeable lenses (65mm, 100mm, 150mm, 250mm). But later 6 x 9cm cameras, such as the **6 x 9 Professional** and their 6 x 7cm siblings, had fixed lenses. The **GX617**

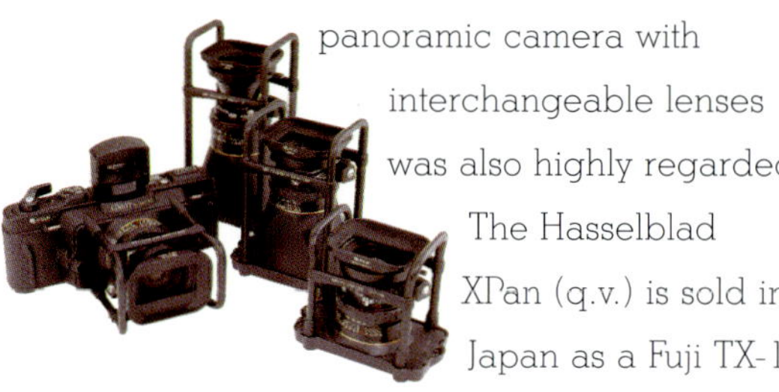

panoramic camera with interchangeable lenses was also highly regarded. The Hasselblad XPan (q.v.) is sold in Japan as a Fuji TX-1.

As well as 80/2.8, 95/2.8 and 100/2.8 lenses (including legendary Zeiss Planars), other lenses for the

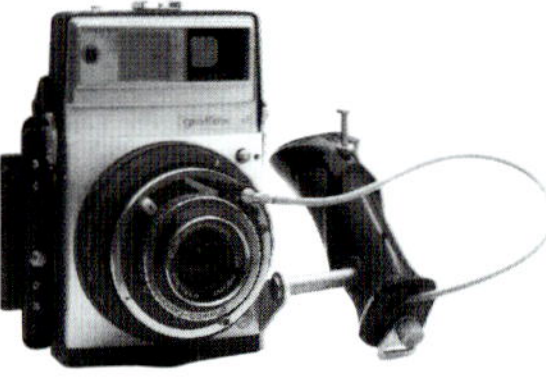

Graflex XL

included 58/5.6 Rodenstock Grandagon, 95/3.5 Rodenstock Ysarex, 100/3.5 Zeiss Tessar, 150/4.5 Rodenstock Ysarex,180/4.8 Zeiss Sonnar and 270/6.6 Rodenstock Rotelar. The combined range/viewfinder is big, bright and easy-to-use, but as far as we know covers 6 x 7cm only: we have never seen a 6 x 9cm version. The XL Super Wide-Angle had no RF but came with a 47mm Schneider Super Angulon (either f/8 or the much better f/5.6), and the XL Standard was a rangefinderless XL. All accept ground-glass backs and standard Graphic-fit backs.

The **Hasselblad XPan**, jointly developed

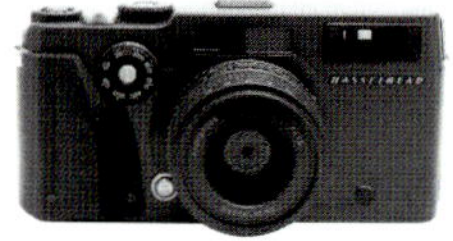

with Fuji (it is sold in Japan as the Fuji TX-1), was first

announced at a press conference in July 1998 and was launched at photokina that year. Focusing is mechanical (with an excellent rangefinder), but film advance is via the 'electric thumb': the film is wound fully out of the cassette when it is loaded, and 24 x 36mm and 24 x 65mm can then be selected and mixed at any point until the film is finished; the film is wound in either direction to accomplish this. The very wide vertical-run shutter is electronically governed, allowing aperture-priority exposure automation (with override), or manual exposure, all via through-lens metering. Lens options at the time of writing were 30/5.6 (normally used with a special centre-grad filter), 45/4 and 90/4.

Hensoldt is well known for microscopes and field-glasses, but the staggeringly rare **Hensoldt Reporter** is one of the greatest 'might-have-been' cameras of the 1950s. This one was kindly loaned by Paul-Henry van Hasbroeck.

The **Horseman 612** is an outstandingly compact and very simple direct-vision 6 x 12cm camera (56 x 112mm). Several interchangeable wide-angle lenses are available – a big order from Horseman was apparently responsible for the introduction of the Rodenstock 35/5.6 Apo-Grandagon – and the camera is made in both 'shift' and non-shift models.

The history of **Kiev** cameras is reasonably fully recited in the main text; and, of course, they accept Voigtländer lenses. The relationship between Kiev and Contax is

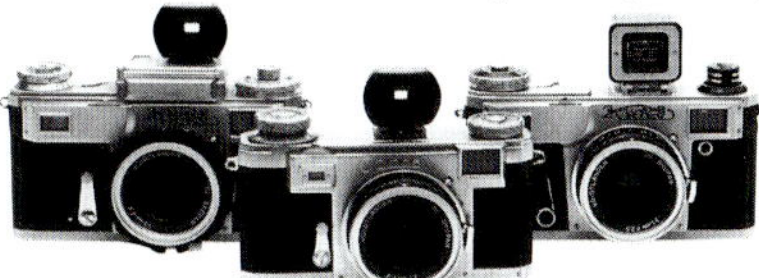

shown here clearly enough, with a Contax IIa in the middle and Kievs either side.

Konishiroku (Konica) is arguably the oldest-established continuously operating photographic company in the world, founded in 1874. The IIIa is typical of the many excellent fixed-lens, leaf-shutter, rangefinder cameras they made in the 1950s and 1960s, while the **Hexar-M** is the nearest you will get to a fully automated Leica – though focusing is still manual.

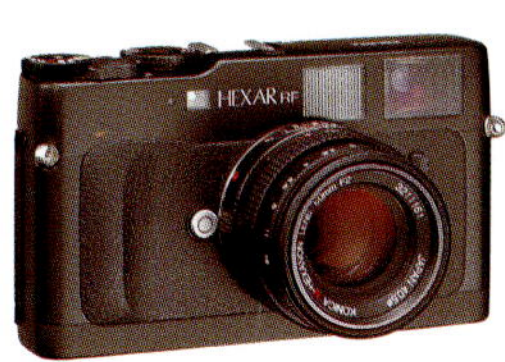

Leica cameras have been comprehensively covered in the text; notes worth adding are that the **Ur-Leica** dated from about 1912, a year after its builder Oskar Barnack joined Leitz; the **Nullserie** had a non-self-capping focal plane

shutter, so the lens had to be covered (with the bung) while winding on; the **Leica A** could unofficially be fitted with a Meyer lens (on the Elmar's multi-start thread) by the late 1920s; the **IIIa** was

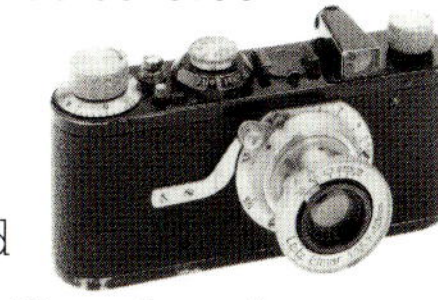

the first with 1/1000 second top speed; the **IIIf** was the first with flash synch; the **IIIg** was actually released

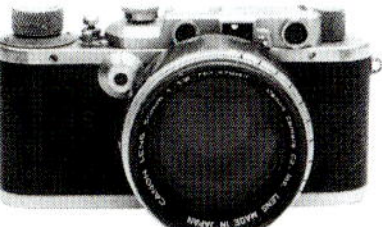

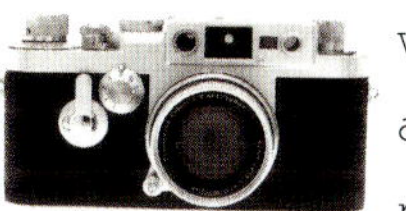

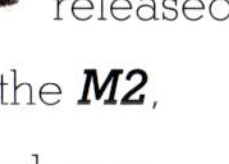

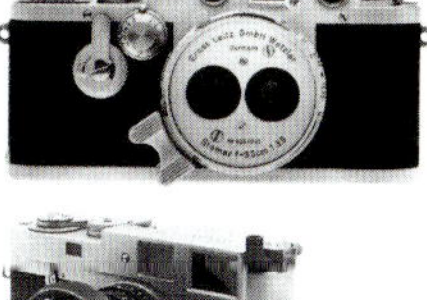

after the M3; the **M2**, often described as a 'lower-cost' Leica, now fetches as much as an M3 because more people want the 35mm viewfinder frame; the M4-P (1980) was effectively an M4 with two more viewfinder frames (28mm and 75mm); the **MP** is a rare collectable variant with a trigger base; the M6 managed to

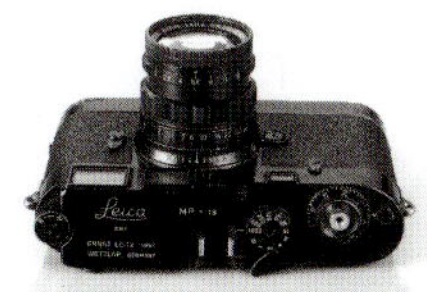

fit through-lens metering into the classic shape; and the M6ttl and (superficially identical) **M7** were current at the time of writing.

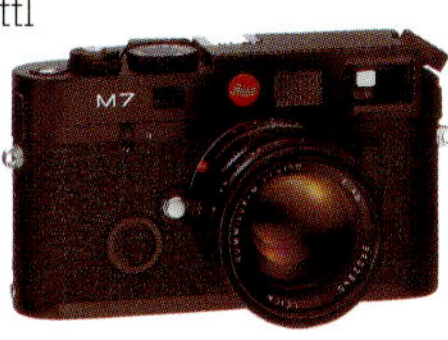

As far as we know, there was only one model of **Leningrad**, built from about 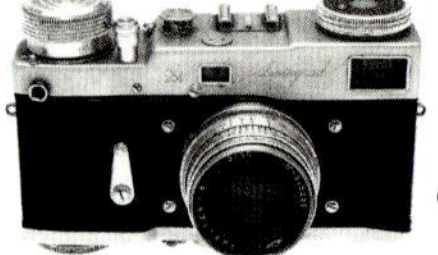 1956 to 1966. It was the most expensive Soviet camera of its era. With built-in spring film advance (3 fps for 12 frames), bright, multi-frame engraved finder (35–50–85–135), 57mm rangefinder base and Leica screw-fit lenses – the only Leica-fit camera with a built-in auto-film advance – the specification is very attractive. Unfortunately it is less usable than it looks. The alloy of which the chassis is made has a nasty habit of cracking; the sprocketless film transport results in very uneven spacing; and the camera jumps badly when the wind-on operates.

Linhof cameras are widely acknowledged as among the finest ever, and the Technika 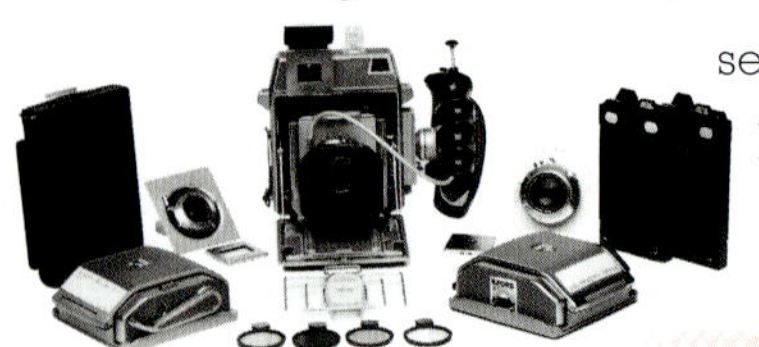 series has been built in a number of formats: 'baby' (roll film and small cut film) like this **Super Technika IV**, 4 x 5in (9 x 12cm), like this **Super Technika III**, and even 13 x 18cm (5 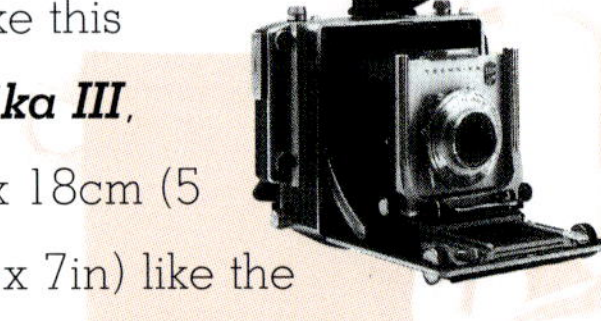 x 7in) like the **Technika V**. Super Technikas have rangefinders; plain Technikas don't.

In 1995 the Mamiya 7 replaced the former 6 x 6cm RF camera, thereby knocking the bottom out of the market for the old camera in no time. As well as the extremely wide 43mm lens option, the 7 (like late Mamiya 6 models) also offered the option of a panoramic 35mm format the full width of the 120 format. This should be the wedding photographers' camera par excellence.

The original 1962 fixed-lens version of the Mamiya Press seems to have owed a great deal to the Graflex XL, above, a debt that grew larger rather than smaller as the design progressed. Interchangeable lenses arrived in 1965 and the camera remained in production for well over a decade more. Some models have back movements (which, if employed, make the optional ground-glass back essential), while others do not.

Univex **Mercury** cameras were made in two versions: the 1938 I (for Mercury-unique paper-backed 35mm film) and the II (which took conventional 35mm cassettes). The huge hump featured a rotary shutter – the format was 18 x 24mm – and this was the company that then introduced the hot shoe, in 1939.

Walter Zapp made his first prototype stainless-steel **Minox** sub-miniature in 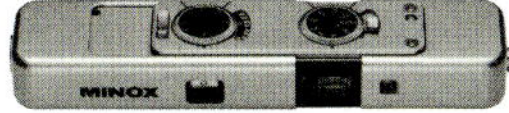 1936, but series production began in 1938. Up to 8,000 of the first 'Made in Latvia' series (1938–40) were made, followed by up to 3,000 in 40/41 (engraved 'Made in USSR') and another 5,000 to 6,000 before production shifted to Germany in 1948. The first metered model (B) appeared in 1958 and automation followed with the LX/TLX in 1978. Today's sub-miniature models still look suprisingly similar.

The **Minox 35** was introduced in March 1975 and has changed 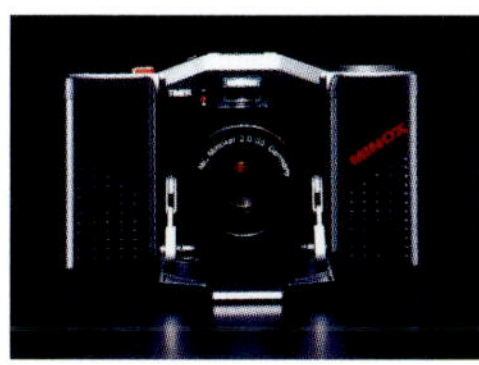 surprisingly little since; it features aperture-priority automation (without manual override), and a folding flap that covers the retractable 4-glass Tessar-type lens. Batteries for early models are no longer available, but Minox sells an inexpensive adapter that allows the use of later batteries.

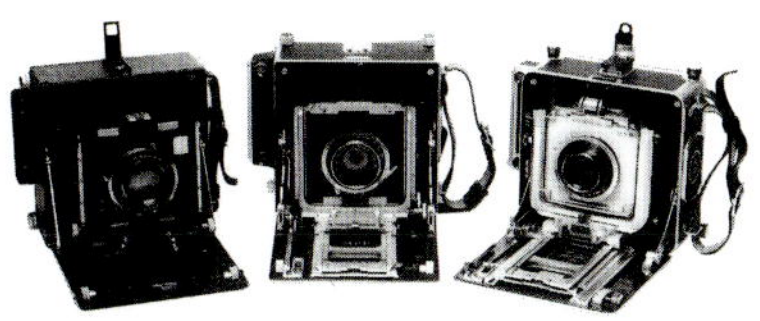 **MPP** (Micro Precision Products) Micro-Technical cameras are adequately covered in the text. The one that is generally most esteemed by aficionados is the Mk. VII,

with the full international back, though late Mk. VI cameras had the same, and the Mk. VIII – the only one with a fabricated, rather than cast, body – sells at a slight premium, simply because it is newer. The wood-bodied Micro-Press, with limited movements, a fixed back and double instead of triple extension, is not widely sought after.

The pre-war Zeiss **Nettax** 35mm was often referred to as the 'poor man's Contax', though 'poor' is a relative 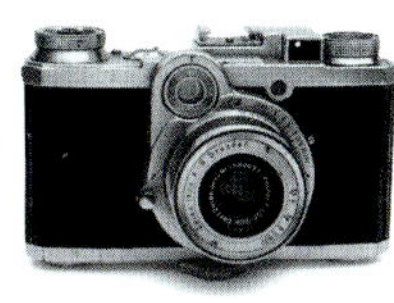 term here. It featured a rather small range of **interchangeable lenses**, each with its own front rangefinder group, all of which are very rare today. 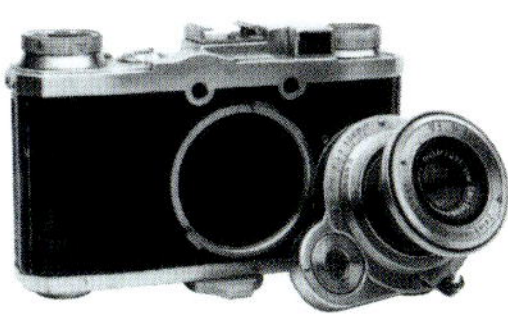

Nicca made a series of Leica-compatible rangefinder cameras before being subsumed into Yashica; 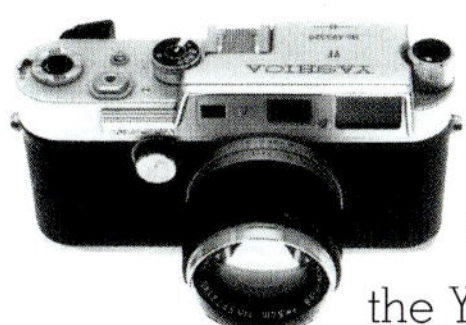 the Yashica YF incorporates both the Yashica and Nikka names. Although very usable, this camera is worth more to a collector than to most users.

Nikon rangefinder cameras are adequately covered in the text, where there are pictures of the **S3** with a Micro-

Nikkor and an **SP**. Allegedly, Nikon lost money on every one of the 'Millennium' re-released S3 cameras they sold, even at the stiff price they commanded.

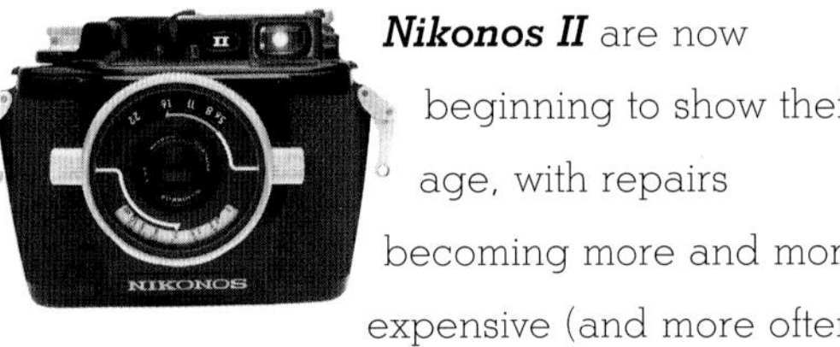

Nikonos cameras are covered reasonably well in the text; older models like this **Nikonos II** are now beginning to show their age, with repairs becoming more and more expensive (and more often needed) and a lack of availability of some parts, including the viewfinder O-ring.

The **NPC 195** doppel-klapp was a reincarnation of an earlier Polaroid 195, which had become very highly sought after. Introduced in 2000, it was the progenitor of a 4 x 5in doppel-klapp from the same company.

Olympus cameras are pretty well surveyed in the text. This **Pen W** was the only black-bodied Pen DV camera,

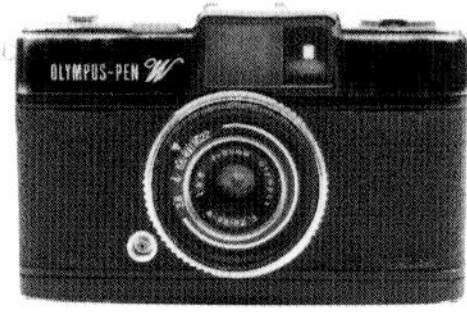

and boasted a remarkably good 6-glass 25/2.8 lens, roughly equivalent to 35mm on full frame.

The pre-war Voigtländer roll-film **Prominent** was staggeringly complicated, with just about every conceivable feature for its day (introduced 1932) including an exposure meter. Trying to use one today makes you appreciate the strides that have been made in ergonomics in the last few decades. The post-war 35mm **Prominent** was introduced some 20 years after its namesake and again was one of the finest cameras of its day, with arguably the most advanced lenses of the time, but the viewfinder is squinty by modern standards and the leaf shutter imposes considerable constraints on the lens designs.

The Krauss **Peggy** was one of the very first CRF 35mm cameras,

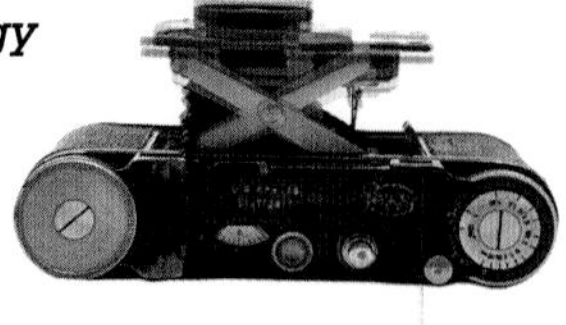

introduced in 1931. The ergonomics were not too good – the RF and viewfinder are at opposite ends of the top housing – and the cassettes were unique and not interchangeable with the Kodak design, which must have contributed to the camera's demise in 1934.

The first non-RF *Plaubel Makina* appeared in about 1920; this CRF version dates from the 1930s, and a substantially similar camera was 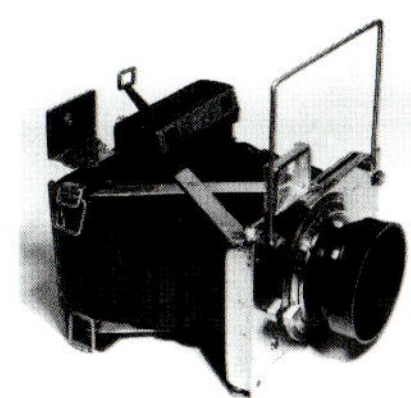 produced until 1960. Interchangeable lenses are wildly inconvenient: front and rear elements must be replaced separately in the fixed shutter. It looks beautiful, but every one we have ever used has been a terrible disappointment. On the bright side, they don't cost much. The later (1975–1986) Japanese version with the 80/2.8 or 55/4.5 Nikkors are much more sought after, but slightly fragile.

The ancestry of the *Polaroid 600SE* is 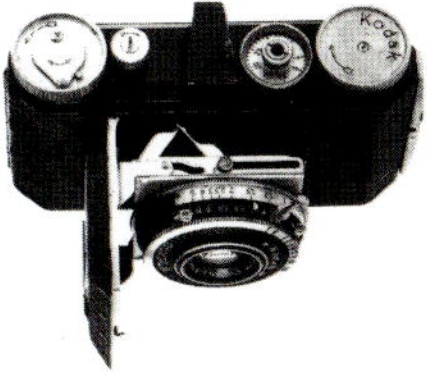 mixed: ultimately, it descends from the Graflex XL via the Mamiya-Press. The plain fixed-lens S is less sought after. It and the NPC 195 are the most usable Polaroid cameras for professional use. The NPC 4 x 5in adapter for the 600/600SE was still in production at the time of writing (the camera was discontinued in about 2000) but roll-film adapters are hard to find. Other lenses are the 75mm and 150mm.

Retina cameras are pretty well covered in the text. Even ancient Retinas, such as the *Retina I*, remain usable to this day – a post-war IIa with an f/2 lens can be particularly delightful – as do their cheaper cousins, the Retinettes, though earlier models with uncoated lenses are best used only with black and white. The IIc/IIIc (small c) sell for quite a bit less than the *IIC*/IIIC (big C), but the uncluttered viewfinder of the earlier model is more pleasant to use with the standard lens, and the interchangeable lenses (actually interchangeable front components) are hardly worth using at all. To collectors, though, the big-C series are the most sought after. There are two series of lenses, from Schneider and Rodenstock, and they should not be interchanged.

Robot cameras are covered reasonably fully in the text. The *Robot I* is best left to 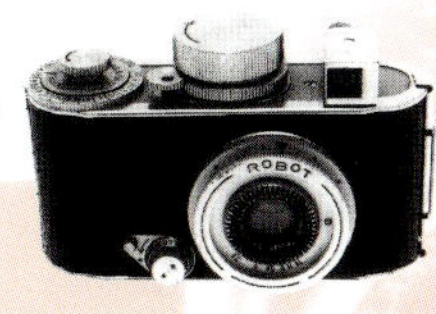 collectors, partly on price, partly on the (non) availability of cassettes, while 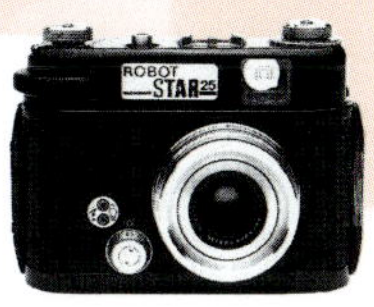 the *Star* is one of the most affordable and usable of the classic 24 x 24mm series.

First introduced in 1966, the Rollei 35 remained in production at the time of writing, though it had been through many incarnations: throughout the 1990s, special-finish models were aimed more and more at collectors, and less and less at users. Most had coupled CdS meters, though a few had uncoupled selenium meters. Lenses ranged, in ascending order of desirability, from Triotar through Xenar and Tessar to Sonnar; German-built models are more desirable than Singapore-built. Incredibly compact, fully mechanical (apart from the meter), with no automation, these are among the most desirable of fixed-lens DV cameras. Over three million had been sold at the time of writing.

Samoca

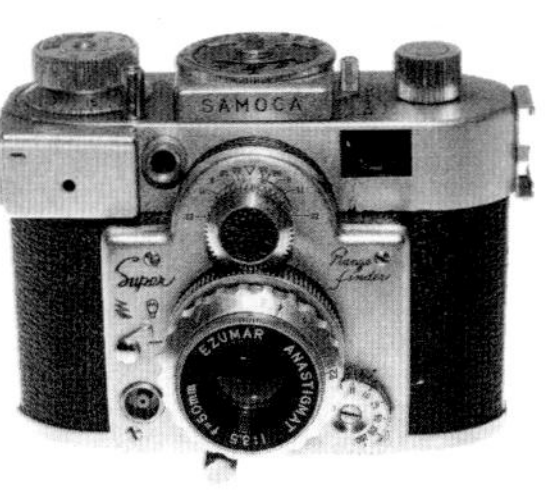

started making 35mm cameras in 1952; the Samoca 35 Super (1956) was the first coupled-rangefinder model. Even the shutter (1/10 to 1/200) was made by Samoca.

When Leica switched from the 39mm x 26tpi screw mount to the 4-claw M-bayonet, they made the film-to-flange register 1mm less (27.80mm instead of 28.80m) to allow the use of ***screw-to-***

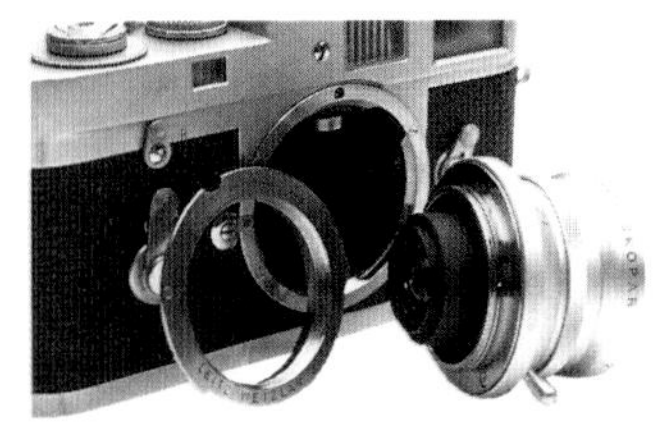

bayonet adapters, which also automatically key in the appropriate viewfinder frame: there are three models, for 28/90, 35/135 and 50/75. Leica's own adapters were for a long time hard to find, but now they have been supplemented by Japanese models from a number of manufacturers – not all of which accept all screw lenses, or will lock securely into all M-mount bodies.

Speed Graphic cameras were made in 4 x 5in, quarter-plate (3¼ x 4¼in) and (as here) 'baby' or '23' versions. Among 'babies', the ones that accept roll-film

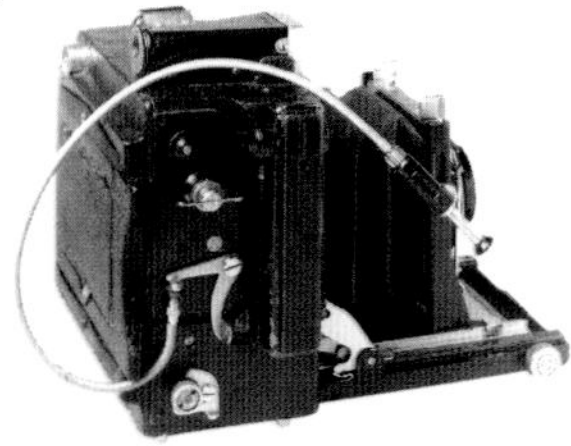

backs are much more usable than the ones that rely on 6 x 9cm or 2¼ x 3¼in cut film. Plain non-Speed models had no focal plane shutter. Century models are moulded bakelite, in 23 format only; Speed and Crown models are wood-bodied; and Super and Super Speed models are metal-bodied. Movements on all models are limited, but a drop baseboard allows the use of wide-angles, and double-extension bellows allow extreme close-ups or use of long lenses .

Stereo attachments have been made for a suprising

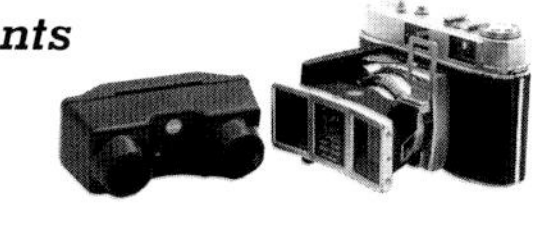

variety of cameras and are covered reasonably well in the text.

The ***Super Ikonta*** from Zeiss was available in 6 x 9cm (as here) as well as in smaller guises; like many cameras of its time, the film gate could be masked down to 645 for 16-on-120, though the mask has often been lost over the years. Red window film advance, uncoated lenses (except in late and very expensive models) and a front-strut system that was marginal even when new, especially on the big 6 x 9cm cameras, mean that we would rather leave these cameras to collectors.

Swing-Lens panoramic cameras are not covered in the text at all; they are thrown

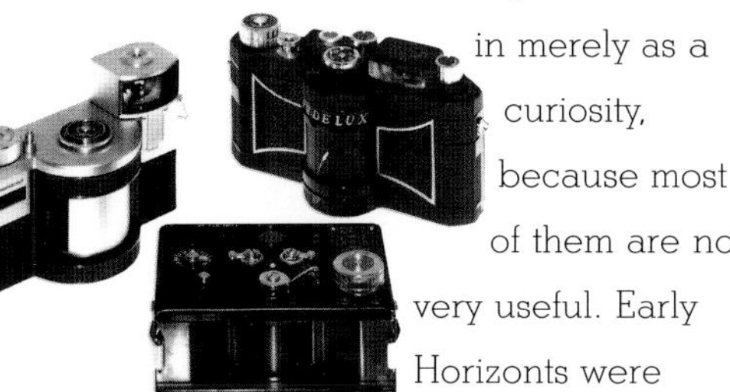

in merely as a curiosity, because most of them are not very useful. Early Horizonts were hopelessly unreliable; if you want to buy a late one, make sure it comes from someone who rebuilds them before sale and offers a guarantee. The FT-2 is more of a collector's camera than a user, and although the Widelux was less prone to striping than the Horizont, it still required frequent servicing. Probably the best are Noblex (not illustrated).

Soft-focus lenses have been deservedly rare in 35mm – most work far better in larger formats – and of the few that have appeared, most have been for reflexes. This rare and collectable 1930s Leitz ***Thambar***

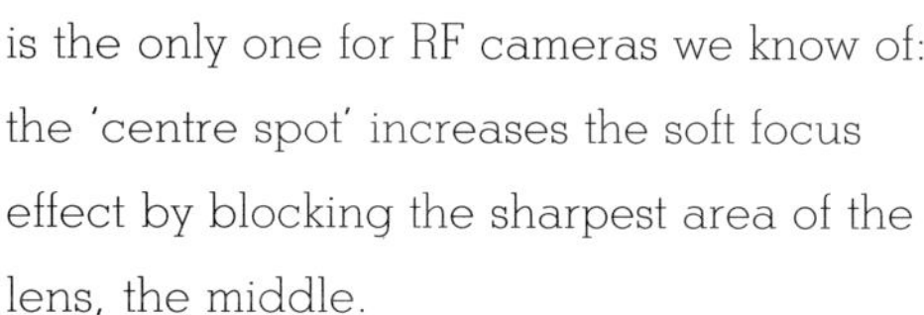

is the only one for RF cameras we know of: the 'centre spot' increases the soft focus effect by blocking the sharpest area of the lens, the middle.

Voigtländer's ***Vitessa*** was made in two distinct series. The first was the 'bomb doors' model with the unique folding mechanism that gave it its nickname and a unique plunger-type wind-on. The latter was rigid-bodied and had interchangeable lenses, but is nothing like as interesting.

The **Yashica YF** was a short-lived camera (1959/60) which is an intriguing Leica 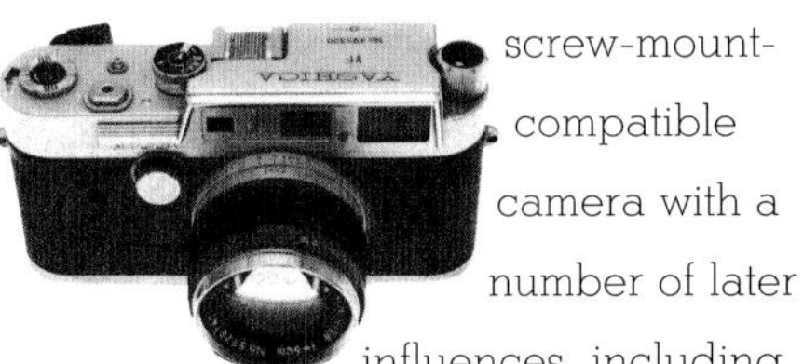 screw-mount-compatible camera with a number of later influences, including lever wind, opening back Leica M-style, and parallex-corrected bright-lines for 50mm and 100mm lenses. The 50/1.8 Yashinon is the most usual lens, but there were also many Nikkors offered as original equipment. After the Canon 7/7s it is one of the most modern of old RF 39mm x 26tpi cameras.

Some Zeiss cameras other than the Contax are covered in the text, such as the **Nettax** and Ikonta/Super Ikonta, but there were countless other models from the most 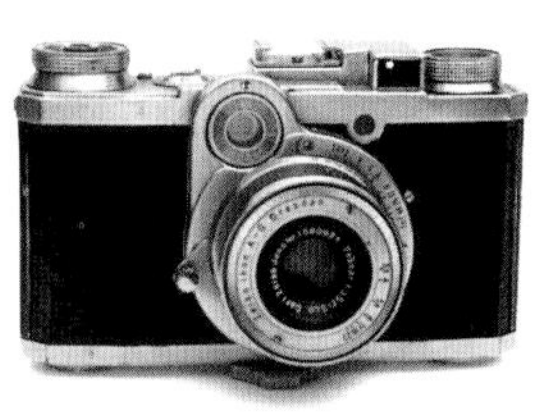 basic box cameras (Baldur, Box Tengor and more) though square-format (24 x 24mm) 35mm Tenaxes, doppel-klapp press-type cameras, rigid-bodied Ermanoxes with staggeringly fast lenses such as a 135/1.8, and more. The company seemed totally unaware of the concept of market positioning, and made far too many models, but because the very best were always among the finest cameras ever made, even the most dismal box cameras attract disproportionate admiration from collectors, because of reflected glory.

Zorkii cameras were generally more advanced than their Fed siblings (see above), but they were again 39mm x 26 tpi Leica compatible. 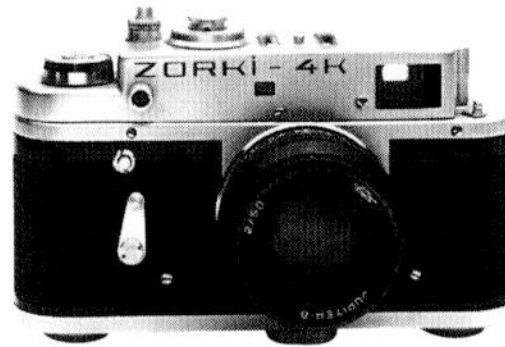 The 4K with the lever wind (1972–1978) is generally reckoned to be one of the most usable Russian cameras; some even accord it 'classic' status. Its predecessor, the knob-wind 4 (1956–1973) is also found in huge numbers.

APPENDIX LENS FITTINGS

The following list covers only 35mm cameras and is not complete: there is always some other obscure make to be unearthed. Some are noted from experience; some are from memory (it's been years since we handled a Hensoldt Reporter); and some are from other sources, though all have been cross-checked both to books and to the Internet as far as possible. Even so, with well over three dozen RF cameras it's probably the most comprehensive list that you will find anywhere in one place.

Alpa: 35mm models had an Alpa-unique bayonet, while modern roll-film models use an Alpa-unique 'box panel' fitting.

AKA (Akarette/Akarelle/Arette): Unique breech lock.

Ambi Silette (Agfa): Unique bayonet fitting.

Bessa (Voigtländer): Bessa-L and Bessa-R (1990s) are Leica screw mount compatible; Bessa-T and Bessa-R2 (early 2000s) are Leica M bayonet compatible. R2S is Nikon S, R2C is 'classic' Contax.

Canon: Unique fitting until about 1942, then Leica screw compatible. Some late Canons had an additional (external) bayonet mount, used for mirror boxes and the 50/0.95.

Casca (Steinheil): Unique bayonet fitting.

Chiyoka/Chiyo Tax, Chiyotax: Leica screw compatible.

Contax: There are two series: Original (circa 1932–1962) and New (G1, G2) – quite apart from Contax reflexes. With the original mount, the inner bayonet accepted 50mm lenses only; the outer bayonet was for all other focal lengths, plus mirror boxes. Since 1994, Contax G-series lenses are a unique bayonet, all autofocus except 16mm.

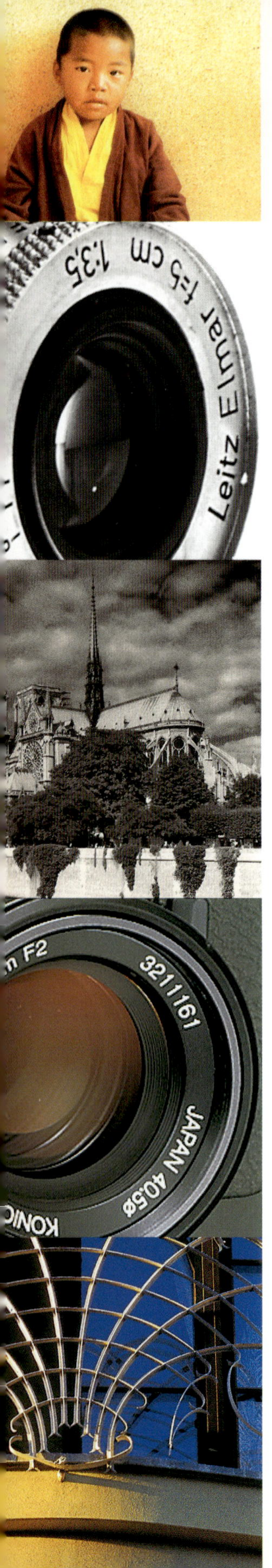

Detrola: Unique screw fitting; though may be cross-compatible with Perfex, also reported as a 38mm screw.

Ektra (Kodak): Unique breech-lock fitting.

Fed: Leica screw compatible.

Finetta: Unique clip-in 'pincer' mount.

Foca: Unique screw fitting, 36mm not 39mm, though it is often reported as 'Leica mount'. Bayonet-fit lenses for Focas are probably only for reflexes.

Foton (Bell & Howell): Unique screw fitting.

Fuji: The XPan (see Hasselblad, below) is badged as a Fuji in Japan.

Hasselblad: The XPan has a unique 3-claw bayonet.

Hensoldt: Unique fitting.

Honor: Leica screw compatible.

Kardon: Leica screw compatible.

Kiev: Nominally Contax (original) bayonet compatible, though some lenses seem to work better than others. Always check carefully to make sure that any given lens couples fully to the rangefinder.

Konica Hexar-M: Leica M bayonet compatible.

Kristall: Reported as Leica screw compatible, but we are not sure.

Leica Screw: Introduced as 39mm x 26tpi in early 1931; register standardized at 28.8mm a few months later. It has subsequently been adopted by many others, some of which are still in production. Some Leica screw mount 'compatibles' seem to be 39 x 1mm instead of the Leica standard 39mm x 26tpi, resulting in stiff or sometimes impossible fitting. Others (especially early Japanese lenses) may have a different thread pitch, with the same result. Some early Russian reflexes use Leica thread but had a considerably longer register, so Leica lenses will not focus to infinity.

Leica M-fit: The Leica 4-claw bayonet was introduced with the M3 in 1954 and has been used with all subsequent M-series and the CL.

Leningrad: Leica screw compatible.

Leotax: Leica screw compatible.

Lordomat: Unique captive-screw breech lock.

Melcon: Leica screw compatible.

Meopta: Leica screw compatible.

Mercury: Unique fitting.

Minolta CL: Leica M bayonet compatible. Some 1950s Minolta cameras are reputedly Leica screw fit.

Nettax: Unique bayonet fitting.

Nicca: Leica screw compatible.

Nikon (S-mount): Contax (original) bayonet compatible, but some longer Nikkor lenses are engraved N or C for Nikon-only and Contax-only compatibility.

Nikonos: Unique bayonet fitting.

Paxette: Leica screw, but not Leica register, so not Leica compatible.

Peerless: Made by Nicca, so Leica screw compatible.

Perfex: Unique screw fitting; though may be cross-compatible with Detrola, also reported as a 38mm screw.

Periflex: Most are Leica screw compatible, but the late Interplan series was also available with 42 x 1mm (Edixa/Pentax screw) and with Exakta bayonet.

Prominent 35mm (Voigtländer): Two unique bayonet fittings in front of the leaf shutter, the inner for 50mm, the outer for all other focal lengths and mirror boxes.

Red Flag (China): Leica M compatible.

Reid: Leica screw compatible.

Retina: IIc/IIIc and IIC/IIIC models had interchangeable front components. All other Retinas are fixed-lens.

Robot: All except the Royal series have a Robot-unique 25mm screw fitting; Royals have a different Robot-unique fitting.

Vitessa (Voigtländer): Unique fitting.

Werra: Unique fitting (but most were fixed-lens anyway).

Witness (Ilford): Leica screw compatible, but also accepted unique 39mm x 26tpi interrupted screw lenses like the breech of a heavy gun for faster fitting and removal.

Yashica: Leica screw compatible.

Yasuhara: Leica screw compatible.

Zorkii: Leica screw compatible.

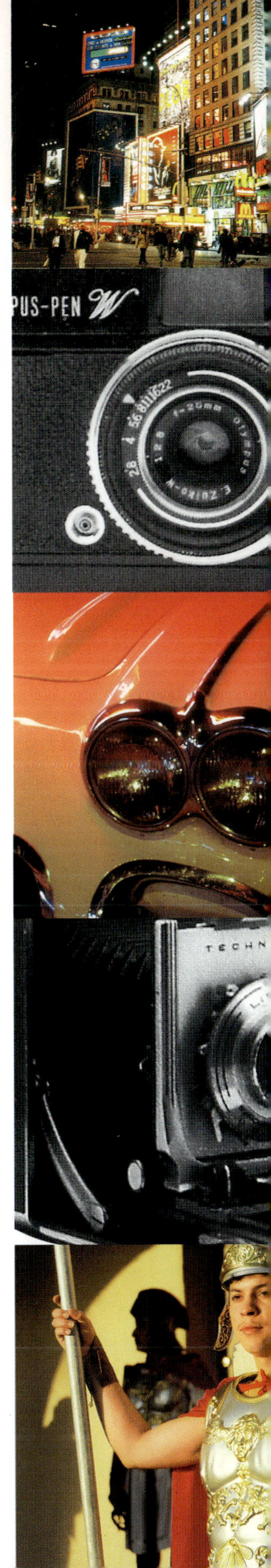

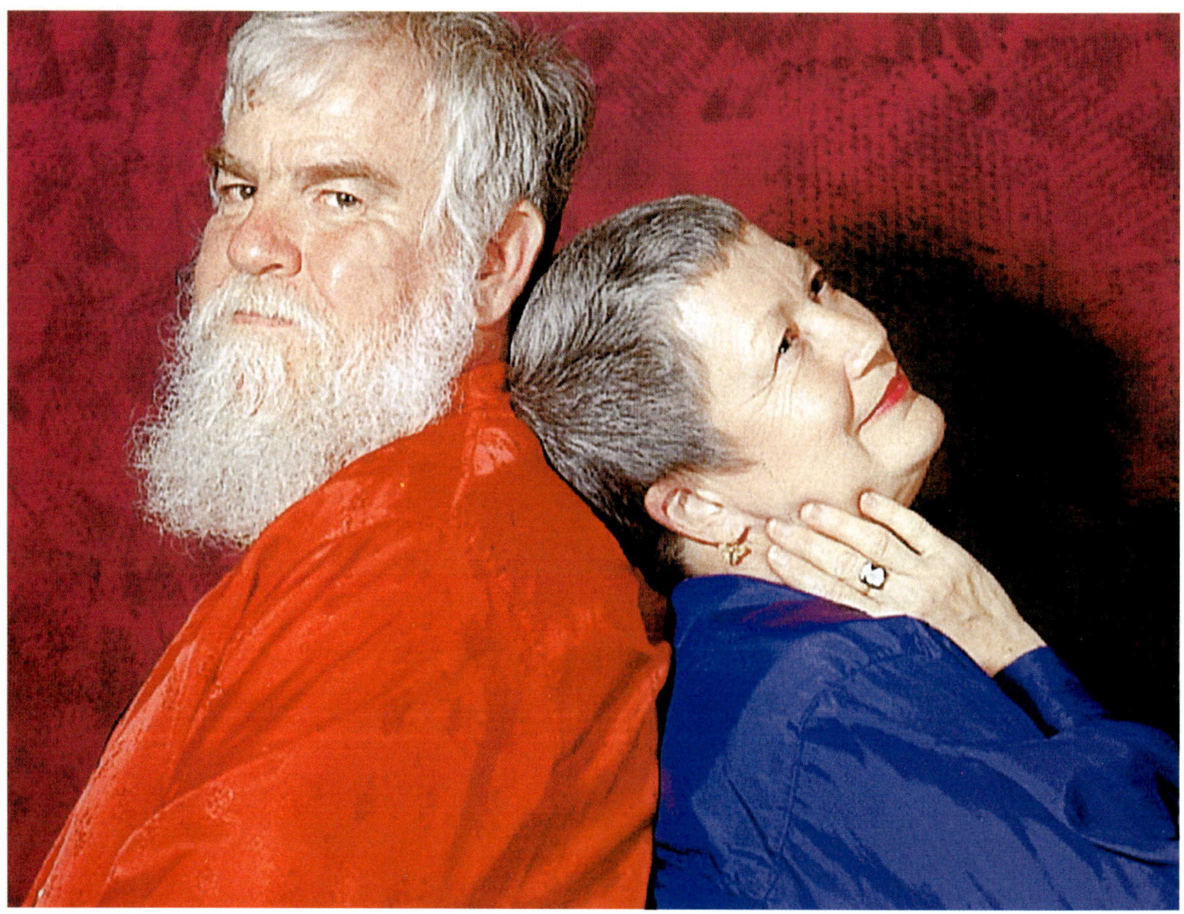

Roger Hicks is a Cornishman who took up photography seriously in his teens, when living in Bermuda. His first job as a professional photographer was in 1974 at a London advertising studio, and since 1982 he has been a full-time freelance photographer and writer.

Frances Schultz was born in Rochester, New York and took up photography in self defence shortly after meeting Roger in May 1981; her first published picture was a book cover. Since 1990 she has been a full-time freelance photographer and a leading writer on darkroom subjects.

Between them, Roger and Frances have over 50 years' experience in photography. They are regular contributors to the magazine *Black & White Photography*, also published by the Guild of Master Craftsman, and have many other photographic titles to their credit.

They travel extensively and are currently based in the Loire Valley, after living in Brisol, Central California, and Kent.

INDEX

Dolls' Houses and Miniatures

Crafts

Gardening

VIDEOS

MAGAZINES

Woodturning ◆ Woodcarving ◆ Furniture & Cabinetmaking ◆ The Router
New Woodworking ◆ The Dolls' House Magazine ◆ Outdoor Photography
Black & White Photography ◆ Travel Photography
Machine Knitting News ◆ Business Matters

The above represents a full list of all titles currently published or scheduled to be published.
All are available direct from the Publishers or through bookshops, newsagents and specialist retailers.
To place an order, or to obtain a complete catalogue, contact:

GMC Publications,

166 High Street, Lewes, East Sussex BN7 1XU, United Kingdom

Tel: 01273 488005 Fax: 01273 478606

E-mail: pubs@thegmcgroup.com

Orders by credit card are accepted